Glyn Dŵr's War

War

The Campaigns of the Last Prince of Wales

G. J. Brough

Walcs Books
Glyndŵr Publishing
2002

ISBN 1-903529-069

Publications from Wales Books (Glyndŵr Publishing) rediscovering our hidden past, appraising the present and safeguarding the future will be featured on our website . We have also founded cysgod.com, a shelter organisation to stimulate new research on Wales, and to link Welsh societies across the world.

PUBLISHED BY WALES BOOKS

2000-2001
The Secret Vale of Glamorgan - T.D. Breverton 228pp, illustrated
ISBN 1 903529 00X

The Book of Welsh Saints - T.D. Breverton 614pp hardback, illustrated
ISBN 1 903529 018

The Dragon Entertains : 100 Welsh Stars - Alan Roderick 230pp, illustrated
ISBN 1 903529 026

100 Great Welshmen - T.D. Breverton 366pp, illustrated
ISBN 1 903529 034

A Rhondda Boy - Ivor Howells 144pp, illustrated
ISBN 1 903529 050

100 Great Welsh Women - T.D. Breverton 304pp, illustrated
ISBN 1 903529 042

2002
From Wales to Pennsylvania : The David Thomas Story - Dr. Peter Williams 220pp, illustrated ISBN 1 903529 085
Glyndŵr's War – the Campaigns of the Last Prince of Wales - G.J. Brough, illustrated ISBN 1 903529 069

The Path to Inexperience – T.D. Breverton, illustrated
ISBN 1 903529 077

The Welsh Almanac – T.D. Breverton, illustrated
ISBN 1 903529 107

The Book of Welsh Pirates & Buccaneers - T.D. Breverton, illustrated
ISBN 1 903529 093

Forthcoming Books
Owain Llawgoch : the History of a Legend - Bryn ap Dafydd
The Quilt of Dreams - Marcella Davies
The Castles of Wales Vol 1 : Glamorgan – Lise Hull
Another 100 Great Welshmen - T.D. Breverton
Wales & the Welsh : the New A-Z - T.D. Breverton
Madoc : the Evidence - Bryn Griffiths
The Glamorgan Seascape Coast – T.D. Breverton
Arthur ap Meurig ap Tewdrig – T.D. Breverton

This book is dedicated to
Mary, Frederick, Sarah Angharad and David Huw
without whom none of this would have been possible or worthwhile
and, not least, to
'the rebellious people of Wales'.

Published in 2002 by Wales Books (Glyndŵr Publishing),
Porth Glyndŵr, Sain Tathan, Bro Morganwg CF62 4LW
www.walesbooks.com

A CIP catalogue record for this book is available from the British Library.

ISBN 1 903529 069

Illustrations and artwork arranged by Simon Fry
Maps and Internal Artwork: Simon Wyatt
Cover Illustrations: Paul B. Davies.

Printed and bound in Wales by
J & P Davison, 3 James Place
Trefforest, Pontypridd.

Glyn Dŵr's War
The Campaigns of the Last Prince of Wales

PUBLISHER'S PREFACE

On 1 January 2000 Owain Glyn Dŵr was named the most influential Welsh person of the millennium by BBC News Online and Ceefax services after a poll conducted the previous month. He headed a list of luminaries that included Aneurin Bevan, Gwynfor Evans and Lloyd George. Earlier, on a wider stage, a hundred influential, international leaders ranked him 7th when asked for their views by the Sunday Times of London.

In this *Top Ten Makers of the Millennium*' poll, Gutenberg and other inventors ranked highly as did Shakespeare; Elizabeth Tudor was in 4th place. We can understand that the flowering of the Elizabethan era should be recognised through its queen of Welsh descent, but Owain Glyn Dŵr? Even those aware of his name may know little of his life, his achievements and what he represented to his countrymen in the 15th century. He has been described variously as '*this wonderful man, an attractive unique figure in a period of debased and selfish politics*' (G.M. Trevelyan); '*a man of genius and courage*' (H. Martin) and '*the symbol for the vigorous resistance of the Welsh spirit to tyranny*' (J.E. Lloyd).

'*Glyn Dŵr's War – the Campaigns of the last Prince of Wales*' tells the enthralling story of a rebellion ignited by greed and injustice and the emergence of the heroic figure of Owain Glyn Dŵr. He was the bards' '*mab darogan*', the son of prophecy, who would reclaim Welsh independence lost in 1282 with the murder of Llywelyn ap Gruffydd. An earlier 'mab darogan' and sole descendant of Llywelyn II, Owain Llawgoch was assassinated in France in 1378, on the orders of the English crown.

Twenty-two years later, some of his battle hardened captains returned to Wales to support Glyn Dŵr in his fight to free a suppressed nation. He was also the only Welsh prince to elicit spontaneous and passionate loyalty from every corner of Wales.

The early part of the book gives a glimpse of Welsh military history up to the dawn of the 15th century. Wales is depicted as a small, well-developed nation with strong cultural traditions, conscious and proud of its identity and striving for liberty against incredible odds.

This unique account examines the events and pressures that provoked Glyn Dŵr into violent action against the Kings of England, and its aftermath. It chronicles the development of the war between the Welsh rebels and the

Norman-English crown, demonstrating the sensational military successes and political accomplishments of the Welsh under Glyn Dŵr's dynamic leadership. The English administration in Wales was brought down and, for a while, Welsh independence was revived. Fidel Castro, a successful and respected revolutionary of our era has described Owain Glyn Dŵr as one of the greatest freedom fighters of all time. Other guerillas throughout the world have admired his achievements and emulated his tactics. Historians, too, recognise his leading role in the development of guerilla warfare.

The romance and fascination of Glyn Dŵr is that from 1400 for over a decade, he led a fiercely sustained rebellion with no standing armies and few resources against the most powerful military force in Europe, or indeed, the world at that time. Most uprisings were usually brief and, in Wales, no war had lasted as long, let alone one so enduring and fierce. Yet, by 1417 Glyn Dŵr had vanished forever. Even so the English Crown sent messengers with pardons for him. Only years later, in 1421, did his named heir, Maredudd, accept a pardon. In this unjust war, not sought by Glyn Dŵr, many family members and friends were killed or captured, but he was never taken nor betrayed.

Not for him the brutal public death of Braveheart, William Wallace (a Scot of Welsh descent), nor a known grave to desecrate. Glyn Dŵr, the essence of Welshness, is one of the greatest heroes in two millennia of British history: a cultured and learned linguist, a lawyer and not least a warrior. He had fought valiantly for the Crown before his betrayal by Earl Grey and the King of England. Glyn Dŵr had no secret agenda; he wanted only justice for Wales and to defend this right against invaders.

Recognised as their only prince, he exuded leadership and charisma so that all, including nobles and clergy, flocked to his banner despite huge odds stacked against them. They died in the cause. In him, all knew that they had a worthy hero and that their ill-fated revolt had been a moment of glory, a time of national completeness and fulfilment. Glyn Dŵr re-united Wales both politically and symbolically: his uprising left an imprint on Welsh consciousness and a fervour to be rekindled in later eras.

The book concludes that for his achievements and more than any other leader, Owain Glyn Dŵr, descended from Welsh Princes and Kings should be acknowledged as the last Prince of Wales.

The author of this book, G.J. Brough, spent his formative years in Wales, was educated at universities in Wales, England and most recently at the Sorbonne, Paris.

Always interested in history, he became aware of Glyn Dŵr many years ago and his fascination deepened with research. Impressed and enthusiastic about this great Welsh historical figure yet frustrated at the lack of will to promote Owain Glyn Dŵr and Wales, there was no alternative for him but to write this book.

> *'A vineyard placed in my care is Wales,*
> *My country*

To deliver unto my children
And my children's children
Intact, an eternal heritage'

Saunders Lewis.

WALES BOOKS (Glyndŵr Publishing) founded in 2000 is dedicated to promoting, in several ways, the small, undervalued country of Wales – a venerable, cultured nation whose humanitarian laws, codified in medieval times, were the most enlightened in the world – especially regarding the meting out of justice and the equal status of women. It has also the oldest Christian community with more churches per capita than anywhere else in Europe. The story of Wales is that of endless defence and stubborn resistance by a small, under-resourced nation against those who wished to extinguish its distinctive identity. That is why, as with all nations, the preservation of its ancient language, first written in 600 A.D (predating French and English by centuries) is vital. Interestingly, in Wales during the Middle Ages the word for language *'iaith'* was also used to denote 'nation'.

The first of our aims is to present a fair and factual account of Welsh history to counter-balance any biased versions, or entire omissions in the media and sadly, even in school text books. For instance Owain Glyn Dŵr and many other Welsh heroes should be as famous and as well documented in history books as Robert the Bruce, William Wallace and so on. We seek to right this imbalance with our publications.

Y gwir yn erbyn y byd
The truth against the world

Iolo Morganwg

Without a knowledge of our rich past, the present cannot be understood. As one of our modern heroes, Gareth Edwards, recently said *"To know where you're going, you've got to know where you've come from"*. This knowledge gives us a sense of our place in history, of belonging to Wales, of our Cymreictod, and thus armed, perhaps we will see that, as Paul Flynn predicted, *"the greatest days of Welsh history are before us."*

Secondly, we want to publicise the splendour of Welsh culture, an appreciation of which is essential for preserving the very life of the nation. As Iolo Morganwg recognised, the continuity of Wales lies, above all, in its literary traditions. Against all odds, even though its demise was confidently predicted in the 14th century, Welsh – the oldest living European language, denigrated and outlawed at times, has survived.

Rydym ni yma o hyd!
We are still here!

Dafydd Iwan

We can delight not only in today's songs, but in the lyrical images of the past, conjured by Aneirin, Taliesin, Dafydd ap Gwilym, Henry Vaughan, Ellis Evans (Hedd Wyn) among others.

However, linguistic changes occur as a result of social and economic influence over the years. To safeguard and strengthen the language it would be essential for Welsh to be used in the community in everyday life. Despite the fact that English is the common language, the Welsh are not English and Wales is not England.

Thirdly, we seek to respond to those interested in reading about Wales and/or wish to explore a small, beguiling country. It has lovely landscape enriched with holy places (there are more than 900 saints), museums and castles. Ironically, the castles – those emblems (like the coal mines) of past struggles – are now flourishing tourist attractions.

Fourthly, we aim to encourage research and to continue publishing more books on Welsh topics. Suitable manuscripts are invited which should be based as far as possible on proven facts, not academic theory, or speculation. Particularly welcome would be submissions on overlooked figures such as Richard Price, Owain Llawgoch (a commemorative statue will be unveiled at Mortagne-sur-Mer on 31 August 2003) and numerous others. We also believe that a true appraisal of Iolo Morganwg would lead to his long overdue rehabilitation.

Finally, we are a self-financing, independent enterprise where profits from the sale of affordable books are ploughed back to further our aims. All our publications have a real purpose in addition to presenting Wales to its people and the world. We would like to support tourism and economic regeneration, to re-institute feast days and traditional events, to highlight those that already exist and even to stir the passive Welsh psyche! At this late stage, can we revive our national heritage or are we, as Gwyn Alf Williams put it, *"nothing but a naked people under an acid rain"*? The spirit of Cymru lives still but like its language, its countryside and economy it is in a critical situation – still waiting for a secure future.

One of the most underprivileged areas of the British Isles, it consistently qualifies for Objective One funding, no source of pride but which may yet make much needed resources accessible.

Time is of the essence. Will our fledgling Welsh Assembly, despite its early set-backs and current limitations of power, bring about a Welsh renaissance? This is the first time since Owain Glyn Dŵr's last Parliament at Harlech in 1406, that the Welsh people and their political representatives have the opportunity to make patriotic decisions for Wales. Cymru am byth!

T.D.Breverton

AUTHOR'S PREFACE

Thanks to Terry Breverton for his time, advice and help, Simon Fry for about a million things, Simon Wyatt and Paul B. Davies (Art Work), Jim Rowlands of Paris and Graigfechan, Robin, Anne Pilling, M and D and the rest of you who have helped in one way or another – you know who you are!!

G.J. Brough

Glyn Dŵr's War

The Campaigns of the Last Prince of Wales

Glyn Dŵr's War

Table of Contents

FOREWORD

Wales is a land blessed with a host of heroes, but none of them has the aura of Owain Glyn Dŵr. None captures the imagination and fires the emotion of this ancient nation as he. His name rolls off the tongue of all Welsh people, yet who knows what he achieved? This book will tell you.

His epic story should be more widely known. It is astonishing how few details are common knowledge, even in Wales. The aims of this book are to enlighten and inform readers of his life and deeds, and to make this knowledge accessible to all, where necessary, bypassing academic convention and traditional discussion points. In order to prepare any reader for the detailed account of Glyn Dŵr's war, there are two preceding sections. The first is an abridged history of the Welsh in battle, from the time of the Romans through to 1400, to help the modern reader understand the mood and mindset of the nation at that time. The second is a brief evaluation of the opposing forces on the eve of battle in 1400. This explains the enormity of the task which faced Glyn Dŵr and his supporters, rebels against the Crown of England.

Amazingly, since he disappeared into the mists of legend in the early fifteenth century, Glyn Dŵr's exploits in the name of Welsh independence have been well hidden. The whole story, embellished in part by myth, shows the pride and bravery of the Welsh nation at a key moment in their long history. The real Owain Glyn Dŵr cuts an awe-inspiring figure on the pages of history. Widely recognised as a superb military tactician and the father of a national movement, he was also a man of vision, charisma and courage.

It should be noted in advance that there is much that is imprecise or uncertain when dealing with medieval history. It is detective work carried out under difficult conditions. Much of what we believe to have occurred is obscured by a lack of irrefutable proof. There are no witnesses alive to cross-examine. Often, events are recorded, or alluded to, long after they took place, by distant chroniclers lacking impartiality. Equally, those more closely involved in events unashamedly represented their own stances, adding to the difficulties of anyone trying to piece together any factual account relating to the medieval period. Also, a modern reader has a different worldview, and should not assume that people of that period had the same norms and accepted truths as are common today. Some of the plethora of folk tales associated with Owain Glyn Dŵr have been referred to or included in this book for interest's sake. So many places, from Glyn Dŵr's heartland in the north, to the Vale of Glamorgan in the south, have some part in Glyn Dŵr's story. There are too many such places to include in this book. Some commonly believed inaccuracies have been discussed and dispelled. On certain matters opinion has been offered with the benefit of hindsight.

This book is only the skeleton of the story. In completing this synopsis of Glyn Dŵr's war, I consulted many sources of information, from some of which I drew extracts, acknowledged here. I unreservedly recommend these to anyone interested in further reading on this subject. *"The Revolt of Owain Glyn Dŵr"* (OUP) by R.R. Davies is a must for anyone intent on exploring the depths of the matter. *"Owain Glyn Dŵr and the War of Independence in the Welsh Borders"* (Logaston) by Geoffrey Hodges is also illuminating, and includes some interesting anecdotes relating to the conflict. For a more general account of the country and its history, *"A History of Wales"* (Penguin) by John Davies is without peer. For an insight into Wales and the character of its people, consult *"The Matter of Wales - Epic Views of a Small Country"* (Penguin) by Jan Morris. Some interesting facts concerning Wales in the early Middle Ages emerge from *"A Mirror of Medieval Wales. Gerald of Wales and His Journey of 1188"* (Cadw) by Charles Kightly. In addition, I found the Owain Glyn Dŵr Society's website useful, and the Cambria Magazine extracts contained therein. Furthermore, a number of webpages by David Fortin of the Catholic University of North America provide a wealth of information on a number of Welsh historical topics, and are well worth perusal.

From his numerous books and essays, Terry Breverton's own solid library of work on Wales and all things Welsh provides ample interesting reading and brings to light a range of historical revelations. A number of the medieval manuscripts are included by courtesy of the Owain Lawgoch Society and the National Library of Wales. Certain points, particularly those concerning Roman involvement in Wales, were drawn from *"When was Wales?"* (Pelican) by Gwyn Alf Williams. *"In Search of Owain Glyndŵr"* (Blorenge) by Chris Barber contains noteworthy information concerning Glyn Dŵr's campaigns and contains a useful reference section detailing most of the places touched by the war, including those not mentioned in other works, mainly due to their vast number or obscurity. A number of interesting fifteenth century documents are revealed in *"Owain Glyndŵr. Prince of Wales."* (Christopher Davies Ltd) by Ian Skidmore, and Dafydd Johnston's translations of *"Iolo Goch : Poems."* (Gomer) provide an invaluable insight into the work of Glyn Dŵr's household bard. Information concerning medieval Welsh heraldry was gleaned from *"Historical Heraldry of Britain"* (Phillimore) by Sir Anthony Wagner, *"Medieval Heraldry"* (William Lewis) by E.J.Jones and *"The Development of Welsh Heraldry, Volume I."* (National Library of Wales, Aberystwyth) by M.P. Siddons. Finally, a good deal of the research for this work was undertaken while a student at Universite Paris III, La Sorbonne Nouvelle, under the guidance and tutelage of Professor Franck Lessay, whom I respectfully acknowledge.

Geoffrey Hodges proposed that Owain Glyn Dŵr's rebellion should, more correctly, be called a war. He argued that rebellions and revolts are fitful by nature and are characterised by sporadic, even random action, whereas a war is a more constant effort, with defined goals and strategy. Welsh attacks were indeed sporadic during the early days of the campaign, but soon intensified. At a certain point, detailed later in this book, the English civilian administration in Wales collapsed in the wake of several crushing Welsh military victories. Wales succumbed to Glyn Dŵr's insurgents. The Crown of England relied solely on the military to maintain its tenuous presence in Wales. That intensification of the conflict can be identified as the period when rebellion matured into war. I concur with Hodges' suggestion. Chroniclers of the time did not hesitate to call it *"the war between the Welsh and the English"*, and contemporary society can also consider it so.

This book has not been written in support of any political party, nor does it seek to further any contemporary stance. It is accepted that in seeking to redress the balance of the conventional view of Welsh history, this book goes against the 'received wisdom' of the past. It is up to the modern reader to consider a more balanced perspective than was previously available. Some of the information contained in this book will be revelatory, showing that Welsh history to date has not been written in an impartial way, nor has it been written by sources complimentary to Wales. One must ask why this is so.

NOTE: The numbers in squares upon the year-maps of the campaigns, are cross-referenced with corresponding dates in the text of the book, to enable the reader to see how the war of independence ebbed and flowed across Wales and into England.

The Five Native
Clans as Named
and Mapped by
the Romans

DECEANGLI   DEVA

ORDOVICES

CORNOVII

DEMETAE

SILVRES

MARIDVNVM

ISCA

VENTA
SILVRVM

The Welsh in Battle up to 1400.

The world beyond Wales's borders hardly knows of its existence, let alone anything about its history and culture. This can be explained in part by the curious fact that even the Welsh have not been taught their own history. It seems equally curious that, like its history and culture, Welsh military prowess is also so unfamiliar, when other nations revel in their histories, both in victory and defeat. As the subject of this book is a war in Wales, this first part aims to give a fleeting glimpse at warfare involving the Welsh from Roman times, and briefly set the tone of social discontent up to the eve of battle in 1400.

Cambria

From the very beginning, Welsh skill at arms has impressed all those unfortunate enough to be on the receiving end of their wrath. The 'Britons' we read of in British history were the ancestors of the Welsh, and the Welsh alone. They won the respect and admiration of the first continental invaders to follow in the wake of the Celts: the Romans. The Britons were famed for scorning armour and taking to the battlefield naked. If it was your time to die, they reasoned, then it would come whether you were in battle or at home in bed. To them, wearing armour was pointless. They reassured themselves with the knowledge that a solid stroke with their razor sharp curved *macheira* swords would pierce armour and kill the wearer just as efficiently as it would a naked opponent.

The first Roman invasion, led by Julius Caesar, took place in 55 B.C., but did not penetrate beyond the south - eastern coastal region of what is now England. Eighty eight years later, in 43 A.D., during the reign of Emperor Claudius, a real invasion force, intent on conquering as much land as possible, attacked Britain. Initially, it comprised of over forty thousand soldiers. Over the decades, this immense Roman invasion force won supremacy over the majority of the mainland. Even after conquest and settlement, unlike in much of the Empire, the British people were far from calm. In order to subjugate and defend lowland Britain, one-tenth of Rome's overall military strength had to be deployed, on a province that covered just one-thirtieth of Roman imperial territory. There is a proliferation of Roman literature proclaiming the Britons as fearsome warriors. Individually or in small numbers they were without peer, but in a massed battle they lacked the rigid discipline of the legions, a necessity for large-scale victory. We know of two revolts of particular note, led by Welsh-speaking Buddug and Caradog, more commonly known as Boadicea and Caractacus.

It is worth bringing to light the fact that the Britons of modern-day Wales were not conquered as traditional history tells us. The southern and northern coastal strips were invaded and, in places, built upon. Anglesey, sacred home of the druids of Britain, was put to the sword some twenty years after the initial Roman invasion of the British mainland. The hilly interior and inland valleys were always the traditional homelands of these Britons however, not the sparsely inhabited coastal areas. The wild interior bears little evidence of Roman visitation, only occasional temporary structures and signs of road building, in some cases inexplicably incomplete. In these areas there is no history of conquest by Rome, but rather of a difficult coming to terms with one another. These Britons certainly traded with the Romans, but they also fought them. Two of the four Roman legions on the British mainland were deployed around the borders of Wales, first at Wroxeter and then at the new forts of Caerleon and Chester, in an attempt to contain the Welsh.

We are told that Britain was peaceful by 60 A.D., yet Wales was unconquered and still fighting. Of the five native clans mapped on this land only one, the Silures, was brought to an uneasy peace in 75 A.D., just a generation after they had destroyed the entire XXth (Augusta) Legion in battle. The Roman historian Tacitus wrote of the Silures *"...they are a naturally fierce people...warlike, stubborn, with swarthy features and curly hair."* He added that *"...on the Silures, neither terror nor mercy had the least effect for they persisted in fighting."* Tacitus also described the destruction of the XXth Legion as *"Rome's greatest defeat in Britain"* and told that after peace had been reached between the Silures and the Empire, they were accorded the status of "Civitate Peregrine", non-citizens of the Empire, but honourably associated with it. In 78 A.D. Tacitus claimed that *"almost the entire race"* of Ordovices were massacred by the Romans. Peace reigned in the area that is modern-day Wales, the Romans apparently happy to let the native tribes go about their business, once they felt sure enough that they had no intentions of invading the more settled areas to the east. The Welsh, for their part, seemed to have been content to remain ensconced on their lands while the Romans went about their imperial business beyond their borders. This is a behavioural pattern that would be repeated by the natives' descendants in Wales throughout the history of Britain.

The Romans recorded Wales as 'Cambria', clearly a romanisation of 'Cymry' or 'Cymru'. This shows us that a notion of nationhood existed, 'Cymry' meaning kinsman, countryman and friend. 'Cambria' was at peace with the Roman Empire, hardly subjugated, unquestionably the weaker of the two, but it was not brought under the imperial umbrella in the same way as the rest of occupied Britain.

The Romans dealt with these difficult kingdoms through trade and influence, underpinned with the threat of the legions, but did not romanise the area, possibly through choice, more probably through inability. A little publicised fact is that Hadrian's Wall was built to keep out these Welsh-speaking Britons, not the Scots. The Scots began filtering into the western islands and peninsulas from Ireland in the fourth and fifth centuries. It was not until the sixth century that they established a mainland powerbase in modern-day Argyll. From there they launched attacks on the Picts in the east. The Picts had encountered and fought the Romans, but the Scots were many years too late to do so, and were not in the right geographical location. It is worth reappraising the extent to which the Britons were romanised. When the legions withdrew, their language, law and customs went unpractised by their former subjects. Their technology was used, notably the roads, but much of it fell into disuse. That is not to say that the Romans were not appreciated by the natives, even after their withdrawal. In the year 469, after the alleged Saxon invasion of Britain, the Britons of south - east Britain sent a contingent of troops to Gaul to assist the Emperor in shoring up his crumbling authority. They went unmolested, it should be noted, by the so-called Saxon invaders in the areas they passed through. It is interesting to note that the first 'Anglo-Saxon' invaders, traders or settlers were neither Angles nor Saxons, but Jutes from southern Denmark. Towards the end of the fifth century, the Gauls in modern France were overwhelmed by another Germanic people, the Franks, led by Clovis. During the period which followed, Britons began to take up residence in Armorica, modern Brittany.

The royal dynasties of Wales: Gwynedd, Dyfed, Powys, Morgannwg - Gwent and Ceredigion -Ystrad Tywi, can all be traced to a time prior to the Roman withrawal, and match the geographical territories of the five clans mapped by the Romans. The fact that these areas still had kings throughout this period surely denotes at least a measure of independence from centralised Roman rule. Dynasties would rise and supercede their original limits; Dyfed, Ceredigion and Tywi would be united under the House of Deheubarth, to whom Morgannwg and Gwent in time swore fealty, and eventually all of Wales would come to be ruled by the foremost of Welsh royal houses, Gwynedd.

Wales

The so-called 'barbarian invasions' by the Angles and Saxons have been altered by generations of historians and writers, seemingly seeking to prove English ascendancy from the very moment of their arrival. They were referred to as 'barbarians' not because of any modern interpretation of 'toughness' we associate with the word, but because they could not read or write, and their cultural output was somewhat limited. They began arriving from Germany and the Low Countries from the fifth century onwards, but the concept of 'England' was not a solid one until Aethelstan was declared and recognised as 'king of England' in 924, some five hundred years after their initial arrival. The idea that these Angles, Saxons, Jutes, Frisians and others, invaded and manfully pushed back the Britons into modern-day Scotland, Cumbria, Wales and Cornwall has no credibility at all. Prolonged fighting did occur between

the British and these Germanic peoples and flared sporadically for some five centuries, but at the time of the arrival of these illiterate, pagan Germanic folk, the Britons of Wales were more interested in pursuing a feud with the Irish in the east of Ireland than fearing the newcomers, essentially traders and settlers, as potential invaders.

Indeed, traditional history records that Saxons and others were invited to Britain by the Council of the Kings of Britain, headed by Vortigern, to work as mercenaries to deal with the Picts in the far north. It is quite probable that the immediate forebears of many of these Saxons had served in Britain under the Romans. Surviving Roman military records show that many of the soldiers who served in Britain towards the end of the Roman period were Germans from the near continent. Those Saxons hired by Vortigern, led by Hengest and his brother, Horsa, were eventually granted Kent as a wedding gift for Hengest's daughter, with whom Vortigern had allegedly fallen deeply in love. Thus, the Germanic toe-hold in Britain was established. It was not long before the newcomers showed their colours during the infamous 'Treachery of the Long Knives'; a peace banquet between Saxons and Britons where weapons were forbidden.The Saxons drank only water, pretending that they, like the Britons, were drinking wine, and had smuggled or hidden weapons about the hall, which they used to kill the flower of the British nobility on Hengest's signal, late into the banquet.

Later, there certainly were battles and protracted warfare between the newcomers and the natives, including the Scots and the Norse who often allied themselves with the Welsh-Britons. This period provided a rich body of legends and literature, a number of original manuscripts still exist today. Welsh literature of the time mainly takes the form of praise poems describing heroic figures, both mighty and tragic, events and places. One famous poem written around the year 600 by Aneirin was called 'Y Gododdin', and described a battle between the Britons and the Saxons at Catraeth (Catterick). (Recent research places this battle elsewhere, as the place seems to have been derived fron cad-traeth - battle on a shore). Everyone died save one Welsh warrior, who returned home to lament the tragic victory.

About a dozen works by the poet Taliesin have survived and depict the style and era of the praise poets. In literary circles, the period is known as the 'The Age of Saints' and the 'Golden Age of Heroes', and its most famous figure is King Arthur. This was the original Arthur, a Welsh warrior-king, not the chivalric prince of later versions. Famed for leading his people, the 'Brython', into battle against their hated enemy, the Saxons, it is ridiculous that later writers acclaimed him as an English icon, when he made war on their forebears.

The 'English' did not even exist at that time, nor would they for hundreds of years. At one golden moment, recorded as 633 A.D., the Welsh king, Cadwallon, ruled over the whole island, the kingdoms of the Germanic newcomers included, having won his crown in a series of battles. It is from this period that we also learn of another important figure in Welsh history, the king Cadwaladr, or Cadwaladr Fendigaid (the Blessed), Cadwallon's son.

It is recorded that, in the seventh century, he was the first to use the legendary red dragon symbol of Wales on his war banner. The peoples of the western fringe of Europe still sent the bodies of their saints and revered figures to Ynys Enlli, the island of Bardsey off the Welsh coast. It was a religious centre of the Celtic world, a few miles from Môn, Anglesey, home of the Druidic religion. Priests and prophets from Brittany, Galicia, the Hebrides, Ireland and Wales were interred on the island, reputedly the burial ground of 20,000 saints.

It was not to last. By the end of this period the Welsh-speaking kingdoms of The Old North: Gododdin, whose capital was at modern Edinburgh, Ystrad Clud or Strathclyde at Dumbarton, Rheged at Carlisle and throughout Cumbria, Elmet at Leeds and others, became detached from their Welsh roots. The Welsh-speaking kingdoms of The Old North were absorbed or replaced by stronger powers in those areas, generally by the Scots, Danes and the Angles.

It is from this period that we gain the word 'Wales'. The significance and origin of this word is a disputed topic. Some writers claim that it was a standard term used by these Germanic peoples to describe the inhabitants of areas under Roman influence. They cite other examples:- the Walloons in modern Belgium and the Vlachs in Romania, as proof of this. Although possible, this surely does not apply to Wales, largely unconquered by the Romans? The Romans used the word '*Celtai*', but the word 'Celt' comes from the Greek '*keltoi*' meaning 'those who are different'. The Greeks noted with admiration and curiosity the way 'the Celts' interacted with other nationalities in large, cosmopolitan ports of the ancient world. The Greeks struggled to define them precisely, describing a quirkiness, a certain flamboyance and ready wit, as well as a warmth and friendliness, especially between themselves. Celtic warriors wore jewellery, warpaint and some had braids in their hair, yet were far from being either strutting peacocks or aloof.

They also noted the Celtic skill and capacity for fighting and respect for their religion, the beliefs of which stemmed from gods of nature. The German word '*waleseer*', meaning 'foreigner, stranger, those different from us' may well be a germanification of the Greek term for the Celts. Therefore, in calling the Britons '*waleseer*', the Angles, Saxons and others may have simply been referring to the natives as Celts and not, as popular history would have it, as '*foreigners*'. Irrespective, the Welsh have, for many years, regarded that as a slight, but in fact they should revel in it, for it recognises their unquestionable distinction from other peoples. As with so many historical things, ultimately, we do not know the answer. The Saxons tried repeatedly to invade 'Wales', as they were now calling it, and failed. One of their leaders, Offa of Mercia, built a huge defensive ditch with a few guarded crossing points to protect his people from predatory raids by the Welsh. This long earthwork defence, 149 miles long, twice the length of Hadrian's Wall, stretching from the Dee to the mouth of the Severn, was called 'Offa's Dyke', harking back to similar structures in the Low Countries, from where a number of the peoples who constitute the 'English' came. Offa ruled Mercia from 757 until 796, when he was killed in battle with the Welsh.

The great terror of the age, the Vikings, did not have as much of an impact on Wales as elsewhere. In 856, the Vikings landed on Anglesey and were met by King Rhodri and the Welsh. Rhodri killed the Viking king in hand-to-hand combat, and, in the ensuing battle, the Viking army was slaughtered. The Vikings learnt from this, and although they would harass the coasts in the future, they would not attempt to invade again. Rhodri won international acclaim and plaudits, and was referred to as 'Rhodri the Great' by foreign powers. During the ninth century only three kings were so honoured; Charles of France (Charlemagne), Rhodri of Gwynedd and Alfred of Wessex. Rhodri ushered in a new era of Welsh rulers, he became the first High King of All Wales. Interestingly, just eighteen years later, Mercia and much of modern-day England was conquered by the Vikings. Wales, mostly united under Rhodri's rule was not invaded or conquered by the Vikings as were the English, Scots and Irish.

Rhodri's grandson, Hywel Dda or King Hywel the Good, reunited Wales during his long reign, and as well as being the first and, arguably, only authority in these islands to codify civil law, he was an able diplomat. More so than elsewhere, Welsh rulers enjoyed good relations with the Vikings in England, Ireland, Scotland and the Hebrides. There were marriages and alliances between the ruling houses of Gwynedd, Dublin and Norway. Welsh nobles frequently stayed amongst the Vikings of Dublin, and it was not uncommon for Welsh and Norse contingents to be found in each other's armies. However, the Vikings were not one united people, and other Norse raiders, Danes in particular, struck at offshore Welsh monasteries and other similarly vulnerable targets, with particular vigour in the last fifteen years of the tenth century, during the reign of Maredudd ab Owain, Hywel Dda's grandson.

The Vikings did have trading posts and permanent representation in a number of coastal locations, but, unlike elsewhere, they achieved no major penetrations or settlement in Wales. The lack of Viking place-names in the only language applicable to Wales of the era, Welsh, underlines this fact. The words Anglesey, Bardsey and Swansea are Viking in origin, and entered the English language thus, though these places retain Welsh names to this day; Ynys Môn, Ynys Enlli and Abertawe, unrelated to their Viking or English names. A poem written in south Wales, dated 930, indicates a close relationship of past alliances and co-operation between the Welsh and the Vikings. Entitled 'Armes Prydain' (The Prophecy of Britain), it called for an alliance of western and northern peoples against the English. One stanza reads thus:

"The muse foretells they will come in hosts: Riches, prosperity, peace will be ours,
Magnanimous reign, benevolent Lords, And after disruption, all regions settled.

Men bold in battle, wrathful, mighty, Keen in combat, unbudging bulwark,

Warriors as far as Caer Weir will rout foreign foes, will bring celebration, devastation done.

And concord of Welshmen and Dublin's men, Gaelic men of Ireland, Mona and Scotland,

Cornishmen and Clydesmen at one with us, Remnants will the British be when they triumph.
Long it is foretold, in time will come, Monarchs possessing noble lineage,

Northmen in pre-eminent place among them, Amid the vanguard, will launch the assault."

Although Aethelstan declared himself 'King of England' in 924 A.D., others had previously referred to themselves as 'King of the English', notably Offa of Mercia in a letter to Charlemagne. Realistically, Aethelstan was the first to have any claim to both sovereignty over English territories and the acknowledgement of other English 'kings' and leaders. Though his achievements were arguably greater, Alfred the Great, King of Wessex only, had not enjoyed the same measures of unity and territory as would his grandson, Aethelstan, to enable him to lay claim to 'England' before his death in 899. Even allowing for the Danish occupation and colonisation of the north and middle of England, the English ruled most of the south and centre until 1016. In that year the Danes led by Cnut, or Canute, defeated them in battle and he was crowned 'King of All England'. English rule of mostly occupied 'All England' lasted from 924 to 1016, a grand total of ninety-two years. The Danish and English factions vied for power until the English regained control under Harold Godwinson, just in time to lose it utterly to the Normans in 1066.

While the English tussled with Danes for the crown of England, Gruffudd ap Llewelyn, grandson of Maredudd ab Owain, had been energetically uniting Wales. His troops defeated the English led by Leofric, Earl of Mercia and husband of the famed Lady Godiva, at Rhyd-y-Groes, near Oswestry, in 1039. He then unleashed a successful campaign on the border, during which Hereford returned to Welsh hands. By 1057 he had completely unified Wales. The country enjoyed an all too brief seven years of unity before Gruffudd ap Llewelyn, the self-styled "Shield of the Welsh", was killed by internal enemies in1063, who took their cue from an English seaborne attack led by the ill-fated Harold Godwinson.

'La Natioun del Walsherie'

The arrival of the Normans profoundly affected the world view of the people of Wales. Previously, the Welsh had been engaged in a world which faced mostly north. The powers with which the Welsh most commonly dealt were the various Norse nations, the Scots, the Irish, the peoples of England and, to the south, their cousins, the Bretons and the Cornish. The new dominant force in Europe, the Normans, brought Wales into a different sphere of affairs, that of continental Europe to the south and east, and away from the Viking-dominated world. It is noteworthy that the Normans, though Norsemen in origin, seem to have severed their ties to their Northern brethren, less than two hundred years after settling the Seine valley in France.

The Normans arrived at the Welsh border during a very unstable period for the Welsh. This may well be the basis of a reputation for murderous in-fighting. From 1070 to 1081 the factions of the three Welsh kingdoms - Gwynedd, Deheubarth and Powys - fought a series of highly damaging fratricidal wars, which took a heavy toll on the native nobility, with many losing their lives. Even so, the Normans approached the Welsh with extreme caution. They communicated cordially and respectfully with the rulers of Wales and met them as equals. Initial Norman military incursions were repulsed with the invader sustaining heavy losses. Chroniclers for the de Braose dynasty later recorded with amazement how: -

> *"...one of our soldiers, in a battle against the Welsh, was struck by a Welsh arrow in the thigh. It penetrated through his padded cloth hauberk and right through his leg armour, and this same arrow then passed on through his saddle flap and deep into his horse, mortally wounding it. Another soldier was likewise hit by an arrow which penetrated through his hauberk and leg armour and into his saddle. When he reined his horse round in a half circle, moreover, a second arrow shot by the same archer hit him in the other thigh, so that he was firmly fixed to his horse on both sides..."*

Norman chroniclers and monks described the Welsh of this period. Interestingly, they depicted them as wearing striped, multicoloured plaid cloth, and sketched them with bare legs, wearing lengths of this cloth wrapped around them in a kilt-like fashion. It was recorded that the Welsh cut their hair to shoulder length or shorter, brushed their teeth and shaved their faces. Moreover, before battle, many warriors shaved their heads completely *"...for ease in running through thickets..."* to avoid snagging their hair or beards on branches or brambles. The Normans also noticed how the Welsh seemed undeterred by the fact that they were mostly on foot and unarmoured, and readily charged into ranks of heavy cavalry. Their first assault was usually preceded by terrifying yelling and long, high-pitched horns, then volleys of arrows. Even as they closed for hand to hand combat, the Welsh hurled javelins and other missile weapons on the run. In flight, they fired arrows over their shoulders at pursuers, and in a stand-off glowered and taunted the Normans in a way they had not encountered before. The Norman chronicler Giraldus Cambrensis later committed many of these findings to parchment. He wrote at length on the subject of the people of Wales and their character, and how they differed from the English and the Normans. On this particular military point he wrote:

" *They* [the Welsh] *are passionately devoted to their freedom and to the defence of their country: for these they fight, for these they suffer hardship, for these they will take up weapons and willingly sacrifice their lives ... It is a*

*remarkable fact that on many occasions they have not hesitated to fight
without any protection against men clad in iron, unarmed against those
bearing weapons, on foot against mounted cavalry. They are so agile and
fierce that they often win battles fought against such odds ... The English fight
for power; the Welsh for liberty; the one to procure gain; the other to avoid
loss. The English hirelings for money, the Welsh patriots for their country...
if they would become inseparable, they would be insuperable ..."*

The Welsh also noted how the enemy went about fighting, and contrasted
the difference in warfare one could expect in Normandy and Wales;

> *"There they fight on plains, here in rough terrain;*
> *they fight in fields, we in woods;*
> *there armour is honourable, here it is a nuisance;*
> *they win by standing firm, we by agility;*
> *they capture the enemy, we cut off his head;*
> *they ransom prisoners, we slaughter them."*

In order to reward his faithful nobles after the conquest of England, William,
Duke of Normandy, granted them any part of Wales that could be taken by
force. These men and their noble families became known as Marcher Lords,
and came to play a crucial role in the next phase of Welsh history. They could
establish kingdoms of their own, loyal to, but beyond the grasp of their
Norman king of England. They simply had to dispossess the natives. Their
initial invasions were repelled, even though the Welsh were still recovering
from the recent civil conflict which claimed so many of their nobles,
commanders and fighting men. Rhys ap Tewdwr of Deheubarth was
recognised as the leading Welsh noble by William the Conqueror, the first
Norman King of England, when William I made a personal visit and
pilgrimage to Saint David's in 1081.

King William I's death in 1087 spurred the Normans into making further
incursions into Wales, as it appeared that the new king, William II, would not
have such a firm grip on the kingdom and its nobles as did his father. Rhys
ap Tewdwr, father to 18 children, was killed in battle fending off the
Normans at Brecon in 1093. The Normans began to edge along the
borderlands, built fortifications at Brecon and crept along the southern coast
into Glamorgan. The Earl of Shrewsbury went on a more daring mission and
marched from Shrewsbury to Pembroke, claiming land and erecting motte
and bailey castles along the way, as well as a large stone castle at Pembroke.

The Normans had taken England in one day. Thirty years after their
arrival, and after a number of humiliatingly defeated attempts, they were
finally making progress west of the border, but Wales was far from being
theirs. They encountered the Welsh at a particularly weak and divided time
in their history, and assumed it was always thus. So when, in 1094, Gruffudd
ap Cynan, leader of the House of Gwynedd and born of Rhodri the Great's
bloodline, escaped from a Norman prison and rallied his countrymen, the
Normans were unprepared for the events which followed. Gruffudd ap
Cynan added forceful impetus to a nationwide counter-attack, initiated by

other nobles. His mother was a Viking noble from Dublin. Gruffudd did not hesitate to elicit Viking support and brought Norse troops into the fray against the English Crown.

The Normans were shocked at the intensity of the campaign. They suffered rout after rout. Royal English troops were sent to shore up their forces in Wales in 1095 and 1097 only to suffer the same fate. The Normans were swept out of almost all of Wales, but desperately held on to southern Dyfed around Pembroke, the coastal part of Glamorgan and segments of the border, all of which were supplied and supported from the sea and mainland England during the fighting. In 1098, the Earls of Chester and Shrewsbury struck at Gruffudd himself, in a counter-attack launched along the north Wales coast. The Earl of Shrewsbury had the singular pleasure of being killed on a beach in the Menai Straits by the King of Norway, Magnus Barefoot, who led a force against them. Records show that, as the Vikings closed on the shore in their longboats with King Magnus standing at the prow shooting arrows into the Normans, the Anglo-Norman army panicked and were *"fearful like women"*. The Vikings, fighting on the side of the Welsh, decisively crushed the English there, ending that war.

Norman-held areas in Wales saw another wave of newcomers. The rulers of these areas moved in serfs and peasants from England, Flanders and France to settle on and work the land. They acquired more territory through selective land purchase and, by judicious marriages with native nobility, sought to give their descendants a claim to the land through right of inheritance.

The twelfth century saw a cultural flourishing in Wales, with a tide of music, poetry and books, such as *'The Black Book of Carmarthen'* and *'The Book of Aneirin'*, the latter named after the Golden Age poet. Geoffrey of Monmouth wrote *'Historia Regum Britanniae'* in 1138, in which he laid out the history of the Britons and their royal succession, as he understood it, dating back to Brutus, the mythical progenitor of the race of Britons. It was Geoffrey of Monmouth who embellished and altered the story of a wise man and seer from the Golden Age of Heroes, known as Merlin Silvester, and created the famous Merlin the Magician figure at the court of King Arthur. This spawned the interest in King Arthur that has occupied such a prominent place in European literature ever since. Geoffrey of Monmouth's work was romanticised by many European writers, almost immediately after its completion by the French poet, Chretien de Troyes.

1176 witnessed the first royal eisteddfod - a cultural festival of poetry, music, singing and, in those days, skill at arms too - in Cardigan, presided over by Rhys of Deheubarth, grandson of Rhys ap Tewdwr. It was recorded in *'Brut y Tywysogion'* (The Chronicle of the Princes) thus;

"At Christmas in that year the Lord Rhys ap Gruffudd held court in splendour at Aberteifi ... And he set two kinds of contests there: one between bards and poets, another between harpers and crowders (fiddlers) *and pipers and various classes of music craft. And he had two chairs set for the victors."*

Religious orders were taking root and spreading all over this vibrant Wales, and began to tell the rest of the world about this *'natio'* as they called it. However, the subject at hand is the Welsh at war and the twelfth century saw three of Wales's most powerful rulers - Rhys of Deheubarth, Owain Gwynedd and Llewelyn ab Iorwerth. There were others celebrated alongside these great men. Iorwerth ab Owain ambushed and killed the notoriously cruel Norman lord, Richard de Clare, and all his retinue in Grwyne Fawr in Gwent in 1135. The place is marked by a cairn in a place named thereafter Crug Dial, 'the Cairn of Revenge'. Hard campaigning in the west saw the Welsh break Norman power there by 1136, with the exception of Pembroke, which remained a foreign toe-hold in Wales. Another story relates how, in 1158, Ifor Bach, Lord of Senghenydd, stole into Cardiff castle one night, swam the moat, climbed the walls of the Norman lord's tower, and quietly killed guards on the battlements before entering the Norman lord's chamber. Ifor Bach tied up the Norman lord, William of Gloucester, and his wife, then smuggled them out of the castle, lowering them down the wall while trussed up in sacks, swimming the moat with them still tied and later ransomed them, much to king Henry II's annoyance. Henry II had acceded the throne of England in 1154, the titular king of everything from Scotland to Spain.

Owain Gwynedd in the north was respectful of the new king of England, but defiant. Owain was the son of Gruffudd ap Cynan, and had reconquered much of the north for Gwynedd and seized parts of the neighbouring kingdom of Powys, which, in turn had seized English land, including Oswestry. It was one of Owain Gwynedd's sons, Madoc, who sailed west with a thirteen-strong fleet and laid a strong claim to having discovered and settled in America. Centuries later, native Americans able to converse in Welsh related the tale to arriving Europeans. Madoc, who had spent many years among the Vikings of Dublin, allegedly took some of them with him on his voyage. It is widely accepted that the Norse were the first Europeans to travel to north America. Using their knowledge, ships and maps, Prince Madoc may have led the first large-scale European settlement on that continent, centuries before other Europeans even dreamed of such voyages of discovery.

Another Madoc, King of Powys, sought English help to reclaim his lost lands. In accepting English overlordship, he hoped to gain their military backing to further his own schemes. Eliciting English support to strengthen their position in Wales became the favourite trick of the kings of Powys. This ancient kingdom had been submerged by Gwynedd and Deheubarth for two centuries and its leaders were keen to rise to their former status, but they were playing with fire and would eventually get burnt. In 1157, Powys, traditionally the weakest of the kingdoms, assisted Henry II's passage to Gwynedd to bring Owain to order. Before Owain yielded, pragmatically but temporarily, intense fighting in the south stopped Henry II's armies in their tracks. In the north, Henry II's forces suffered a crushing defeat at the battle of Coed Eulo on the north-eastern border. Around Anglesey, more fighting claimed the life of his son, also named Henry, in a naval defeat which greatly reduced English naval capability for a time. Owain ceded territories in the north-east of Wales at the peace made with Henry II in 1157.

Between 1158 and 1165, Rhys of Deheubarth resisted Henry II's attempts to subdue the south, inflicting heavy loss on the English royal armies in a number of battles.

A Flemish invasion force was slaughtered as it landed at Mwnt, probably in 1165, allegedly with estimated casualties of four thousand men, the whole invasion force. It was remembered for *"the memorable and sanguinary resistance opposed by the natives to a body of invading Flemings, who had effected a landing on part of the beach, called Traeth y Mwnt, and in the desperate battle which ensued, these invaders were defeated with dreadful carnage and their dead bodies were strewn in heaps on the sands ..."*

Rhys' forces slaughtered a number of English and Flemish communities in the west in that year, determined to stamp out their notion of establishing a land they called 'England beyond Wales'.

The Welsh, including Lord Rhys ap Gruffudd, Prince of Deheubarth, and Owain Cyfeiliog, Prince of Powys, united behind Owain Gwynedd who, with his brother, Cadwaladr, led them to victory in battle against Henry II at Berwyn in 1165. The Battle of Berwyn is an important milestone in Welsh history. The armies of Gwynedd, Powys and Deheubarth united and, assisted by dreadful weather, smashed the English army, which contained sizeable contingents from Normandy, Scotland and France. They were supported by Danish warships and funded by money-lenders and merchants from London and elsewhere. It seemed as if the whole world had turned against the Welsh, who, united, had defeated their enemies and had driven them from Welsh soil. Owain and his forces recaptured the lands ceded to Henry in 1157, utterly destroying Rhuddlan castle in the process. Following the retreat from Berwyn, Henry II burnt a number of Welsh churches and villages, killed his hostages and prisoners, and blinded two of Owain Gwynedd's sons. In appeasing the native clamouring to avenge this disgrace against God, Owain and Wales, Owain Gwynedd reassured his people saying, " ... *through what they have done, thay have made an enemy of God himself, who can avenge the injury to himself and to us at the same time."* In 1168, Owain Gwynedd corresponded with Louis VII, King of France, discussing friendship and assistance.

In the south, Rhys devastated his enemies to such an extent that they simply wished to leave. He had imprisoned the Norman military commander, Robert Fitzstephen, at the capture of Cardigan, and offered him liberty on condition that he and other Normans left Wales. Fitzstephen accepted and raised a force of Norman troops, who, together with Welsh adventurers, invaded Leinster in 1169. Their battle cry was 'Sain Daui', a Norman reworking of 'Saint Dewi', or Dewi Sant, foremost amongst Welsh saints. The Norman Earl of Pembroke, another Richard de Clare, known as 'Strongbow', also left Wales for Ireland in 1170 and was King of Leinster by 1171. Before his death in 1170, Owain Gwynedd had increasingly referred to himself as 'Prince of the Welsh', instead of 'King', the first to do so. Welsh noble society underwent another important reform.

Since the time of Rhodri the Great, slayer of Vikings, Wales had evolved from a land of many petty kingdoms, to a land of five and then three powerful kingdoms; Gwynedd, Deheubarth and Powys. On the death of Owain Gwynedd, his second son and successor, Dafydd, took the title 'Prince of North Wales'. In response, Rhys of Deheubarth, the most powerful, feared and respected man in Wales called himself 'Prince of South Wales'. All other lands, including once great Powys, would hereafter be subservient lordships on the fringes of the two principalities which ruled Wales.

It is clear from documents of the time the Welsh were gaining a fearsome reputation abroad. Henry II wrote to a Byzantine Emperor, telling him:

" *A people called the Welsh, so bold and ferocious that, when unarmed they do not fear an encounter with an armed force, being ready to shed their blood in defence of their country, and to sacrifice their lives for renown ...the Welsh are a wild people who cannot be tamed.".*

The Archbishop of Canterbury reported to the Pope of the tenuous hold that the church had over the Welsh, saying:

" *The Welsh are Christian in name only ... they are barbarians."*

He was not making any accusations of illiteracy, given Welsh literary and musical output of the time, but of the existence of a semi-wild, native version of Christianity which he abhorred as much as he abhorred the natives. There is much evidence that Christianity in Wales was mixed with or replaced by druidic practices, which were still important amongst the Welsh. It should be said that the monasteries within Wales played a significant role in this mixing of old and new religious practices.

Richard the Lionheart, renowned fighter and King of England between 1189 and 1199, took many Welshmen with him on the Third Crusade and recalled in glowing terms their natural prowess as warriors and constant readiness for war. Though sometimes scornful, he wrote of them;

> *"For though they may be routed today, ... tomorrow they are ready for another campaign, quite undaunted by their losses... they are deterred neither by hunger or cold, fighting does not exhaust them, nor adversity cause them to despair: after an overthrow they immediately rise again, ready to face the hazards of warfare once more..."*

He also noted that they tended to shun armour, which reminds us of their ancestors going to war naked against the Romans. The Crusades opened up a whole new international theatre of war for the Welsh, who exploited this opportunity to the full. Professor R.R. Davies evocatively described the Welsh as *"the Gurkhas of medieval Europe"*. It is an image supported by a good deal of evidence. Their impact on the battlefield was felt far and wide.

Not only were the Welsh making their presence felt on foreigners abroad, but also on foreigners in Wales. King John noted in anger and dismay that an

A Land of Many
Kingdoms with the
Three Major Kingdoms

môn

rhos

tegeingl

rhufoniog

GWYNEDD

penllyn

edirnion

meirionnydd

arwystli

POWYS

ceredigion

gwortheyrnion

maelienydd

elfael

buellt

ewias

DEHEUBARTH

seisyllwg

brycheiniog

erging

ystrad
tywi

dyfed

gwent

glywysing

gwyr

morgannwg

increasing number of Normans in Wales, seduced by the people and culture of the land were 'going native', or, "becoming cymricised", as Gwyn Alf Williams put it. Some stayed loyal to the Anglo-Norman kings in England, but many became cymricised in their thinking, language and culture. The monasteries were a case in point, planted into Wales to bring the natives to peace and understanding. By 1212 King John was calling them *"our [England's] enemies"*, so fervently pro-Welsh had they become. Impressed by Welsh music, literature and eisteddfods, the monastic orders were the first to record that the Welsh, only just being revealed to the outside world in any detail, had a very well-defined concept of their *'natio'* and *'patria'*. They wrote that there was a unified concept of Welshness. Irrespective of factional feuding,- common in any society throughout history, a thoroughly mature idea of the Welsh nation had already existed for a very long time.

The monks recorded that the Welsh would sometimes refer to themselves as *'Brython'* (Briton), but more frequently *'Cymro'* (Welshman). The monks often wrote in French, calling the people of Wales *'Galois'* or *'Galeys'* and, at times, interestingly mixed French and English, naming the country *'La Natioun del Walsherie'*.

It was not just the religious orders that were seduced by Wales, indeed, the descendants of the Norman nobleman, Gerald of Windsor, and his Welsh wife - the famously promiscuous Nest, daughter of Rhys ap Tewdwr, King of Deheubarth, were the Fitz Gerald dynasty. They had the following rallying cry:

> *"Who penetrate the enemy's strongholds?"*   *" The fitz Geralds!"*
> *"Who protect their native land?"*   *"The fitz Geralds!"*
> *"Who do the foemen fear?"*   *"The fitz Geralds!"*
> *"Who are assailed by envy?"*   *"The fitz Geralds!"*

One of the Fitzgerald dynasty, Giraldus Cambrensis, showed where his sympathies lay when, in 1188, he wrote;

> *" Our British race ... defending their liberty against both Saxons and Normans by continual rebellion, has up until today thrown off the yoke of servitude by strength and arms."*

Llewelyn the Great

At the very end of the twelfth century Wales was again divided between warring factions. In 1194, Llewelyn ap Iorwerth manoeuvred into a position to inherit the throne of Gwynedd by defeating his uncle Dafydd in battle. By 1196, the 24 year old Llewelyn I was on the throne but was not universally recognised until the death of his cousin Gruffudd in 1200. In 1197, Rhys of Deheubarth, Prince of South Wales, died and his sons wrestled for power in the south. This internal conflict broke the power of Deheubarth forever, leaving Gwynedd the major power in the land. In 1198, Gwenwynwyn of Powys was eager to prove himself, claim a princely title and show that Powys was a match for anyone, even Gwynedd. He went to war with the Marcher dynasties of Mortimer and de Braose, and lost a bloody battle at Painscastle. It was William de Braose, who, in 1175 arranged a feast to celebrate peace between the beaten Marcher dynasties and the Welsh nobles of the south - east at Penpergwm.

Abbey Cwm Hir courtesy Lise Hull

Treacherously, as at Hengist's feast, the guests, led by Seisyllt ap Dynwal, were attacked and massacred by de Braose's troops. All but one of the seventy Welshmen died, Iorwerth ab Owain dramatically escaping after a bloody fight. Llewelyn I was shrewd, swearing an oath to King John in 1201, and marrying his illegitimate daughter Joan in 1205. He then annexed southern Powys and northern Ceredigion after defeating Gwenwynwyn and his allies in battle and putting them to flight. Llewelyn I also had a score to settle with the Scots, who had sent their royal forces to help Henry I and Henry II attack north Wales. The Welsh had borne a grudge ever since. He led a Welsh contingent on King John's invasion of Scotland in 1209. After observing them in a number of actions, King John decided that the Welsh were his most dangerous enemies and took an army to Gwynedd in 1211 to remind Llewelyn I who was king.

The minor Welsh lords backed away from supporting Llewelyn, judging that it would be better to have a distant overlord who would not interfere with their own affairs, rather than the aggressive, burgeoning power of Prince Llewelyn I of Gwynedd in the next valley. With his support waning, Llewelyn had little choice but to concede to King John, who promptly began building castles throughout Wales, his intention to subjugate the Welsh then obvious. In defiant refusal to accept the actions of King John, the lords who had left Llewelyn unsupported, flocked back to him. The Welsh went into immediate revolt in 1212, destroying the castles King John had just built and assaulting English border strongholds. King John offered one shilling for the head of every rebel. Records show that he was obliged to pay out the princely sum of six shillings in the south during this period. Llewelyn opened negotiations with Philip II, Phillippe Auguste, King of France and gained the support of the Vikings of Dublin. The barons of England also revolted against the Crown, and, after Llewelyn seized Shrewsbury in May 1215, he was among them at Runnymede when John was forced to sign the Magna Carta in that year. The Lords of Powys, the middle border, Gwent, Morgannwg and Deheubarth proclaimed him their prince. The following year, Llewelyn the Great held a

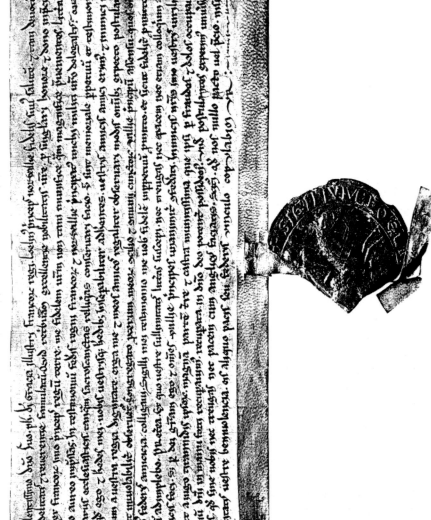

The Treaty between Llywelyn I and the King of France

TRANSLITERATION OF TEXT IN LATIN
CONFEDERACIO LOELINI PRINCIPIS NORWALLIE CUM DOMINO REGE FRANCIE.
Circa AD1216

Excellentisimo domino suo Philippo, Dei gracia, illustri Francorum regi, Loelinus princeps Norwallie fidelis suus, salutem et tam devotum quam- debitum fidelitatis et reverenffle famulatum, quid retribuam excellentie nobilitatis vestre pro singulari honore et dono inpreciabili, quo vos, rex Francorum, imo princeps regum terrej me fidelem vestrum non tam mun fice quam magnifice prevenientes, litteras vestras, sigillo aureo impressas, in testimonium fedris regni Francorum et Norwallie principatus, michi, rniliti vestro delegasti;s, quas ego in armatiis ecclesiasticis, tanquam sacrosanctas relliquias conservari facio, ut sint rnemwiale perpetuum et.tes'dmonium inviolabile quod ego et heredes mei vobis vestrisque heredibus inseparabiliter adherentes, vestris amias amici erimus et inimici inimicis. Idipsum a vestra regia diglutate erga me et meos amicos regaliter observari, modis omnibus expecto postulans et expeto, quod ut inviolabiliter observehr, congregato procerum meorum concilio, et cornmuni cunctorum Wallie principum assensu, quos omnes vobiscum in hujus federis amicicia colligavi, sigilli mei testimonio me vobis fidelem in perpetuurn promitto, et, sicut fideliter promitto, fidelius promissum adimplebo. Preterea ex qou vestre sullimitatis litteras suscepi, nec treugas nec pacem, nec etiam coll quium aliquod cum Anglicis feci. Sed, per Dei gratiarn, ego et ornnes Wallie principes unamiter confederati, inimicic nostris, imo vestris, viriliter restitunus et a jugo tirannidis ipsorum magnam partem terre et castra munitissima, que ipsi per fraudes et dolos occupaverant, per auxilium Domini in manu forti recuperavimus, recuperata in Dornino Deo potenter possidemus, unde postulantes expetimus universi Wallie pnncipes, quod sine nobis nec treugas nec pacem cum Anglidc faciatis, scitwi quod nos, nullo pacto vel precio, nisi precognita voluntatis vestre benevolencia, eis aliquo pacis seu federis vinculo copulabimur.

ENGLISH TRANSLATION
THE COVENANT OP LLYWELYN, PRINCE OF NORTH WALES, WITH THE LORD KING OF PRANCE.
Circa AD1216

To our most excellent lord Philip, by the grace of God, the illustrious King of the French, Llywelyn, Prince of North Wales, his friend, sends greeting and such devotion as the debt of fealty and respectful service, which I will repay the excellency of your nobility, on account of the singular and priceless gifts, which you, King of the French, even prince of that country of kings, outstripping me, your friend, not more munificently than magnificently, have sent me by your knight, your letters, impressed by your golden seal in witness of the alliance of the kingdom of the French and the principality of North Wales, which I, before an assembly of clergy, even upon the sacrosanct relics swear to observe as they will be a perpetual memorial and an inviolable testimony, that I and my heirs, cleaving inseparably to you and your heirs, shall be to your friends' friends, to your enemies' enemies. This itself therefore stipulating, I expect and ask from your kingly dignity to be royally observed in every manner towards me and towards rny friends, and in order that it may inviolably be observed, having called together a council of my chieftains, and with the common consent of all the princes of Wales, all of whom I have joined with you in the friendship of this treaty, I promise you, under witness of my seal, fidelity in perpetuity, and as I thus faithfully promise I will carry out my promise more faithfully. Moreover, since I received letters of your excellency, I have made neither truce, nor peace, nor any negotiation whatever with the English. But, by the grace of God, I and all the princes of Wales, unitedly confederated, will manfully resist our enernies, even yours, and by the help of God and with a strong hand, we will recover from the yoke of the tyrants themselves the great part of the land and the strongly fortified castles, which they by fraud and guile have occupied. And being recovered, we will powerfully hold [them] in the Lord God, whence stipulating, we, the princes of all Wales, desire that without us, neither truce nor peace will ye make with the English, [for] let it be decreed, that by no pact or reward, unless by the foreknown kindness of your wish, will we be joined to tbem in any peace or treaty.

parliament, at Aberdyfi. He took the Anglo-Norman castles at Cardigan, Carmarthen and elsewhere. Brecon, Swansea and Haverford all came under sustained pressure from Llewelyn.

The English made peace at the Treaty of Worcester in 1218, which recognised Llewelyn's authority, but officially took away his claim to certain parts of the country. In practice though, these areas still recognised him as Prince of Wales and paid homage accordingly. The English plotted against him though, and within five years of the Treaty of Worcester again made war on Wales under the auspices of individual Marcher action, backed up by royal forces. They began by attacking and seizing Welsh castles and land. Llewelyn's appeals for rectification of this injustice through the proper channels proved fruitless. Military action was again called for. An invading army under Justiciar Hubert de Burgh was smashed at Ceri in 1228. In 1231 Prince Llewelyn led his forces on another successful campaign, winning victories at Neath, throughout Glamorgan and at Brecon. King Henry III appealed to Anglo-Norman nobles in Ireland to come to his aid against Llewelyn of Wales, offering them whatever lands they could take as reward.

This strategy failed completely, as the nobles in Ireland had no desire to take to the field against the Welsh under Llewelyn, and none came. The English were forced to cede land to Llywelyn by treaty in 1234. At that point, he held even more land than he had during King John's reign. Members of the Anglo-Norman aristocracy desired to marry into his royal line, and did so. The fact that leading members of the French-speaking dynasty of Norse origin, which held sway from Scotland to parts of the Mediterranean, wished to be part of his House and line, serves as a measure of how successful and respected Llywelyn was. He hanged one of them, his son's father-in-law the powerful Marcher lord, William de Braose, for trying to seduce Llywelyn's wife, Joan.

When Llewelyn's son, Dafydd, became prince on Llewelyn's death in 1240, Henry III immediately moved against him, thinking him less formidable than Llewelyn the Great, as Llewelyn I came to be called. Dafydd fought back though, and the war between them was surprisingly fierce. Even though Henry III had the stronger forces, he did not go for an all-out attack - his best chance of victory, and so failed to defeat Dafydd. Majority opinion suggests that Henry could well have won, but at too great a cost, indeed, if at all. Wales had been the graveyard of many English armies in the past and the spectre of defeat loomed large over the whole venture. It had been Llewelyn the Great's last achievement, to have his son recognised as his sole successor under the 'primogeniture' inheritance system, where the eldest son is the sole inheritor, rather than the traditional Welsh system of 'gavelkind', where all lands are divided among family members. Dafydd died suddenly without issue in 1245 and technically the land could be claimed by the crown. Some evidence suggests he was poisoned by Crown agents, we can not be sure, but the timing of his death, and that of his wife shortly after, was extremely convenient for Henry III of England.

Llewelyn II

However, by 1246, Gwynedd had independently chosen a new ruler, a grandson of Llewelyn the Great through another of his sons. Llewelyn ap Gruffudd became Prince Llewelyn II. Henry III made peace and recognised his position in Wales. He insisted, though, on retracting Gwynedd's borders and attempted to treat it like a lordship in England. Clearly, this was a peace which would not last.

In 1255, Llewelyn went to war against his brothers, Owain and Dafydd. At the battle of Bryn Derwin, he defeated and imprisoned them for a time, to allow them to cool their heels. He was then the sole ruler of Gwynedd. Welsh inhabitants of neighbouring territories claimed to be 'oppressed by the king of England' and requested Llewelyn II's intervention in their lands. He duly did so in 1256 and then went to war in the rest of Wales. His allies in Deheubarth won a crushing victory over Henry III's armies near Llandeilo in 1257, where Henry III's general, Stephen Bauzin, lost nearly three thousand men on the battlefield. Henry III counter-attacked in Gwynedd in the same year, but failed to achieve the success he needed. By 1258, Llewelyn and his allies had not only reconquered those parts of Wales outside direct Welsh rule, but the native nobility had sworn allegiance to Llewelyn II in a ceremony, and proclaimed him head of state. Llewelyn II's regime then set about developing and implementing the apparatus of modern statehood. While Henry III was busy with Simon de Montfort and the Barons' Revolt, Llewelyn consolidated his powerbase within Wales. From 1262 onwards he pushed ever forward, invading Maelienydd and part of the border Marches, dispossessing elements of the powerful Mortimer family. His brother, Dafydd, having been freed from prison, deserted the cause, but other lords rallied to his banner later in the year. In 1263, he moved south and swept into Brecon and Abergavenny.

During this campaign in the south, Llewelyn suffered a defeat at Blorenge, but the people of the area came over to his cause and asked him to be their sovereign. Simon de Montfort, acting head of the English government, having defeated Henry III at the battle of Lewes in Sussex the previous year, recognised Llewelyn II as Prince of Wales and rightful leader of the Welsh nobles in 1265. Llewelyn married Simon de Montfort's daughter, Eleanor. At the time it was a shrewd decision. When Henry III regained control of England, with de Montfort's defeat and death at the battle of Evesham later in 1265, the wisdom of the marriage may have appeared questionable. Henry, too, made peace with Llewelyn at the Treaty of Montgomery in 1267, effectively a ratification of the accord with de Montfort. Henry III's forces at Evesham had been led by his son, Edward, the future Edward I. There was more fighting in south Wales from 1267 to 1271, as Llewelyn II captured tracts of lands from the Marcher lords of the south. Llewelyn was gaining both land and enemies, and his treacherous brother, Dafydd, again deserted him.

Llewelyn the Last (Llewelyn II) courtesy Martin Green

By 1276 a dispute with Edward I, king since 1272 but who only returned to England to be crowned in1274, again threatened to bring war between Wales and England. English writers and historians make the charge that Llewelyn II repeatedly provoked Edward by not attending his coronation and by 'ignoring' five summonses to come to court and pay homage. In fact, Llewelyn had agreed to pay homage but sought to delay doing so until a more favourable time. By that he meant that he did not feel safe presenting himself at a court where vengeful Marcher lords defeated and dispossessed by Llewelyn were congregated. Edward's royal court also harboured Llewelyn II's perfidious brother, the hot-headed Dafydd, and another noble from Powys whose plot to assassinate Llewelyn had already been uncovered. In 1275, a year after his coronation, Edward I moved provocatively against Llewelyn, capturing and imprisoning Llewelyn's wife as she sailed to safety in France. She was still a prisoner while Edward I, still demanding homage, gathered an army in 1277. Given these circumstances, Llewelyn's reticence is understandable. Llewelyn II, Prince of Wales, wrote three times in three months requesting a peaceful solution and a realistic scenario in which he could pay homage to the seemingly deaf and blind Edward I.

In the spring of 1277, in spite of Llewelyn's pragmatic, peaceful overtures, Edward I, spoiling for a fight, set out with an army of sixteen thousand men, over a hundred of which were nobles. To put this into perspective, William of Normandy arrived at the battle of Hastings two hundred years earlier with twelve thousand men and twenty nobles. This was the biggest Anglo-Norman army ever seen in Britain. Edward's army was supplied and reinforced from Dublin and Chester. English armies despatched on *'chevauchées'*- large sweeps by mostly mounted armies- to fight in France during the Hundred Years war rarely numbered more than six thousand men at a time.

By November 1277, Edward's sixteen thousand-strong army had fought their way into Gwynedd and made Llewelyn sign the Treaty of Aberconwy to bring an end to a conflict he was determined to avoid in the first place. According to the terms of the treaty, Llewelyn was shorn of several of his conquests and agreed to grant land to his now reconciled brothers, Owain and Dafydd. Edward I claimed to have gone to war with Llewelyn II, at great expense to the English crown, in order to protect and ensure the interests and rights of Owain and Dafydd, who, under ancient Welsh inheritance law were entitled to some of their father's estate. Such an absurd, flimsy and patently untrue 'justification' from Edward I was hardly worth proclaiming, and would be laughable if the consequences had not been so serious. Llewelyn was allowed to keep the title 'Prince of Wales' and the homage of most native nobles, whom he consulted at the parliament he summoned, called 'Y Senedd', the Senate.

Edward I now began his infamous castle building programme in Wales and oversaw the imposition of punitive anti-Welsh laws which created a two-tier system in the country.

Castles were built in a girdle around around the coastal fringe and borders, called "The Iron Ring of Castles" in an attempt to place a defensive cordon around the uncontrollable interior. By 1278, the Welsh outside Llewelyn II's lands were pleading with him to release them from the state of servitude which they suffered under the king's law. Dafydd, by all accounts a firebrand, almost ignited conflict in 1280 with his spirited protestations in defence of Wales and its people in the face of English oppression. Edward I's policies and behaviour towards Wales provoked the Welsh time after time, even on a daily basis. In March 1282, the Welsh erupted in rebellion, led by Dafydd in the north east. In just five days the revolt spread from north east to south west and Wales was once again consumed by ferocious warfare. Llewelyn II stayed uncommitted to the rebellion until his wife died giving birth to their only child, a daughter, Gwenllian, on 19th June 1282.

In this troubled state of mind, grieving the loss of his wife, Llewelyn did not hesitate to declare war on England and superbly marshalled Welsh forces. The Welsh took a number of Edward's fortresses by storm, some of which he had only just built. They trounced a large English army under Gilbert de Clare and repeatedly thrashed attempted English invasions in the centre of the Marches and on the high ground along the border. In November 1282, Llewelyn's army slaughtered the army of Luc de Tany, Seneschal of Gascony, as he launched an attack on Llewelyn II at Aber. De Tany was acting on Edward I's orders, and the attack took place during a truce called by Edward, King of England.

Even putting the treachery of de Tany and Edward aside, the negotiations during the truce went badly. The English ambassador and Archbishop of Canterbury, John Pecham, could not understand why Llewelyn and the Welsh were in revolt. He tried to buy off Llewelyn with offers of land and high positions in England, and of course, a large sum of cash if he would just surrender his territories to the Crown. Pecham had missed the point entirely and wrote to the nobles of Gwynedd, somewhat arrogantly, telling them;

> "... [you live] *in your little corner of the world. The rest of humanity scarcely knows that you are a people."*

Pecham scoffed in correspondence to English counterparts;

> *"The Welsh, being sprung by unbroken succession from the original stock of Britons, boast of all Britain as theirs by right."*

During the negotiations, Llewelyn explained that the Welsh did not wish to be oppressed by Englishmen and their laws, but wished to live by their own customs and laws, under their own leader, in their own language, in their own country. To English amazement, Llewelyn flatly rejected their offer. The nobles of Gwynedd, calling themselves the '*Walenses*', also sent the English a letter which indicated the depth of their convictions. The letter is a classic and should be a national treasure. There are numerous translations from the original latin text, some translations vary considerably from one another, one version, amongst other things, stated that:

> " *The Prince can not throw aside his inheritance and that of his ancestors in Wales ... the people would rather die than do homage to the English, whose language, way of life, laws and customs are unknown to them ... his* [the Prince of Wales'] *council will not permit him to yield ... the Welsh will not do homage to any stranger ... English treatment and ways are harsher than those of the Saracens ..."*

This declaration by the nobles of Gwynedd is a gritty precursor to the Scots' Declaration of Arbroath in 1320. The themes expressed are very similar, as is some of the wording. That is not to detract from the Scots' fine reputation. Theirs is another story.

By 11th December 1282, Llewelyn II had moved south with a few retainers to meet a large part of his army, massing for an attack on the middle of the border. At Cilmeri, on the banks of the river Irfon, he was ambushed as he drank from a well at dusk. He was hit in the side with a spear as he fought with a number of men, brought to the ground and killed. He was decapitated and his head taken to London and set on a spike for all to see. His body was buried in Cwm Hir abbey, near Cilmeri. There is debate as to whether it was just a chance skirmish or an assassin's ambush. Some historians claim that the

English were simply spearmen on patrol, but then why was such a group of men patrolling there precisely ? They were in Wales, in the vicinity of a large Welsh army. How would simple soldiers have recognised Llewelyn II ? Common soldiery had no access to their leaders, nor foreign heads of state. The Norman lords and knights present, Mortimers chief among them, claimed they knew exactly who their opponent was, and that some of them had nobly defeated Llewelyn in a duel. We know he was not defeated in a duel, that being a one-on-one fight, and could not have been killed by the nobles alone, unless these nobles fought with simple peasant's spears instead of swords, as Llewelyn's side bore a spear wound.There is some credence to the story that Llewelyn was undertaking a secret meeting with the Mortimers and went unarmed, as agreed, in good faith. Once there, he and his eighteen retainers, were ambushed and killed by the nobles Roger and Edmund Mortimer, John Giffard, Roger L'Estrange and their troops.

The evidence indicates he was rushed by soldiers and nobles alike in a desperate fight, typical of an ambush. Edward I bankrupted England in pursuing this pointless war, and pressed on with even bigger armies than in 1277. Dafydd took over the mantle of command and after months of bitter fighting, was captured and hung, drawn and quartered at Shrewsbury in October 1283. Dafydd's head was also set on a spike in London, tradition has it, next to that of Llewelyn, remembered by poets as *"the dead lion"*. Edward I and his vast smothering armies began a vindictive campaign against the demoralised and defeated Welsh. More of his punitive laws, enshrined in the 1284 Statute of Wales Act, added to in the 1294 Statute of Rhuddlan, and huge fortresses simply worsened the situation, keeping raw wounds open. England was dragged deeper and deeper into debt pursuing the conclusion of Edward's campaign in Wales and exorbitant castle building programme.

The Norman-English under their French-speaking king not only massacred Llewelyn's soldiers who, on hearing of his death sought only to return to their homes, but thousands of Welsh men, women and children in many locations throughout Wales. Thus began the occupation of Wales.

Occupation, Apartheid and Rebellion

Edward's determined policy of castle construction went ahead at massive expense. It was all very necessary, claimed the authorities, whose chief architect, Master James of Saint - Georges - d'Esperanche from Savoy, justified it with the glib tautology " *because Welshmen are Welshmen*". The cost of the wars against the Welsh added up to over a third of a million pounds, which is almost incalculably high in today's money. England was bankrupt and heavily committed with troops in Wales before Edward I made war on Scotland and France. On top of that, the annual cost of maintaining castles and garrisons in Wales, before accounting for other operations, such as bringing a thirty-five thousand strong army to Gwynedd to deal with the rebellious natives in 1295, was almost double the annual sum of taxes gleaned from the country. Llewelyn II's entire extended family was persecuted, imprisoned and murdered. His daughter, Gwenllian, was sent to a priory in Lincolnshire, where she lived as a nun until her death in 1337. While the adults of Llewelyn's line were treated without mercy, many of the children were also tortured to death. Some of the children of the royal family were suspended in cages outside towns and castles and starved to death in public. Some though were simply imprisoned until death.

One of Llewelyn's nephews was imprisoned at the age of seven and locked in a box, " *like a mouse*", at night. At the age of thirty, he arranged to have a letter sent to Edward I, King of England, asking permission to play on the grass he could see outside the cell he had never been allowed to leave. One branch of the family escaped to France however, having lived for many years in the south east of England. Edward I carried out numerous massacres of hundreds of people at a time, all across Wales. English records claim to have mainly killed Welsh men, in an attempt to cut off *"the flower of Welsh manhood"*, and destroy the next generation. Many hundreds of women, children and old people were also executed in Edward's reign of terror. So appalling was the extent of these massacres, that even John Pecham, Archbishop of Canterbury, wrote to Edward, reproaching him for the excessive killing.

Edward I is warmly remembered in England as a conqueror. Closer analysis in the context of lasting military achievement, unbridled by jingoism, must surely reappraise him as somewhat of a fool. Edward I, an illiterate monoglot French-speaker, had the most powerful and well-equipped army in Europe at his disposal. He organised a very costly campaign against an enemy which repeatedly stated its desire not to fight and agreed to the terms demanded before he attacked in 1277, on the supposed premise of defending two men's rights under ancient Welsh inheritance law. Again in 1282, he spent more money than had ever been spent before on a campaign, against the same enemy, not brought to peace but pushed into rebellion by the ridiculous terms of a treaty which had concluded an unwanted war just five years earlier. The massive outlay, and ultimate cost to England, was surely not worth the final reward. Wales was unlikely to invade England, threaten the Crown or cause any problems beyond its own borders. Moreover, Wales was not of strategic importance, nor did it provide any great wealth or prize at the end of a campaign. This was not the case with Scotland and France however, but having found Wales a much tougher and draining opponent than expected, England's capacity to make war on these larger enemies was severely reduced. The damage subsequently inflicted on these other countries by Edward I, 'Hammer of the Scots', was not enough to prevent the Scots and, over the course of the years, the French, from having the last laugh, by reclaiming all that the English had taken.

In addition, until Llewelyn II's death in December 1282, enormous English armies had been consistently humiliated in battle by considerably fewer Welshmen. This humbling of the English went on for some time, across the whole of Wales, a poor country with a small population. So, in looking at

Edward's achievements objectively, we can say that he subdued a nation which was no threat to his, sacrificing thousands of his men in so doing, as well as ruining his country financially and gravely weakening its ability to realise lasting victories against other enemies. Without a doubt, these are not the achievements one associates with a great monarch. One must therefore conclude that, for all his strutting, aggression, and bluster, Edward I failed to measure up against any foreign power even approaching the size and eminence of England.

Edward's second campaign has been called 'the conquest of Wales', though 'occupation' would be a more accurate term. Away from the columns of armoured troops and beyond the castle walls, the king's writ counted for little. Wales was not assimilated by England, as was Cumbria, for example, it was not united to England and the Welsh were not equal or loyal subjects of the Crown. It is usually written in general histories, amid the mourning of the bards and the grief and suffering of the people, as their ancestral lands were carved up and divided amongst greedy foreign aristocrats in the wake of Llewelyn II's death, that the Welsh were simply swallowed up in defeat. Few things could be further from the truth.

The Welsh rebelled unsuccessfully but violently in 1287 and again, spectacularly, in 1294, led by Madog ap Llewelyn and a high proportion of the surviving nobles, followed by vast numbers of Welsh deserters, conscripted and armed by Edward. After initial defeats for the Crown, Edward I sent an army of thirty-five thousand men to win the peace in 1295. Near Maes Maidog in Caereinon, they massacred at least five hundred sleeping villagers on the night of 10th March, 1295. Strangely, there is no memorial for them, and this is not commemorated nationally.

After 1282, taxation of the Welsh rose by 600% in many cases. Settlements were obliged to pay a high levy, even if an area became depopulated. Under the crushing weight of their financial burdens, the people starved to death in their thousands. The 1284 Statute of Wales enshrined the first of many anti-Welsh laws, to which more and more were added, and which, by the time Owain Glyn Dŵr was defying the King of England, were suffocating the nation. There were many, but the following selection, which stood by the time Glyn Dŵr had risen, or were introduced then, covers the main constraints on the Welsh.

> The Welsh were forbidden from holding any civilian or military office.
> The Welsh were forbidden from trading outside English towns or trading centres.
> The Welsh were forbidden from owning land or property in Wales without proper licence, and were barred from owning land or property in England itself. Equally, they were banned from owning land or property within any English settlement.
> They were forbidden from carrying arms.
> Courts were not allowed to convict any Englishman, for any crime,

on the word of a Welshman. No Welshman could take any Englishman to court, or any other legal action against any Englishman.

Inter-racial (Welsh and English) marriages were forbidden. Any Englishman married to a Welshwoman was obliged to discard her or relinquish his entitlement to the position and privileges granted to him under English law.

The Welsh language was forbidden in public.

If caught in English towns after dark, Welshmen were to be executed without judicial recourse.

The Welsh were forbidden from 'holding assemblies', or meeting in groups in public.

NOTE: This was of extreme importance in the attempted dismantling of Welsh culture and social structure. Traditionally, Welsh communities held a village or regional parliament, known as a **'Cymanfaoedd'**, in which grievances were aired, matters discussed, justice delivered and the course for the common good decided as a community. These meetings would usually be held on a hilltop, or some other wild place, which was obviously highly suspicious to the English.

The people of Wales had restrictions imposed upon their movements. Bards - native tellers of folk tales, perpetuators of legends and disseminators of news - under suspicion of being fomentors of revolt and insurrection, were banned and faced prison and execution if caught.

The wealthiest amongst the Welsh could seek amendment to their status under issue of a licence. This, in effect, meant that they could apply to become English.

In another age, this would be labelled 'apartheid' and condemned as evil. Still the English could not understand why the Welsh did not wish to become English, but instead rebelled against them and desired the unshackling of their own nation. When it suited the authorities, these rules were set aside and reimposed at their whim. Land purchased by Welshmen during a lax period was seized and reappropriated by the government at times of crisis without compensation to the buyer who, after all, had broken the law. The Irish had similar laws imposed on them almost a century later in the 1366 Statute of Kilkenny. The message to the Welsh and Irish was clear, there was no place for them in any measure; politically, practically or historically. This ethnic divide was institutionalised and enforced by parliamentary law.

It is true that Welshmen did subsequently leave Wales to fight for the crown of England. For the Welsh, recruitment into royal armies would serve as an escape from a life of misery and oppression, just as it would for those Scots Highlanders who joined up en masse following the defeat of the Jacobite rebellions.

We get an interesting insight into the Welsh in battle from the recorded reactions of their employers and enemies of this period. When fighting in

France, both the English and the French noted their military exploits in effusive terms, talking of their courage, tenacity and apparent lack of concern for their own safety on the battlefield. Even when stood down, away from conflicts, they proved very difficult to control and were allegedly prone to going on drunken rampages, pillaging and vandalising all they could. On one famous occasion in 1294 they also mutinied in droves from Edward I's armies. Once armed by the Crown, they refused to embark for France and instead joined the rebellion which had just exploded across north Wales. Both the French and the English remarked the unyielding savagery of the Welsh in battle. They expressed this as both good and bad, on the one hand, it made them highly effective soldiers who tended not to surrender, but on the other it meant that they did not take prisoners and killed those that were taken. This went against the grain of contemporary warfare:- the French, English and Scots were happy to take each other prisoner for ransom and exchange. Ransom was, after all, one of the chief sources of income for the medieval commander. The Welsh however, were born, bred and blooded in the harsh realities of racial warfare: they had never enjoyed the luxury of surrendering *and* living, so, in return, had never extended such a courtesy to their enemies. For them, there was no option, so there was no dilemma.

They campaigned with the English in France and Scotland, notably at Stirling Bridge in September 1297. At that battle, we gain an insight into the character of William Wallace, leader of the Scots rebels. During the pre-battle parley, Wallace spoke to friars sent over by the English to demand the rebel surrender. There are several slightly differing versions of what he said, though the central themes are common to all recordings. One version reads:

> *"Return to thy friends, and tell them we come here with no peaceful intent, but ready for battle, determined to avenge our wrongs and to set our country free. Let thy masters come and attack us; we are ready to meet them, beard to beard."*

The Scots present admired the stubborness and ability of the Welsh in battle. They also noted, as had many others, that the Welsh wore no armour. As Edward I's army and its Irish contingent were routed off the field in disarray by William Wallace and his rampant Scots, the Welsh still held their positions. The Welsh and the Scots stopped fighting, exchanged pleasantries and the Welsh walked off with honour, leaving the field to the Scots. On leaving Scotland defeated, Edward I is supposed to have said, " *It is a good job a man does, to be shot of such shit.*" The Welsh were also involved at Bannockburn in 1314, where Robert the Bruce memorably defeated the English. The night before the battle, Edward II's Welsh contingent seized the English army's alcohol supply. They consumed it heartily then went wild, pillaging baggage wagons in a drunken rampage. Most of them missed the battle, sleeping off their indulgences of the night before several fields away. Those who could be roused and corralled to the battlefield were still drunk, and left the scene without being threatened or engaged.

After the 1284 Statute of Wales, the Welsh repeatedly petitioned the Kings of England, especially between 1305 and 1330, to be restored to Welsh law. Their appeals were repeatedly ignored, and in 1316 they rose in rebellion again under Llewelyn Bren, great-grandson of Ifor Bach. At the same time in the north, the Welsh under Gruffudd Llwyd were negotiating with Robert the Bruce and his brother, Edward, who, leading the Scots in Ireland, was seeking to build a 'Celtic Alliance' and hoping to include the Welsh. The Welsh were favourable to the idea of involvement and awaited the next move. Gruffudd Llwyd was jailed for two years in 1316 for his actions. The Scots' venture in Ireland collapsed soon after and with that, hopes of an alliance. Gruffudd Llwyd led a brief revolt in 1322.

From 1301 onwards, the Welsh continued to express their bitter discontent that the title 'Prince of Wales' had been usurped and awarded to the heir to the throne of England. It was, and still is, an honourary title awarded by the Crown, without consulting the people of Wales. At the beginning of the fourteenth century, parliament heard that Wales was rife with *"unlawful assemblies"*, particularly at monasteries, abbeys and fairs, where the people were being incited into rebellion.The 1320's and 1330's saw more petitions to restore Welsh law and conflict between Marcher lords in Wales, who vied for power at court, in England and in the Marches. One Marcher noble, Roger de Mortimer, in consort with his lover, Isabella, the French Queen of England was powerful enough to orchestrate the murder of Edward II, King of England - and first English Prince of Wales - in 1327. The English authorities monitored Wales very closely. Records show that English forces went to a state of alert in 1335, 1337, 1345, 1369 - 70, 1376- 77 and 1384 - 86, where military operations were undertaken, including the bolstering of castle garrisons, naval patrols, watchmen in town streets and along town walls. During these clampdowns, the anti-Welsh laws were rigorously enforced.

In the 1340's Wales again erupted into rebellion, causing the English to panic. Their fear is almost tangible in these extracts from official letters and dispatches of the time:

" *If the Welsh have their way, there will shortly be not a single Englishman left alive in Wales.*"

" *The Welsh are now more prone than ever to rise against the king - the English of Denbigh dare not leave the town.*"

"*The Welsh are becoming arrogant and cruel and malicious towards the English.*"

One called for immediate military assistance, fearing that " *the English will be exterminated from the land.*"

The English were puzzled by the unquenchable thirst for rebellion amongst the Welsh. They attributed it to *'light-headedness'* and a propensity for violence and hatred. Yet it is precisely because of English arrogance, cruelty and malice - to use one plaintiff's words, that the Welsh struggled so hard to free themselves. As John Davies has so succinctly put it, the English occupying parts of Wales were afflicted with *"that mixture of arrogance and paranoia which is characteristic of privileged racial minorities"*.

Wales, as elsewhere, was hit hard by the Black Death which killed at least a third of the population. It struck Wales in 1348 - 50, 1362, 1369 and 1379, sapping a nation's energy to do much, let alone rebel. Yet from the 1340's to the 1360's especially, Wales was a vibrant culture in those places untouched and untouchable by their eastern neighbours. The poetry of Dafydd ap Gwilym, musing at life, nature, Wales and women, wooed Europe with its skill and beauty. Welsh nobles devoted their time and patronage to furthering the arts in this exceptional flourishing of creativity. The Welsh were well represented in France, particularly in Bordeaux, and although Welshmen in France played a key role in much crowed-about victories for the English at Crecy in 1346 and at Poitiers in 1356, and would do so again in 1415 at Agincourt, they were increasingly finding their way into French armies, and going to war against the English.

'Mab Darogan'
'The Son of the Prophecy'

The latter part of the fourteenth century brings us another fascinating character in Welsh military history. Owain Lawgoch, or Owain of the Red, or Bloody, Hand, was the leader of two Welsh mercenary contingents in the French army during the Hundred Years War. Known to the French as *'Yvain de Galles'*, or Owain of Wales, his military exploits were to take him all across Europe, and have a lasting impact on the places in which he fought. He was even recorded in folk legend and literature in such places, particularly Brittany, France, Italy and Switzerland. In the latter, he is remembered as *'Duke Yvo'*, and features heavily - along with his Welsh lieutenants - in the work of the French writer, Froissart. A consummate war captain, Lawgoch is worthy of a higher place in Welsh folk history than he currently holds. His great-uncle was Llewelyn II, to whose title Owain Lawgoch was the legitimate heir. He made vocal claims outlining his plan to return to Wales and assume his rightful inheritance. The nobles of Wales corresponded with him, promising support. One of them, Gruffydd Sais, was executed for so doing in 1369.

Lawgoch raised an army and gathered a fleet at Harfleur in 1369, but could not put to sea due to a prolonged period of fierce storms in the Channel. The force was dispersed after weeks in port waiting for the storms to abate, and the men were contracted to fight elsewhere. The French gave him a substantial sum of money to raise an army of invasion in 1372. The condition was that he first assault the English-held Channel Islands, which the French had failed to retake in decades of trying. Owain of the Bloody Hand was master of the islands in a few brutal days, capturing the English war hero named Captal de Buch in the process. The surprised and delighted French immediately recalled him from Guernsey, and the invasion of Wales was 'postponed'. Such a valuable asset was best put to use in France, they realised, and ordered his immediate redeployment against the English at La Rochelle. His military career continued in France, while Royal promises of a real invasion fleet bound for Wales kept him in their service.

The English had to act and again resorted to underhand means. They hired a Scottish traitor called John Lamb, who joined Owain's army and wormed his way into his retinue. As the French laid seige to Mortagne-sur-Mer in Gascony in 1378, John Lamb led a team of killers who assassinated Owain Lawgoch, probably as he slept in his tent. The other three murderers with Lamb were killed in their bid to escape. The royal line of the House of Gwynedd seems to have been extinguished in the male line with his death. He was buried in a church on the banks of the Garonne in France. However, the Owain Lawgoch Society, following recent valuable research believes that he married while in France and may have produced heirs. Their interesting findings should shed light on this Welsh hero, and bring him closer to the forefront of Welsh national consciousness.

The last quarter of the fourteenth century was a time of upheaval and painful change all across Europe. The Great Schism saw a bloody rift in the Catholic church and the establishment of a second Pope at Avignon in France. Plagues, war and economic collapse generated tension and hardship across the continent. 1381 saw the Peasant's Revolt in England. In May of that year, a Royal Commission was established to review " *the condition of Wales and its people.*" Its findings led to the hurried military operations of 1384 - 86 which saw the repair and rebuilding of a number of castles and brought English troops to Wales. Although the operation peaked in 1386, it continued on a noticeable scale until 1397. Rumours of Welshmen taking a Castilian spy on a tour of Welsh castles in 1387 again brought English troops and tension to Wales.

Towards the end of the fourteenth century native frustrations in Wales were again rising to the surface. The whole country was taxed into crippling poverty and manacled by racist laws, which reminded the Welsh of their inferior and subservient status every day. The commons were starving, their language, history and culture proscribed. The nobles were also dispossessed of their land, titles and weapons. Those seeking to pursue the traditional means of advancement - high military rank and the accompanying trappings, official positions and titles, land and property ownership, a career in the clergy - or even living a life worthy of their family name, found all paths blocked. It was not until 1395 that the Church appointed its first Welshman, John Trefor, into a position of authority in Wales. He had spent long enough abroad to be considered free of the 'stigma' of being Welsh. The Welsh were legally barred from holding positions of authority in public office or administration, in their homeland as elsewhere. They did hold such administration positions though, when an Englishman could not be found to fill the role. Those that did however, trod a fine line and were rarely well received or treated by their English employers, and to a lesser degree by their fellow countrymen. The latter understood that it was one of the few doors open to Welshmen, and any nation prefers to be dominated, bullied and mistreated by one of its own, rather than by any foreigner.

Wales, as has been shown, was a warrior society with a developed and distinct hierarchy. The traditional way for men, especially nobles, to honour their ancestors' deeds and clan lands was by going to war. Medieval Wales was a highly superstitious place, where mythology, folklore and reverence for their ancestors was of paramount and everyday importance. The family line was traced over the centuries right down to mythical figures, and the deeds of every one of them known and recounted. Welshmen of the time had a number of hard choices to make. If they were to make a contribution to the family name worthy of elaborate bardic praise, how should they go about it?

If they went away to fight for the French, or anyone else, against the English, as common sense dictated, they would be far from Wales, their families and clan lands. In fighting for the French they would also be fighting for a country which made all the right noises and welcomed the Welsh with flourishing courtiers and extravagant gifts, but had never come to Wales' aid, despite many promises, including a signed and sealed alliance dating back to 1212 and the reigns of Phillipe II and Llewelyn I. That they had never honoured their promises to Wales, yet had delivered tens of thousands of troops and endless provisions and supplies to Scotland, whose 'Auld Alliance' with the French dated back to 1295, is a damning indictment of French attitudes and inconsistency.

The other alternative was to be recruited into English armies and go and fight abroad. Many Welshmen did fight for the 'Old Enemy'; in the 1380's in wars with the French and the Scots, and in the 1390's in Ireland. They were rarely promoted above the rank of esquire, a few made it to knight but none ever rose higher. The Irish under English colours had the same problem with promotion. The Scots who fought for the English, however, did not. Their nobles were partly of Anglo-Norman lineage, and thus came from a feudal system the English understood. Many were even related to their English counterparts.On his father's side, Robert the Bruce was from solid Anglo-Norman stock, while his mother's lineage was from Gwynedd. The Stewart dynasty was born from the marriage of Robert the Bruce's daughter, Marjorie, and a Norman nobleman called Walter Fitzalan, related to the Fitzalans of Arundel, nobles of the Welsh Marches. Walter Fitzalan bore the title 'Hereditary High Steward of Scotland', which was abbreviated to Walter the Steward, hence Stewart. The son of this marriage became Robert II, the first of the Stewart kings. Maintaining high rank in medieval England cost a large annual sum. Unlike the wealthier Scots, Welsh and Irish war captains were simply not rich enough to do likewise. Society at the time was hardly meritocratic.

These dilemmas and the injustice of the oppressive machinery of state assembled in Wales must have put an enormous strain on Welsh society throughout the fourteenth century. Towards the end of the century, for the generation alive at the time of Lawgoch's murder in 1378, who had not honoured their family names or homeland, the strain must have been intolerable. The bards lamented the bygone days, the heroes of the past, and pleaded with the heavens and Mother Earth to give them the saviour promised by the prophecies, the *'Mab Darogan'*, the 'Son of the Prophecy'. They searched the genealogies for a true claimant to the throne of Wales. They found such a man, and an exceptional man at that. We know him as Owain Glyn Dŵr.

OPPOSING FORCES

The English

Three hundred and fifty years after conquest, those of Norman descent still held the reins of power in England. The French language dominated the country, men of power and influence spoke French not English as a first, and sometimes only, language. They conversed with rulers from Aquitaine to Ireland, often their brothers and cousins, in their common language. By 1400, the English were claiming overlordship of Scotland, Wales, Ireland, Brittany, Normandy, Poitou, Maine, Anjou, Gascony and Aquitaine, even though certain countries, such as Wales, Scotland and Ireland, were far from being willing, or loyal, subjects. The English ruled in a number of ways: by influence, by being the dominant partner in an alliance, by occupation, by treaty or by right of possession, the territory held as part of the Norman inheritance. Their influence extended even beyond these borders. In 1367, the year of Henry Bolingbroke's birth, Castile was attacked by the English who then installed their favourite local despot, the recently deposed 'Pedro the Cruel'. Countries not under English domination had the dilemma of dealing with them, as did those parts of France not already ruled by, or allied to, England.

The English had awesome military capabilities. They could field armies way beyond the size of all opponents except the French. They were equipped with state-of-the-art hardware, from a large experienced navy to some of the most elaborate and immense fortifications the world would ever see, especially those built in Wales to subdue the rebellious natives. On top of this they had offensive and defensive siege technology and gunpowder weapons. By sheer weight of numbers, not generally by military brilliance, they could lean on and grind down opponents. Much is made of the small size of garrisons during Glyn Dŵr's war. In certain cases, for limited periods, castles were held by nominally small garrisons. Many historians note that official records do not show the true figures. The men named in castle garrison lists do not include their retainers, supporters or hirelings, nor the townsfolk or militia sheltering within, all of whom fought to protect their towns and livelihoods as the law demanded, nor the mercenaries hired to fight there. Castles could therefore be maintained with a small official garrison, given the size and involvement of other forces there. Though sometimes undermanned, they rarely stayed shorthanded for long, receiving regular large-scale reinforcement from the authorities, as the record of the war shows.

Nations such as the Bretons and the Flemish, often allied to the English, benefitted from English aid and protection, but suffered from English interference in their internal politics. The year 1378 saw the Great Schism and the installation of a second Pope. Men had to choose between the Pope in Rome and the Pope in Avignon. England, and her allies, supported the Roman Pope, France and hers, the Avignonese. In 1387, the year of the future Henry V's birth, the English again attacked Castile and France.

By 1400, the English had been technically at peace with the French for eleven years and neither side showed any real intention of altering that situation. There were, of course, privateering missions and vendettas pursued during this time by all parties. The King of England in 1400 was Henry IV, Henry Bolingbroke. He had been crowned on 29th September 1399, having deposed King Richard II on his return from another Irish expedition. Bolingbroke levelled the damning accusation of 'absolutism' against Richard, who was deposed and imprisoned. Richard had made himself unpopular in many ways. One of these was by pressurising parliament into doing as he wished, inducing the charge of 'absolutism'. One way of earning this charge was by hiring a force of Welshmen to intimidate disobedient English nobles in 1397. Parliament caved in to his wishes. Richard II had allowed Welshmen to attain and keep positions of military and administrative authority from the very beginning of his reign, even though this went against the laws initiated by Edward I.

The deposed Richard was probably murdered in early 1400 while in custody at Bolingbroke's castle at Pontefract. Bordeaux-born Richard had no children and was rumoured to be homosexual. Indeed, it was only under pressure from his nobles that he married a French princess in 1397. He was almost thirty years old and she was just seven. Henry Bolingbroke was his cousin and had a strong claim to the throne of England. Bolingbroke ruled an England in which the Crown enjoyed a state of territorial solidarity no previous monarch had experienced. This was due to a number of deaths in noble families, particularly Marcher families, after which their lands reverted to the Crown. Unusually for the time, this was not due to skulduggery, but coincidence.

Another branch of the ruling family, the Mortimers, arguably had a stronger claim to the throne than that of Henry Bolingbroke. The fourth Earl of March, Roger Mortimer - named by Richard II as his rightful successor, should the King die without issue - who was friendly to the Welsh, died in Ireland in 1398 at twenty-four years of age. He had two young sons, Edmund, the eldest, and his brother Roger. Their estate and inheritance would be cared for by the younger brother of the deceased earl, who was also called Edmund, and who took the title 'Earl of March' during his nephew's minority.

Henry IV inherited a traditional Norman ruling infrastructure. William the Conqueror had divided England between his family and twenty Norman nobles who had accompanied him on the invasion of England in 1066. He rewarded them by granting them land and gave them free rein to claim any lands they could take by conquest in Wales. Two hundred and eighteen years of conflict and defeats would pass before they could carve up Wales between them in 1284, as they had England in 1066. These lords were known as Marcher Lords and ruled their lands as kings in their own right, beyond the jurisdiction of the King of England. The Marcher States, or Marches, apart from being small kingdoms in their own right, were intended to act as a protective buffer between the King of England and his enemies in Wales. Marcher Lords relied on the king for patronage, and so were compelled to show allegiance to the Crown. This did not always happen of course, and

English nobles had as much a taste for infighting as the nobles of any other nation. They did not attempt to establish old English kingdoms for themselves, such as Wessex or Mercia, which were just as alien to the Normans as Gwynedd or the Danelaw. In times of crisis the king of England could, in theory, call upon other nobles to support him, or in most cases, go and fight for him. Henry IV's father, John of Gaunt, died in 1399. He was a vigorous military commander who had campaigned across Europe with other leading nobles of the time. His reputation and record in military matters were impeccable. His son would be able to draw on his father's ties and friendships during his reign. Although hailed as an excellent soldier, Henry IV was not a wise king, and involved himself in courtly factional squabbles instead of maintaining a regal distance. The infighting and manipulating of the various factions at court was a dangerous arena in which to manoeuvre. Anyone doing so, inevitably, won friends and enemies alike. A king could not afford to have too many enemies in his own court, but, remembering the fate Henry Bolingbroke had engineered for Richard II, he could not afford to ignore his nobles and rule 'absolutely'. Henry IV's son, also called Henry, referred to hereafter as Prince Hal, was but thirteen years old when trouble first flared in Wales in 1400.

There were two other men named Henry in the upper echelons of the English military command. Henry Percy senior, the Earl of Northumberland, was a solid military commander with many years of campaigning experience. His son, Henry Percy junior, known as 'Hotspur' for his reckless heroics on the battlefield, was reputed to be the finest knight of the age. Thomas Percy, the Earl of Worcester, Northumberland's brother and Hotspur's uncle, was perhaps the most respected of the three, a commander of long and glorious standing. Worcester was one of John of Gaunt's favourite commanders and went on Gaunt's expeditions to Castile, France and Scotland. Percy experience was based not only on glorious chevauchées through enemy territory and victories against small, badly-armed forces, but also forged in the painful crucible of defeat. In 1388, Percy-led armies were defeated by the Scots at Otterburn, a battle also celebrated in ballad as 'The Chevy Chase', and the twenty-six year old Hotspur was captured and ransomed. Years before, Thomas Percy himself was captured in heavy fighting in France, before being ransomed. Interestingly, he had been taken prisoner after losing a bloody fight to a Welshman fighting for the French.

The Percy family powerbase was in the north of England, where Henry Bolingbroke landed and gathered support when he returned from exile and seized the throne in 1399. The Percys met Bolingbroke as he landed and actively supported and encouraged him throughout his claim to the throne. The Percys organised and executed English campaigns against the Scots, and held important military commands in Wales. It was the Earl of Northumberland who negotiated with Richard II when he returned from his final campaign in Ireland. Northumberland also led Richard II into the ambush which resulted in his arrest by Bolingbroke. Henry IV would be calling on the Percys in times of trouble.

There were other powerful potential supporters with enormous retinues, both within Wales or along its borders. Apart from Henry's own large extended family, such as John Beaufort, his half-brother and Earl of Somerset, there were the Dukes of Gloucester and York, the Beauchamp Earls of Warwick, the Fitzalan Earls of Arundel, the Earls of Stafford, various Lords such as Charlton and de Grey, and knightly families including the Hanmers, the Scudamores, the Harvards.

The most powerful Marcher dynasty was the Mortimers who, since the time of Edward I had been the mainstay of English military control on the border. They had never been shy when repressing rebellions in Wales and had not dealt gently with the population in times of peace. In short, they had oppressed, killed and looted in Wales for decades. Roger de Mortimer, the first Earl of March, lover of Isabella, Queen of England, brought down and murdered the King of England, Edward II in 1327.

In 1400, the acting Earl of March, Edmund Mortimer, had been born amidst awesome portents, one of which was that his father's horses inexplicably dripped blood from their legs. As an infant, he allegedly showed a sinister fascination for cutting-weapons. He was a military man, but by 1400, in his twenty-fourth year, he had not achieved any major victories nor sustained any such defeats. Perhaps his time was about to come. The Mortimers were related by marriage to the Percys and the Fitzalans of Arundel. Welsh bards however, also recalled their distant blood link by marriage to a daughter of Llewelyn the Great. Roger Mortimer, killed in 1398, was called 'Penarglwydd', or 'Chief Lord', by the Welsh, such was the esteem in which they held him. The Mortimers had enjoyed good relations with their cousin, Henry Bolingbroke, up until he took the throne. However, as an unstable and neurotic usurper of the throne, Henry IV may well come to consider the Mortimers, with their strong claims, as potential enemies. Factional politics and rivalries would again play an important role in events as they unfolded.

By 1400, the English had been enjoying successful, if sporadic, campaigns against the French, Irish and Scots for several years. They suffered the occasional setback, but in general, English - led campaigns increased the rate of attrition on the natives. Their claim of sovereignty over these lands, first made by Henry II in 1154 was nonsensical. Otherwise, why would a sovereign's own armies be campaigning against his own subjects? It was a titular claim, perhaps even a statement of intent, these wars for possession and freedom in Europe dominated the politics and actions of the era. When considering the lasting impact of such sovereignty disputes, it should be remembered that the English monarch only dropped the title 'King of France' in the twentieth century. The small matter of some five hundred years after French victory in the Hundred Years War resulted in the expulsion of the English from French soil.

On balance, England had the men and the commanders, overseas territories and allies, a navy and state-of-the-art castles, arms and armour which vastly outstripped Welsh hardware. The English military machine also had the full gamut of troops to deploy, from spies to garrisons, from light skirmishing footmen to fully-armoured heavy cavalry, from artillery to noblemen with long years of international campaigning experience behind them. The Welsh knew this, yet they still went to war against the English.

Traitors

In conflicts, people choose sides. In all countries, in peace and in war, an element of the population will do anything to further their own personal or family interests above all other considerations. Others, for various reasons, will side with the enemy of their people. In times of war especially, these people are known as traitors. Branding someone as such is, of course, a question of viewpoint.The overwhelming majority of traitors act in their own interests, not through any commitment to a cause, and, as a general rule, they do not like endangering themselves. In Glyn Dŵr's war, traitors are very few in number, but theirs is an interesting story, and warrants being told.

Treachery comes in a number of different forms. For some, there is a fine line between the treachery implicit in non-participation, hesitation and outright refusal to choose sides. In times of conflict, people not directly involved often delay choosing sides for as long as possible. In Glyn Dŵr's war, surprisingly few Welshmen turned out in English colours on the battlefield. Only one Welsh noble actively supported the King of England. He was Dafydd ap Llewelyn, the sheriff of Brecon, also known as Dafydd Gam, meaning Dafydd One-Eye. He holds the perhaps unique distinction of being the inspiration for two parts in the same Shakespeare play. He is certainly the 'Davy Gam' of King Henry V, Act IV Scene viii, and almost certainly 'Captain Fluellen' - an English mis-pronunciation of his surname, Llewelyn, in the same play. Fluellen is the doughty Welsh Captain, much mocked for his quaint manner of speech, his gruff, abrasive attitude and constant readiness for combat, as the character 'Pistol' discovers to his misfortune. Fluellen is noted and praised for his steadfast loyalty to the king of England, hardly a Welsh trait; in fact 'Davy One-Eye' is the only role model for the part. From 1384 onwards the Lord of Brecon was Henry Bolingbroke. When he seized the throne of England in 1399, things looked promising for his loyal Welsh

The Arms of Dafydd Gam

retainer and his family. There are a number of folk tales surrounding Dafydd Gam, two of which are dealt with later in the book. He is described as being a short, squat, ginger-haired man with one functioning eye. We do not know if it was missing or badly injured. Gam held the rank of esquire, as did Glyn Dŵr, but was personally retained in the king's own retinue, and was supposed to have been knighted by the king as the Welsh retainer lay dying on the battlefield.

Other Welshmen are known to have defended the English cause in Wales, but again, so few that they can be named individually. We know this because their names were listed and kept at the castles where they served. Among those on the rosters with Welsh names were men who were half-Welsh, others who had been given Welsh names by their Marcher families, and a few genuine Welshmen. One legend from the war has one brother, a rebel, killing his own brother who was serving in the garrison at Caernarfon, in a desperate sword-fight on the walls. Another killed at Caernarfon was called Hwlcyn Llwyd. He added a new dimension to the scope of treachery as, with two other men, Einion ab Ithel and Hywel Sele ap Meurig, he plotted against Glyn Dŵr. They were not acting on behalf of the English, but for themselves. All related by marriage, they were seeking to benefit from the inevitable power vacuum should Glyn Dŵr fall. As we shall see later, one of them, Hywel Sele ap Meurig, is purported to have tried to assassinate Owain Glyn Dŵr, and paid a terrible price. There were a number of others who simply sought to profit from any opportunity presented, even if it meant unscrupulously changing allegiances, always cautious to keep their options open, ready to change course again, should the need arise. One man who benefitted financially in such a way was Gwilym ap Gruffudd ap Gwilym, a distant cousin of the Tudors of Anglesey. He bought up sequestered rebel lands, having cynically surrendered at the earliest possible moment. He later successfully sought to have his status amended under English law, so that he could be declared an Englishman.

The English sent a number of spies on Glyn Dŵr's trail. Initially, they were tasked with finding him, and later, when his movements became less secretive, they were simply to observe and report. It seems that they met with remarkably little success: for we know of only a very small number who were able to perform their duties adequately, and, to the authorities, Glyn Dŵr remained shrouded in mystery. Flintshire landowners David Whitmore and Ieuan ap Maredudd sat at Glyn Dŵr's parliaments and passed on information about the proceedings to the English. Two other spies played a more risky game. Iorwerth ab Ithel ab Owen acted as a scout for Sir Henry Conway, commander of Rhuddlan castle. Thinking he was leading Conway's troops from Rhuddlan out to ambush the rebels one day, he found the tables turned and inadvertently led the English into an ambush where he was also killed. Maredudd Ieuan Gwyn also acted as a spy for Sir Henry Conway, and paid quite a price for his master, the tale of the event being covered during the account of Glyn Dŵr's campaign.

One fascinating feature of Glyn Dŵr's war is the fact that Englishmen also sided with the enemy of their nation, and fought for the Welsh cause. It is genuinely surprising that Englishmen sided with Owain Glyn Dŵr. Some were certainly coerced, others did so to serve their own personal interests, and others for what can best be described as ideological reasons. Some leading English nobles aligned themselves with the Welsh during the war, which is detailed later. Nobles, of course, stood to gain much should the rebels prove victorious, but it is initially difficult to see why any townsmen, tradesmen or commons would take sides against their countrymen. After all, they held a position of exceptional privilege in Wales, but gave that up and risked death by joining the rebels. Similarly, Welshmen had more to gain in terms of lucrative reward and future comfort by siding with the English, and yet only one, Dafydd Gam, did so.

Some Englishmen served zealously in Welsh forces, earning the bitter hatred of their countrymen. We know of a number of examples where the English authorities executed Englishmen as Welsh rebels. They defected to Glyn Dŵr from all over Wales and the border, but especially from the south and east. Men with names such as Philip Scudamore, John Sparrowhawk, David Perrot, John Fleming, Thomas Huntley, John Merlawe, William de la Mere and Thomas le Ferrour all served. Even women, such as Isabel Lanfey, helped the rebel cause. More often than not these were landed and skilled individuals. David Perrot of Tenby, for example, was an experienced sea captain who guided rebel vessels and foreign warships through the tangle of dangerous reefs around the coasts. Englishmen even crossed the border to join the rebels. The men of Whittington in Shropshire seem to have joined up as a whole unit. Other men from border villages fought alongside the rebels, in accordance with truces made with Glyn Dŵr's men. They did this to prevent further rebel attacks on their villages. This was a perfect role reversal: after 1284, Welshmen had fought for the English to escape the harsh life they were inflicting upon Welsh settlements, and now the Welsh had a small measure of revenge. For the most part, they would claim they had been coerced if caught by the English authorities. Frequently, this was accepted, even though the authorities knew a significant proportion to be lying. The government had little choice but to accept their excuses, for in some cases they were certainly true and, moreover, the risk of executing all but the most notorious rebels was too great.

Foreign Powers

International conflicts, even civil wars, are rarely, if ever, fought out solely between the two protagonists. The goal is victory and most sides will deal with outside forces, in one way or another, to achieve this aim. Each side actively seeks to involve, or negate involvement by foreign powers, to one end or another. Foreign powers, in turn, may seek to become involved or to distance themselves from a conflict, depending on a myriad of factors, the prime being the consideration of their own national interests. All nations occupy a position in an interrelated framework of nations. All actions affect all nations to varying degrees, so all nations inevitably play a role in each other's politics, overtly or covertly, deliberately or unintentionally. Even if one nation refuses to respond to another's appeals, and retains a so-called neutral position, its actions or inactions, invariably play a role, provoking more diplomatic advances from the warring sides. This provides an advantage to one of the protagonists as well as promoting prejudices in the other.

The balance of power between Wales and England was far from equal. England was the eminent power of the time and area; Wales lacked many basic weapons, let alone anything to match English cannons, castles and siege technology. England was a very wealthy country, in both finances and resources, with the ever present possibility of acquiring more from abroad, or from its various territories or allies; Wales, on the other hand, had been financially castrated. The English population outnumbered that of Wales by roughly twenty to one. The twentieth century equivalent would represent a war, modern weapons of mass destruction aside, between Great Britain versus a country four times more powerful than the United States, in terms of population, military and financial capabilities. Even then, in order to accurately represent an equivalent of Wales in 1400, Great Britain would have to be severely impoverished and disarmed, have dozens of powerful American installations on British soil to represent the castles and share a long land border with the enemy. A war between the two, theoretically, would be very short.

Any small nation in such a situation needs to elicit support, aid, or preferably, direct military intervention from other powers. If this were not possible, the next best thing would be to encourage other nations to distract their common enemy by also rising against them, thereby weakening the enemy's potential to act strongly in one area. A last option, though equally beneficial to a small country, would be to become included in the diplomatic agenda of truces and negotiations between their enemy and another nation. There were a number of countries in the immediate vicinity of Wales who could and would have a bearing on the conflict with England. The actions or inactions of these countries would prove crucial to its outcome.

France

The kingdom of France was the other major power of the day, with the same weaponry and massive armies as the English. It was a very wealthy country which had a larger population and surface area than its rival, England, and had as many or more foreign allies. It is true that small allies can be a drain to a country, but an astutely manipulated satellite or ally can only be an asset. However, France, in 1400, was not comparable with its present national boundaries. It was divided roughly down its current middle, from Rouen to the south. Everything east of that line was nominally the possession of the King of France. Most territories west of that were English-held or allied to the English. Some areas, particularly Brittany, played a more subtle game with their allegiances, which changed in accordance with their varying needs. It should be remembered that the English elite at this time were French-speaking, still with strong links to France in terms of blood and land. They had no concept of loyalty to an image of England to which modern readers can easily relate.

They owned England; it made them rich. Going to war was par for the course for men of the day, bringing the nobles glory, and the booty, plunder and ransom they took made them richer still. During the Hundred Years war generations of Frenchmen willingly fought in their thousands for England against the king of France. It is a little considered point that while the Hundred Years war was, undoubtedly, a war between the French and the English. It was not simply a rivalry based on English antagonisms towards the French, or vice versa, as Frenchmen ruled England. Its eventual conclusion was, to a point, a question of Frenchmen uniting with other Frenchmen, instead of collaborating with England. A concept of 'France' as we understand it from its modern incarnation - more than a geographic entity but a country - simply did not exist then.

The realm of France itself was riven with pro- and anti-English factions. To simplify the matter, they can be respectively identified as the Burgundians and the Orleanists. Owain Glyn Dŵr had the misfortune of striking at the English when a cripplingly weak king sat on the French throne. Charles VI is remembered in French history as 'Charles le Fou', or Charles the Mad. He reigned from 1368 to 1422 and suffered long periods of mental breakdown, interspersed with moments of lucidity. This meant that court was pulled in a number of different directions by the different factions. These were led by the king's brother, Louis, the aggressively anti-English Duke of Orleans and in opposition, the king's uncle, the peacemaker, Philip the Bold, and on Philip's death by Charles' cousin, 'Jean Sans Peur' (literally, John Without Fear) both respectively, the pro-peace or pro-English Dukes of Burgundy. It was the Burgundians, Frenchmen, who later captured Joan of Arc and were responsible for her execution in 1431, though, historically, the blame for this has been placed upon the English.

France and England had been at peace, though still posturing and manoeuvring against each other since 1389. France had concluded a truce with the English following the frustrating failure to co-ordinate movements and tactics with the Scots in 1385. France, in spite of its evident difficulties, had the population, equipment and, from time to time, the will to match or defeat England on the battlefield or at sea. In order to succeed against England, Owain Glyn Dŵr needed to obtain the support of such a large power, if not in terms of direct, large-scale military intervention, as Scotland had, and would enjoy, then by supply, or perhaps more importantly in negotiations between England and France. This could be by personal representation or by inclusion as a non-negotiable element insisted upon by the French at future talks, truces and treaties.

Scotland

In 1400, Scotland was still independent enough to stand up to the English. Robert the Bruce, father of independent Scotland, born in 1274, declared himself 'King of Scots' in 1306 and reigned until his death in 1329. Scots had regained their own sovereignty, won mainly through military resistance and maintained through military strength, diplomacy and measured acceptance of English demands. There had been moves to create a 'Celtic Alliance' involving Scotland, Ireland and Wales in the early fourteenth century. It came to nothing in the end, but the idea had been planted in the minds of all, especially the English.

Scots had served in English armies in Wales from the reign of Henry I at the end of the eleventh century. In turn, Welshmen under Llewelyn I had campaigned in Scotland in 1209, and did so again under Richard II of England in the 1380's. The Scots raided Anglesey in 1381, an act which encouraged Welshmen to bolster English numbers for Richard II's Scottish campaign. In spite of these tit-for-tat events, relations between the Scots and the Welsh were good. Scots authors and chroniclers wrote very favourably about *'our cousins'* the Welsh, and would do so even more once war broke out between Wales and England in 1400. Scotland would be the natural first choice of ally for Wales. Scotland was close culturally and geographically, and could call upon elements of a common heritage, as well as having a bitter common enemy. There is evidence of mutual influence too, a fact overlooked today.

The 1282 Declaration of the Nobles of Gwynedd is echoed in the 1320 Declaration of Arbroath, and elements of Robert the Bruce's battle tactics seem to have been used by the Welsh thereafter. They pulled down the walls of captured castles, having burnt and vandalised as much as possible in order to deny the enemy. This mirrored Bruce's actions, most famously at Edinburgh. The Welsh did this in notorious fashion at Radnor in August 1401 and Criccieth in 1404, where they added their own touch, by slaughtering the entire garrison, a number by ritual decapitation.

Scotland enjoyed a stable and highly profitable relationship with France, who supported and supplied them. If either were involved in a war in Wales, it may well bring in the other. The possibility of a combined effort from Wales, Scotland and France in a war against England is thought-provoking. It would almost certainly have led to heavy defeat for England, or at least have forced them to seek terms in the sort of punitive truce they so enjoyed meting out. They realised what would befall them if such a union of their enemies could be brought to life. In order to avoid this possibility, the English acted in an underhand fashion, as they had in the past, and did so again during Glyn Dŵr's war and many times thereafter. They were by no means paragons of virtue: English history is littered with examples of acts of treachery, murder and shadowy dealings perpetrated by them throughout the British Isles and beyond.

In 1400, Scotland was, on paper, in a position to become embroiled in Glyn Dŵr's war. Scotland offered an avenue of opportunity worthy of exploration for Glyn Dŵr and his rebel forces, once they opened diplomatic channels with potential allies. However, Scotland had for a long time been in a state of internal crisis concerning its royal succession, a situation crucially worsened by a series of old or weak kings, which would continue to destabilise Scotland for many years.

Brittany

Brittany was still independent at the outbreak of hostilities in 1400. Often, it had been allied to, and used by, England in its manoeuvrings against France. This suited Brittany: for whilst being a pawn in Anglo-French conflicts, its strong ties to one negated any realistic possibility of invasion by the other. At times, the Bretons operated with French forces. In co-operating with both sides, it proved useful to both France and England, ensuring that neither would wish to see Brittany lost to its rival. That is not to say that it was either side's servant, Brittany defended its own national interests through alliance or neutrality. Although the Bretons were not a major force, and certainly no threat to England or France, their land forces were not to be ignored and their primary strength, naval power, was an important factor in the balance of power in the Atlantic regions.

Being allied to England, and occasionally France, did not alter the fact that the Bretons originally came from Wales and Cornwall, itself a Welsh territory at the time of the Welsh settlement of Brittany at the dawn of the sixth century. In accordance with late twentieth century fashion, some modern Bretons also claim Irish ancestry. There was an Irish element, but this was negligible compared to their, as yet unforgotten, Welsh and Cornish roots. Brittany's everyday language was Breton, twin sister to Welsh, its culture, myths and mentality were still closely linked to Wales. If the Welsh called on them in a war, would the ties of blood and kinship overcome the solid pragmatism of international politics?

Flanders

Flanders became a fiefdom of France in the ninth century. It had been saved from being overrun by the Norse, who seized many of the neighbouring parts of northern France, by the military actions of Baldwin Iron Arm, who became the first Count of Flanders in 867. By 1400, Flanders' position of a loyal and integral part of France had been questionable for some time. The Flemish had been allied to Otto of Brunswick and King John of England in their failed joint - venture against the kingdom of France in 1214. The French king, Philip IV, tried to absorb Flanders and was sternly repulsed at the battle of Courtrai in 1302. In 1323 the Flemish again rebelled against France, only to finally be defeated and restored to French rule in 1329. Flanders became a possession of the House of Burgundy in 1369. In 1384, Philip the Bold, uncle of King Charles VI of France, became the ruler of Flanders.

The Flemish became closely allied to the English as the wool trade proved increasingly profitable throughout this period. The Burgundian rulers of Flanders did nothing to discourage this. In 1400 Flanders was a wealthy and densely populated country. It should be remembered that in 1400, Ghent was Europe's second largest city with a population of 50,000, second only to Paris' 80,000. Its other major cities, Bruges and Ypres each had populations of 35 - 40,000, equal in size to London. These cities wielded impressive authority over their own affairs. They were largely autonomous from the 'Counts of Flanders', and controlled the 'Estates Assemblies'- effectively city parliaments, which were summoned several times a year. Although they paid lip service to their French rulers, in practice it was the Flemish who ran their own country and decided their own future.

During times of conflict, Flanders gave the English an extra point of entry into France. It acted as a potential diversionary target for French attacks as well as being a launching pad for attacks on north-east France and that section of the channel coast in French hands. Many thousands of Flemings moved to England, and elsewhere, to settle on behalf of the English Crown. A large number of them fought for England at sea and on land, some as regular troops, some as mercenaries. They were used by the English to settle and fight in Wales, particularly in the south-west. They were not popular it seems: they were often referred to as *'Flemish dogs'* by all sides in Glyn Dŵr's war. However, they were not all unswervingly loyal to England, a number would defect to the rebels during the war.

Ireland

The Irish would seem to be a natural choice of ally to the Welsh. Geographically, they are even closer than the Scots, and similarly, share a common ancestry with the Welsh. Modern genetic research shows that the Welsh and the Irish are the most closely related peoples in Europe. There was a history of peoples, living in both Wales and Ireland, straddling the Irish Sea. One story supposes that in the year 400, the Demetae, as the Romans recorded them, lived in south- west Wales were related to the Deisi, identified as living in south- east Ireland. One heroic tale from between 380 - 400 tells of the deeds of the British warlord, Cunedda, who came to Anglesey from Rheged and drove out the Irish peoples who were living there, as well as in north-east Ireland at the same time. The Irish, too, had come under attack by the Anglo-Normans, a century after the Welsh, and while the Welsh were still rulers of their own country. Moreover, if the English were at war with the Welsh, and possibly other powers, they would not be able to make war on the Irish or effectively enforce their law in those large areas of Ireland under English rule. Indeed, it would serve native Irish interests to see a protracted conflict between the Welsh and the English.

It should be noted, however, that Irish help was unlikely from the beginning. The Irish were to prove incapable of helping Glyn Dŵr in 1400 or thereafter. Weak, ineffectual and divided, they were never to act outside Ireland. One problem was that, even in areas outside defined English control, Norman nobles had independently seized control or were in some way related to native Irish leaders. Another was that the Irish had had a bitter lesson in Celtic alliances handed to them by the Scots under their Anglo-Norman leader, Edward Bruce, who burnt and pillaged Irish settlements, killing many Irishmen and women before their intended liberation venture collapsed.

There was a precedent for union between Welsh princes and rulers of Ireland.Unfortunately for Glyn Dŵr it was with the Vikings of Dublin, who cared little if the Welsh continued to raid and plunder the native Irish or not, as they had done for so many centuries before. Although a Welsh-English war would benefit the Irish, even if they had been able, they were probably unwilling to fight for the Welsh. The Welsh had made war on the Irish for a long time. Massive Welsh raids across the south and east in particular had plagued the Irish for centuries, some areas even suffered periods of Welsh occupation. Tales of merciless Welsh pillaging and barbarity in Ireland still survive. The earliest recorded wars between the two can be found in the Tales of the Mabinogion, some versions of which are unsparing in their accounts of the destruction of the Irish at Welsh hands. Even as late as 1399, the Welsh were fighting the Irish, mostly with the armies of Richard II of England on his two Irish campaigns of the 1390's. Although the Welsh had enjoyed good relations with the Vikings, in 1400 it was the English who held the vast tracts of Ireland the Vikings had conquered, and more. The English were later able to use Ireland to supply their beleaguered garrisons in Wales from the sea, and eventually to attack Wales from the west.

Castile

Castile, so far from Wales, barely seems worth mentioning. However, John of Gaunt led English armies in campaigns there, and a state of war had existed between the two, on and off, for some time. The English were their next door neighbours in Gascony. Castile, though distant, was a naval power to be reckoned with, which often worked in concert with the French. If the French could be pursuaded to engage on Wales' side, then Castile may well follow. The potential of having another ally, especially a strong seaborne one, was worth Glyn Dŵr's consideration.

The Welsh

Given the potential forces ranged against the Welsh in 1400, it was surely madness to go to war against such an enemy as the English? Madness or not, this is what they did. This small, poor country, utterly devoid of a standing

army of its own was virtually
unarmed in 1400. Banned from
carrying weapons, the small
population lived in the shadow of
some of the mightiest fortresses in
Europe. This small population was
still a warrior society however, and,
while the English had glorious
commanders, castles and cannon,
the Welsh had battle-hardened
fighting companies by the score.
Having served in France for both
sides, in Scotland and Ireland, and
at sea in ships' fighting companies,
Wales had a wealth of crack troops;
experienced, ready, and more than
able to form the core of an army.
Evidence suggests that as Glyn
Dŵr's campaign grew in success,
many of Owain Lawgoch's men
returned to Wales from exile in

*4 Lions Passant of Llewelyn II
Prince of Wales, colours of the House of
Gwynedd*

France with their own warbands, to honour the promises made by Owain
Lawgoch about returning to liberate their homeland.

In many cases, Welsh fighting contingents were involved in some of the
toughest, unyielding actions across Europe. The list of combatants who
repeatedly served in those campaigns makes for impressive reading. Names
which, sadly, mean little to us now, the following are but a few of the most
feared warriors of the age: Hywel Coetmor, Morgan Gethin, Rhys Gethin
and Hywel Gwynedd. The knights: Sir Gruffudd Llwyd, Sir Hywel y Fwyall
(Howell of the Axe), lavishly rewarded for his key role in the capture of the
King of France at the Battle of Poitiers in 1356, Sir Hywel y Pedolau, (Howell
of the Horseshoes), Sir Rhys ap Gruffudd and Sir Gregory Sais, were hard
sergeants in foreign armies. Others too, the Yonge family of north- east
Wales, the brothers Gwilym, Maredudd and Rhys ap Tudor of Anglesey,
Henry Don, or Dwnne, or Dun, and his family from Kidwelly, were all war
heroes of long experience abroad. Henry Don had served with John of Gaunt
in France in the early 1370's and with King Richard II in Ireland in the
1390's, and, although he only held the rank of 'esquire' in English terms, he
had a personal retinue of well over two hundred men, often more than the
lords, earls and dukes who commanded him.

It is typical of the plight of Welsh nobles of the era, though they held lowly
ranks on English muster lists, in their own land they were recognised as
barons, lords or even princes. Like many other Welshmen, Henry Don had
had his lands confiscated for actual or perceived crimes against the Crown.
His were confiscated in 1389 and restored after payment of a fine. The Tudor
brothers were praised as being *'eithefigion'* - which translates as 'the most

The Black Lion Rampart (on silver and red). The colours of Powys (Fadog), Owain Glyndŵr's traditional clan colours

reliable oxen in the plough team', and their coat of arms at this time was still that of three decapitated Englishmen. This was quietly changed to three empty helmets for a rather important event later in the fifteenth century, when one of their number seized the throne of England in battle. The English authorities certainly knew of these men of war, as did the English nobles who repeatedly recalled these Welshmen to fight in their retinues. Foreign nobles were happy to have a few battle-ready Welshmen around as bodyguards, in case they found themselves in a tight spot. There were many, many others; the footsoldiers, the archers, the light skirmishing cavalry, who passed unrecorded by name in campaign accounts and returned home once it was all over. Local nobles and commons trained for, and went off to, war in order to satisfy demanding authorities and the diverse pressures of society in Wales at that time. The ties that bind are formed through kinship and conflict, and here, we have both at the same time. Any Welsh retinue going to war would contain friends and relatives. The Welsh word for 'warband' is a cognate of the word for family or clan, 'teulu', indicating the closeness of the venture.

The Welsh have always believed that God is a Welshman, or, at the very least, on their side. In retrospect, they must concede that He has been biding his time on the sidelines for quite a while now. However, in 1400, strong elements of His representation on earth, the church and the monasteries, certainly were on the Welsh side. Cistercian monasteries, in particular, were vehemently pro-Welsh, exhorting them to independence and, if English chroniclers are to be believed, fomenting rebellion and inciting insurrection. Were they simply reflecting the opinions of their congregations or advancing their own agenda? We cannot say for sure, though the former seems more likely.

Since the murder of Owain Lawgoch and the wars of the 1380's, the bards and poets addressed their hopes and praises to one man, having traced his well-known noble lineage to north- east Wales, and the ancient kingdom of Powys. He was known by several names, depending on who was addressing him, and when. He was Owain ap Gruffudd Fychan, Arglwydd Glyndyfrdwy, Lord of Deeside and Sycharth, and various English spellings thereof, most commonly Owen Glendower. His full name, in glorious Welsh tradition, was Owain ap Gruffudd Fychan (II) ap Gruffudd ap Madog ap Gruffudd Fychan

(I) ap Gruffudd ap Madog, but the Welsh know him as Owain Glyn Dŵr, Prince of Wales.

He is very much a man of mystery. We cannot be sure of where or when he was born or died. There was, apparently, a period of intense meteor storms and comets around the time of his birth. Thus, legends say, destiny marked him for a special role in history. There are a number of places and dates given for Owain's birth. The two most commonly named are Carrog in Glyn Dyfrdwy and Sycharth near the border with England. He had a residence at both places, and after the death of his mother, Elen Goch, Helen the Red, he gained another territory on the coast, Iscoed, which included the inland area north of the river Teifi, between the castles of Cardigan and Newcastle Emlyn.

4 Lions Rampant, House of Gwynedd colours as altered and used by Oeain Glyndŵr. These colours were first raised on 16th September 1400.

Early in his life he was more commonly named Owain (of) Glyn Dyfrdwy,- translated by some as *'Glen of the headwaters of the Dee'*, *'Glen of the Sacred River'* or *'Deeside'*, rather than Owain Glyn Dŵr,- 'Glen of the Waters', which implies that Carrog, rather than Sycharth, was his place of birth. His lands had been passed down the unbroken generations of his family from before 1282, and up until he inherited them, probably in 1370, they had not been interfered with by the authorities nor had they suffered English occupation. Owain Glyn Dŵr was one of the few Welsh nobles not obliged to observe the civic rituals of courts and taxation as were other tenant nobles in Wales. He was part of a small group who did not live in the shadow of an English castle or borough. His were among the last truly independent lands in Wales, native enclaves in an otherwise occupied land. His date of birth is even more difficult to determine accurately than its location. The medieval calendar was a procession of saints' days, each day corresponded to a different saint or event, as is still the case in some Catholic countries. By offering a particular date, medieval chroniclers were making deliberate, overt allusions to character traits that the person in question shared with the relevant saint. This is all too often lost on the modern reader.

Tradition suggests the feast of Saint Matthew, 20th or 21st September, 1349, as his date of birth. It is probably incorrect, but is a date to be remembered. As that date was recorded years after Glyn Dŵr's death, it may well indicate an allusion to the biblical figure, Saint Matthew, who turned his

The three decapitated Englishmen (or Saxons), colours of the Tudors of Anglesey

back on his life of comfort and riches to dedicate himself to his calling, that of following Jesus Christ. The parallel with Glyn Dŵr's sacrifice for his nation is clear. Another date proposed is 28th May, 1354, but again this seems improbable, although it is the traditional and most widely accepted date for his birth. We do, however, have one solid lead on the question of Glyn Dŵr's birth and age. In 1386, shortly before Welshmen were barred from giving evidence in court hearings, Owain Glyn Dŵr was a witness at the scandal trial of the era, the Scrope versus Grosvenor case, a dispute about the right to bear certain heraldic insignia. Another witness at the trial was Geoffrey Chaucer. Glyn Dŵr's age was recorded as " *twenty seven years and more*". It is unclear whether twenty seven was a minimum age required to give evidence at such a trial, and that, in so conforming, he was allowed to continue, or whether "twenty-seven and more" refers to a number of months insufficient to bring the total to twenty-eight years, or whether it was the minimum reliable estimate. In any case, the latest possible year of his birth would therefore seem to be 1359.

Owain Glyn Dŵr's family and fortunes were closely involved with those of neighbouring Marcher magnates. The eminent family in north - east Wales at that time was the Fitzalan dynasty, which controlled the Arundel estates adjacent to Glyn Dŵr's homelands close to the border with England. In 1387, the Earl of Arundel himself had included Owain Glyn Dŵr, and his brother Tudor, in his personal retinue. Among Glyn Dŵr's other neighbours were the Hanmers, a knightly family of long standing. Unlike the Fitzalans, the Hanmers numbered among those Norman families cymricised by their occupation of part of Wales. Sir David Hanmer gave his children both English and Welsh names, by which each community knew them separately, and the Hanmers spoke Welsh fluently. Arundel lordship records tell us that by 1370, Elen, Glyn Dŵr's mother, was a widow. It is possible that Owain was made a ward and entered the Arundel or Hanmer households, probably the former, and was raised in refined gentry society. We cannot say for sure, but this is what the evidence suggests. There he would have received a schooling, probably in Latin, French and English, in all the things a young noble needed to know, including arms and warfare. A French knight, Boucicault, wrote this of Glyn Dŵr and his martial training:

"... cased in armour he would practise leaping on the back of a horse; anon, to accustom himself to becoming long winded and enduring, he would walk and run long distances on foot, or he would practise striking numerous and forcible blows with a battle axe or mallet.

In order to accustom himself to the weight of his armour, he would turn somersaults whilst clad in a complete suit of mail with the exception of his helmet, or would dance vigourously in a shirt of sheel; he would place one hand on the saddle bow of a tall charger and the other on his neck and vault over him ... He would climb up between two perpendicular walls that stood four or five feet asunder by the mere pressure of his arms and legs and would thus reach the top, even if it were as high as a tower, without resting either in the ascent or the descent. When he was at home, he would practise with other esquires at lance throwing and other war-like exercises, and this continually."

Upon achieving his majority, or shortly after, we know that he became an Apprentice-at-Law at the Inns of Court at Westminster. If he followed the usual course of studies, he would have been there for three to seven years in the late 1370's, possibly into the early 1380's. At the end of his studies, he did not stay on in London, as was the normal procedure for apprentice lawyers at Westminster, but returned to Wales before 1383.

The English occupation was barely a century old, a mere freckle on the face of Father Time for such an ancient people as the Welsh. Glyn Dŵr was identified by the seers and the ever hopeful people of Wales as the nation's leading noble, in genealogical terms if nothing else. He was the legitimate heir of the ancient kingdom of Powys through his father's bloodline, and, with a little bardic chicanery, a wealth of other honours were proclaimed to be legitimately his. It was highly irregular that the mother's bloodline was claimed on behalf of the son. In this case his maternal uncle, Owain ap Thomas, heir to the throne of Deheubarth, died without issue in 1360, leaving Owain Glyn Dŵr the eldest male heir to the previous generation's inheritance. Through his mother's line, he could equally claim to have blood from the Royal House of Gwynedd in his veins, even though Owain Lawgoch was undeniably the heir to the title. Interestingly, in 1304, at just six years of age, Owain Glyn Dŵr's grandfather was married to Elizabeth, daughter of John L'Estrange, one of the leading Anglo-Norman Marcher families. This could of course mean that Glyn Dŵr also had Anglo-Norman blood, but the name 'L'Estrange' or 'foreign' could be indicative of something else. It would be pure speculation to suggest that it is linked to the English perspective of 'foreigner' or 'walescer', therefore Welshman, and requires further research.

Owain Glyn Dŵr married Sir David Hanmer's daughter, Margaret, also known as Marged ferch Dafydd, in 1383. In 1384, while probably in his mid- to late- twenties, Owain Glyn Dŵr served in a Welsh contingent at Berwick-on-Tweed along with his brother, Tudor, two or three years his junior, and a number of the finest Welsh soldiers of the era, including a number of Welsh knights. Owain Glyn Dŵr was highly praised for his skill and valour in battle.

A fascinating insight comes to us from this period. Owain Glyn Dŵr, typical for the age, believed and followed the prophecies and legends surrounding the Welsh and, in particular, the mantle that was now his following Owain of Wales's murder. He had his own seer, a soothsayer named Crach Ffinant. This druid, referred to by Glyn Dŵr as ' *our prophet*', accompanied his master everywhere, even into battle. The prophet's role was to quote and interpret the prophecies as they related to Glyn Dŵr, and advise him accordingly. In 1385, Glyn Dŵr went on Richard II's expedition to Scotland, along with his brother, Tudor, Crach Ffinant and other Welshmen, notably Sir Gregory Sais and Morgan Yonge. Two of Glyn Dŵr's brothers - in - law, the English Marcher nobles Sir John Hanmer and Robert Puleston, the latter of whom had married Glyn Dŵr's sister, Lowri, were also present. A number of the most important English nobles and soldiers also went on the Scottish campaign; King Richard II, John of Gaunt, the Earl of Northumberland, Hotspur, Sir John Mascy and Henry Bolingbroke, to name but a few. One record shows that Owain Glyn Dŵr had been retained as *'scutiger'* or shield-bearer to Richard II. The mission was simple and successful. They fought, burned and plundered their way to Edinburgh, then returned home. Glyn Dŵr was again lavished with praise for his feats of martial prowess, proclaimed as " *an exemplary warrior"* and an uncommonly gifted horseman. Following one combat in particular, but clearly referring to other times in his martial career, it was written of Glyn Dŵr:

"*...he was a fierce mighty slasher, he did nothing but ride horses. Best time, in dark trappings, bearing a lance ... and a white helmet ... and in its peak, fine plumed summit, a red wing* [feather] *of the bird of Egypt. For a while he was the best soldier with Sir Gregory ...Great renown for knocking down a horseman did he win ... and felling him splendidly to the ground, with his shield in fragments.*
And the second rout was a grim battle, and his spear shattered from fury; this is remembered as a disgrace today, Candle of Battle, by the whole of Scotland; some screaming, some wretched yonder, every bad man, everyone indeed for fear of him shouting like wild goats, he caused terror, harsh he was to the Scots. Great was the path through the froth of blood, a year feeding wolves; neither grass nor dock grew, nor corn where he had been ..."

In 1386, aged "twenty-seven and more" he gave evidence at the Scrope vs Grosvenor courtcase, as mentioned previously. Sir David Hanmer, Owain's father-in-law, died just before Glyn Dŵr left on another military expedition in midsummer 1387.

That same year, both Owain and Tudor were retained as esquires by the Earl of Arundel, to serve in his personal retinue. In 1387, Owain Glyn Dŵr was involved in a fierce naval battle in the Channel, apparently involving much ship-to-ship fighting, and then took part in the raid on Sluys, burning and plundering the town and a wide area of surrounding countryside. Glyn Dŵr again attracted the attention of a number of English and Welsh commanders during this expedition, for his ferocity and fearlessness in battle. Praise was again heaped upon him, *"Canwyll Brwydr"*, 'the Candle of Battle', a beacon of warmth and comfort to his allies and an incandescent, raging danger to his enemies.

He seems to have led a quieter existence thereafter, not going on the English attacks on Castile from 1387 onwards, but devoted himself to his burgeoning family and the politics of his homeland. Glyn Dŵr's legal skills were put to good use in settling Sir David Hanmer's estates on his return from campaigning. Although again retained in Arundel's personal retinue in 1388, he did not serve in the missions against France and Castile of that year. His name is still on the muster, but inexplicably has a line through it. Unlike thousands of Welshmen, and despite some suggestions, it is very unlikely that he campaigned in Ireland in either of Richard II's campaigns in the 1390's. His former patron, the Earl of Arundel, was executed in 1397 for campaigning against the king.

We do not know for sure what he looked like. There is an image of him on his royal seal, which still exists, and a painting purported to be him as an old man not long before his death. We do not know if it is him or the poet Sion Cent. He is said to have had a number of illegitimate children, presumably before he married Margaret Hanmer in 1383. This is credible, as he was at least twenty-four years old when he married, comparatively late for the time. The earliest birth date given for Glyn Dŵr would make him thirty-four years old in 1383, which may well help to discount it as a likely date for his birth. If what we are told is true, Owain and Margaret had at least eleven children together, six boys and five girls. We know the names of all of the girls and two of the boys. They were Alys, Alis or Alice, Catrin or Catherine, Sioned or Janet, Isabel and Margaret, and the boys were Gruffudd and Maredudd. Catrin was recorded as being blonde and strikingly beautiful, and Owain Glyn Dŵr is once refered to as being *'tall, strong and fair'*. A poet named Lewis Glyncothi fell in love with one of Owain Glyn Dŵr's illegitimate daughters, Gwenllian, and wrote love poetry for her, describing her as *'Gwenllian of the Golden Locks'*, and *'Gwenllian of the house of drifted snow'*. An unverified source gives the other boys' names as Madoc, between Gruffudd and Maredudd, then Tomos, Sion and Dewi. If there were four, or more, other legitimate sons, they may well have been placed with relatives or friends, hidden amongst the community, while their father led the nation in war against England.

In 1400, Owain Glyn Dŵr was in his forties, comfortably well-off, and the owner of some of the finest houses in all Wales. It was an unusual time of life for someone to embark on a rebellion. Was it that the prophecies and the destinies envisaged for him, were gnawing at him, or that, as a Welshman, he was provoked just once too often? Whatever the case, the result was the fire and death which characterised Glyn Dŵr's war.

Glyn Dŵr's War

1400

THE UPRISING

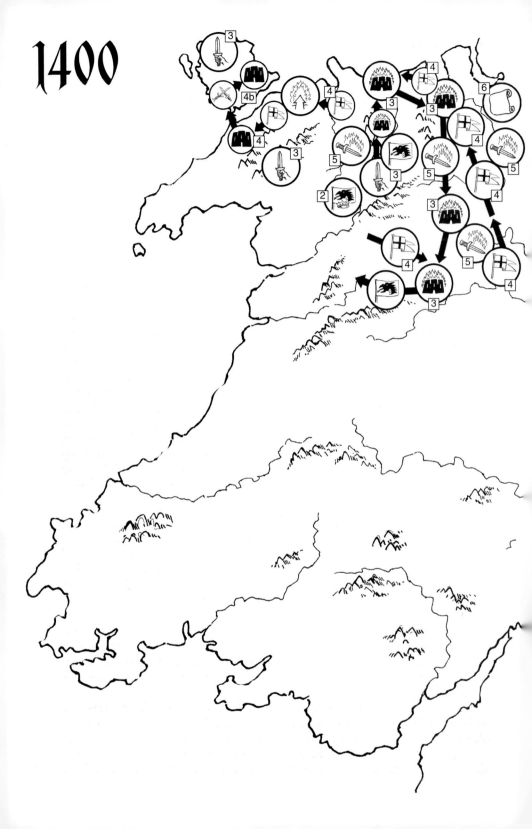

1400

[1] October 1399 to September 1400   The Final Provocation
We are told of three acts which pushed Owain Glyn Dŵr and his supporters
into rebellion. Henry IV's accession to the throne of England in September
1399 was yet another trauma to noble society which had suffered a series of
unexpected crises. A spate of deaths in Marcher society, especially in the
latter years of the 1390's, provoked changes in territorial ownership of
estates, which, in turn, provoked yet more questions of individual, and
family, allegiance. When Henry Bolingbroke was proclaimed king, tensions
rose markedly in England and Wales. While some saw no reason for altering
the delicate *status quo*, Henry's supporters pressed for the reward   they
believed they were due for supporting Bolingbroke in his bid for the throne.
One Bolingbroke supporter, Lord Reginald de Grey of Ruthin, immediateley
began agitating trouble in lands surrounding his own estates in north-east
Wales. In so doing, he hoped to gain new territories and take advantage of
the turmoil of the time.

Chief Marcher and Privy Councillor, Lord de Grey seized villages and land
belonging to his neighbour, Owain Glyn Dŵr, notably Croesau. Owain Glyn
Dŵr, Lord of Glyndyfrdwy, protested strongly through official channels. He
presented himself to parliament to plead his case. The relevant parliamentary
rolls are lost, but contemporary English commentators remarked upon how
harshly Glyn Dŵr was treated at the time, and how he returned to Wales
fuming at Parliament's arrogance and injustice. The Bishop of Saint Asaph,
John Trefor, spoke out in Parliament on Glyn Dŵr's behalf, asking for a fair
hearing and clemency, fearing the event may well push the Welsh into armed
rebellion. Parliament responded by pouring scorn on his appeal, declaring
they cared little for the actions of *"those barefooted clowns"*, the Welsh, who
were, they said, *" a people of little reputation"*. The episode was detailed in
'The Eulogium' a monastic record, thus:

" Owen de Glendour, a Welshman who had been the esquire of the Earl of
Arundel, came to Parliament complaining that Lord de Grey Ruthin had
usurped certain of his lands in Wales, but no argument helped against Lord
de Grey. The Bishop of Saint Asaph gave counsel in Parliament that they
should not entirely despise Owen, as the Welsh might revolt. But those in
Parliament said they cared little for the bare-footed clowns."

The spring and summer of 1400 brought Parliament rumours of Cymro-
Scots collusion, whisperings of letters passing between them and men meeting
"everywhere, to plot sedition". The authorities were concerned enough to put
their men and castles in Wales on full alert, especially at Caernarfon and
along the Menai Straits.

In late summer 1400, a Royal Summons demanding Glyn Dŵr's presence
on Henry IV's campaign to Scotland was entrusted to Lord Grey of Ruthin,
who withheld it. When Grey finally delivered it, Glyn Dŵr was left with just
three days to muster, arm and present himself at the appointed time and
place. Owain Glyn Dŵr sent apologetic messages explaining that he did not

have time to do so, the demand having arrived so late. Reginald de Grey deliberately made matters worse, hoping to take Glyn Dŵr's land once forfeited for treason, by personally telling Henry IV that Glyn Dŵr held the king and his summons *"in contempt"*. The formerly loyal and praised esquire, Owain Glyn Dŵr, was condemned as a traitor when he failed to appear for the Scottish campaign.

English chroniclers of the time of all political colours and persuasions make it clear that blame for this provocative incident fell squarely upon the shoulders of Lord de Grey and Henry IV. Less than a year earlier, in October 1399, on the coronation of Prince Hal as Prince of Wales, a French chronicler named Creton wrote, almost prophetically:

" The King conferred upon him (Prince Hal) the whole of the land of Wales; but ... in my opinion, the Welsh will on no account allow him to be their lord ..."

The scene was now set and Owain Glyn Dŵr quietly gathered his forces around him.

[2] 16th September, 1400   The Coronation

Owain Glyn Dŵr was proclaimed 'Prince of Wales' and crowned at his manor in Glyndyfrdwy on 16th September, 1400. During the ceremony, he unfurled the banner under which he would fight, the Four Lions of Gwynedd. This was an unmistakable claim to the title of the House of Gwynedd. Owain Glyn Dŵr was undeniably the heir to the throne of Powys, the bards had already proclaimed him the heir to Deheubarth also, and now, with support from across the north, he claimed mighty Gwynedd as rightfully his. He inherited his claim to Deheubarth and Gwynedd from his mother's bloodline. As the leading noble of Powys, Deheubarth and Gwynedd, he was indeed the Prince of Wales. He unfurled an amended banner of Llewelyn the Great; four lions rampant, not passant, as they had been when used originally.

This overt act of treason was not merely a wronged noble letting off steam at English injustice. Most, if not all of the powerful or influential men of the area were there in person, or were represented by a family member or agent. This was a joint venture between Glyn Dŵr and other leading Welsh nobles from the beginning. Such an assembly required careful, deliberate co-ordination. Those present included Tudor, Owain's brother, one of his sons, Gruffudd ab Owain, Crach Ffinant, the prophet, three of his brothers-in-law, John Puleston, Gruffydd and Phillip Hanmer, while Hywel Cyffin, or Gethin, the Dean of Saint Asaph cathedral, added a veneer of ecclesiastical authority to the ceremony.

Support also came from beyond those family ties. The native nobility of the north also came to recognise him at Glyndyfrdwy. Nobles who, like Glyn Dŵr, had served in royal armies, and perhaps with him, now paid homage to him as their rightful Prince. Mostly from Powys, they were the 'Barons of the

North'. They represented, amongst other areas, Maelor, Bromfield and Yale, Edeirnion, Dinmael, Flint, Hendwr, Cilan and Crogen. Of them, men of renown like Madog ab Ieuan ap Madog and Ieuan ap Hywel Pickhill were there in person, while Morgan Yonge and his powerful family were otherwise represented. While the nobles acclaimed him, some three hundred warriors sharpened their weapons. They were ready to be led into battle by a Prince of Wales of their own blood and nation, against the old enemy. Prince Hal was titled and recognised by the English as Prince of Wales, but not by the Welsh, who, after a century of occupation, had a native Prince, the 'Mab Darogan', to lead them once again. On the monument dedicated to him at his birthplace in Monmouth, the date given for Prince Hal's birthday is 9th August, 1387. Modern-day historians believe this to be incorrect, and claim 16th September of that year was, in fact, his true date of birth. This makes the date of Glyn Dŵr's coronation all the more significant, and clearly a snub.

[3] The September Rampage (18th - 23rd September 1400) & The Tudor Rising

Owain Glyn Dŵr led his forces on a lightning raid across north-east Wales. Towns were laid waste by fire and sword. Most sources date the initial devastating assault on Ruthin to 18th September. The dawn attack caught the defenders unprepared. Glyn Dŵr's men left the town pillaged and ablaze in the wake of their bloody victory. One source claims that only three houses were left standing in Ruthin in the wake of the rebel attack. In quick succession, Denbigh, Rhuddlan, Flint, Howarden, Holt, Oswestry and Welshpool suffered the same fate. Outside Flint, an English relief column under Sir John Massy was attacked and put to flight. The damage Glyn Dŵr's men inflicted on Oswestry was severe enough to warrant the issuing of new charters by the king for the rebuilding of large parts of the town. Attacks on the castles of the area were not pressed home, this not being the objective of the mission. The intention of this raid was not to capture the castles and hold them, but to have revenge against Grey. Sources tell us that following the last of these attacks, dated 23rd September, Glyn Dŵr and his men melted away into the woods and hills as silently as they had come.

This short but fierce campaign mainly targetted the land, property, soldiers and reputation of Reginald, Lord Grey, whose nose Glyn Dŵr had now very publicly bloodied.

One source claims that the rebels disappeared into the woods on the feast of Saint Matthew (20th/21st September), seen off by a small force led by a Shropshire soldier and landowner, Hugh Burnell. This can probably be discounted for two reasons. Firstly, a number of other sources, known to be reliable, record damage done to towns after this date by Glyn Dŵr's rebels, namely Oswestry on 22nd September and Welshpool the following day. Secondly, Burnell's action can be discounted on the grounds of military unfeasibility. Detailed reports of Burnell's glorious victory were written a

good deal later and bare the
hallmarks of falsification. It
is possible that Glyn Dŵr's
men were seen, booty-laden,
making for the woods and
were pursued, perhaps even
a small skirmish, but the
battlefield victory sometimes
attributed to Burnell lacks
credibility or irrefutable
evidential support. Although
enormous castles could be
held by relatively small
garrisons, beyond their

Harlech Castle coutesy Lise Hull

walls, the English were to learn through painful experience of the need to field
vast numbers of soldiers against small Welsh forces in order to gain any
return for their efforts. It does not tally that a local landowner with a ragged
band of friends and servants should succeed so easily where royal armies,
numbering thousands of men with state-of-the-art weapons and armour, were
to fail.

At the same time, north-west Wales also erupted into violence. The fighting
there was less well recorded at the time, probably owing to its remoteness
and distance from the 'Welsh frontier', as English chroniclers referred to the
border. Two men identified as ring-leaders of the murderous violence were
the battle-hardened Anglesey nobles, Rhys ap Tudor and his brother,
Gwilym. Their family and followers were possibly the most powerful force
in the north-west, and were cousins to Glyn Dŵr.

We cannot say for sure whether this was a co-ordinated two-pronged
thrust against English interests in north Wales. Some sources see it as Tudor
opportunism, some see it as proof of a measure of Welsh unity from the very
beginning. However, we can be sure that when Glyn Dŵr called, the powerful
and influential clans of the north heard him, and rallied to his cause.

[4a] 28th September - 15th October 1400 - Henry IV's Royal Expedition to Wales

Henry IV was returning from a brief punitive campaign in Scotland, arriving
at Northampton by 19th September. While there, he was told of Glyn Dŵr's
coronation as Prince of Wales. The royal response was swift. The king
diverted his thirteen thousand-strong army towards north Wales and reached
Shrewsbury on 26th September, where preparations were made for a Royal
Expedition into Wales. He left on 28th September and began as he meant to
go on, with the execution of eight alleged, but unconvicted, rebels. One of
those executed was a widely respected member of the Tudor clan. The
expedition took him along the north Wales coastal strip to Caernarfon. He
crossed the Menai Straits to Anglesey, then went south to Harlech before

returning through Mawddwy to Shrewsbury on 15th October, 1400.

Along the way, he deposited garrisons at six or more key castles, looted and burnt the Franciscan friary at Llanfaes, as he did to towns and villages, notably Bangor, stole livestock and valuables wherever they could be found, and made summary executions with little heed for judicial luxuries such as burden of proof or fair hearing.

Henry IV's Royal Expedition to Wales was a failure. Those responsible for the uprising had simply melted away into the background and could not be found. The indiscriminate executions, burnings and theft simply consolidated popular support behind the insurgents.

[4b] The Tudors attack Henry IV (1400?)
Sources local to north Wales reported that Henry IV's expedition roused the people of the north beyond resentment to open defiance. At Rhos Fawr, near the fortress of Beaumaris on Anglesey, the Tudor brothers are said to have attacked the king and his retinue, forcing him to flee into the castle. There, he sought shelter until the main body of the army could cross the Menai Straits and catch up with him. He was certainly unforgiving towards the Tudors, but some sources fail to mention this important event, which might lead us to question its veracity.

[5] Early October 1400   Raiding
While the armoured English leviathan lumbered its way along the coast and back, numerous reports from villages in English border counties, as well as Dyffryn Clwyd, tell of violent raids by well-armed, fast-moving Welsh war parties.

[6] 15th October 1400 onwards
Henry IV arrived back at Shrewsbury on 15th October, feeling sure that his mission had been a success. On 23rd October, he stood down a special relief force at Chester and issued a general pardon to all Welshmen who would submit to the king's mercy. Henry IV instructed Hotspur to organise the pardons issued. Owain Glyn Dŵr and the Tudor brothers were deemed traitors, and were not to be pardoned. A few Welshmen did submit, including Tudor Glyn Dŵr, and one of Glyn Dŵr's sons, almost certainly Gruffydd, who could have been at most sixteen years of age. This move was no doubt encouraged by Owain Glyn Dŵr, and was common practice of the time to ensure a noble family's unhindered rights of inheritance. Henry IV awarded title of the Glyn Dŵr estates to his own elder half-brother John Beaufort, Earl of Somerset. However, they were still occupied by rebels and well inside rebel territory. In November, the King's Council considered offering peace terms to the remaining rebels. Nothing more was heard from Glyn Dŵr in 1400.

1401

VICTORIES AND NEGOTIATIONS

1401

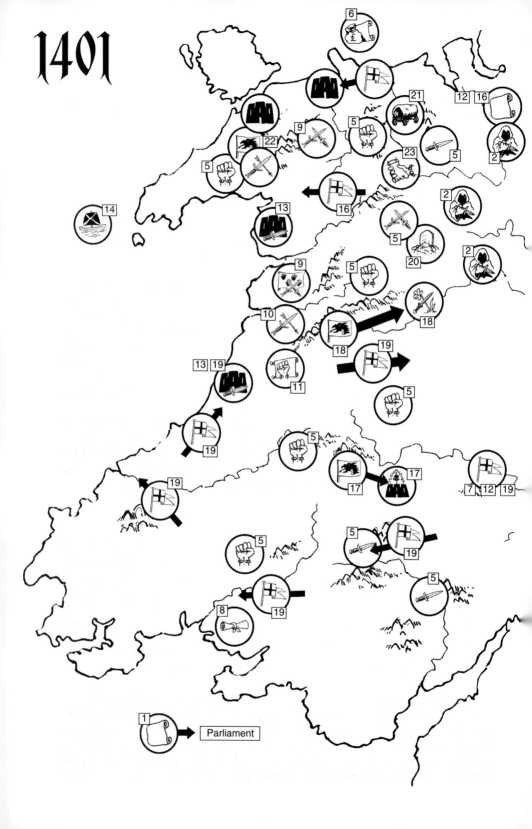

Parliament

[1] January 1401

English Parliamentary Rolls from January 1401 record the virulently anti-Welsh tone of the day. Parliament was told that a number of Welsh scholars and students from Oxford and Cambridge, as well as large numbers of Welsh labourers in England had *'provisioned themselves with armour, bows and swords'* and had *'returned home to make war'*. Moreover, Parliament was informed that bards and friars were inciting revolt within Wales itself, and that all along the border the Welsh were infiltrating English towns and boroughs, taking posts and positions therein. Punitive measures and ordinances against the Welsh were produced and came into force in March of that year. Some of these were mentioned in the earlier section, the Welsh in Battle, but now they were put on or reaffirmed in the statute books, and applied with particular zeal.

It was during this sitting that Parliament outlawed bards, expelled Welsh men and women from English counties, forbade anyone of mixed Welsh and English parentage from serving in towns or garrisons, and ended the rights of English parents to have their children temporarily fostered by Welsh families, previously a common practice. On top of this, Parliament created a clause of 'communal guilt', whereby all Welsh people of an area were responsible for any rebel damage caused. Moreover, the cost, refurbishment and repair of walls, gates and castles was also to be the responsibility of the Welsh populace, not of the English townsfolk resident in Wales.

Existing measures concerning the sale and carrying of arms in Wales were tightened, and strictures on the sale of food to the Welsh were also imposed. The general pardon was reissued to all who would submit, excluding Owain Glyn Dŵr and the Tudor brothers. Parliament resolved to send out spies to try and find information on the rebels, including their whereabouts.

[2] Winter 1400-1401 and Spring 1401

It seems that the Welsh were actively infiltrating English and English-held areas, not only in holding positions of administrative and military responsibility, from which they were legally barred, but also in more surreptitious ways. Spies, agitators and rumour-mongers are believed to have worked their way into towns and boroughs to mobilise the Welsh elements within them, and to scare the enemy populace there. Churchmen and common townsfolk alike were accused of working for *'Owen Glendour, traitor'*. It is also probable that some sort of assessment of a town's defences, population, wealth and immediate military capability would have been noted.

[3] 1st April 1401   The Capture of Conwy Castle

In 1401, 1st April was Good Friday, the holiest date in the Christian calendar. Early in the morning, while the garrison was deep in pious prayer, a local carpenter reported for work on the pretext of carrying out some essential repairs. Once let in, the man, a rebel, quickly and quietly murdered the guards in the gatehouse and let in Rhys and Gwilym ap Tudor and a fifty-strong warband. The Tudors and their men filtered into the castle and seized the armouries before storming into the chapel. There, they captured the entire garrison of some one hundred and fifty men and its commander, Sir John Massy. The Tudors also ransacked Conwy, then torched the town and its bridge.

Welsh rebels now held one of the jewels in the English crown of occupied Wales, Conwy Castle. The capture of this immense fortress must have had its builder, Edward I, turning in his grave. The Tudors were not thinking of the liberation of Wales at this point, but were seeking pardons for themselves for the previous year's fighting. This surprise attack had more of an effect than they imagined. This tactical move caused shock-waves not only throughout England, as they intended, but also throughout Wales. Suddenly, the Welsh realised that these fortresses were not impregnable, for there was Conwy for all to see, in Tudor hands and the garrison held to ransom.

[4] April, May and June 1401

Prince Hal, Hotspur and a force of over five hundred men conducted the siege of Conwy with artillery and attack engines. The Tudors humiliated them, repulsing their attacks time and time again, and inflicted heavy casualties, obliging Prince Hal to bring up reinforcements. The English soon gave up trying to storm the castle and settled in for a prolonged siege, intent on starving out the rebels.

In the end, however, Prince Hal and Hotspur were obliged to seek a negotiated settlement. They lacked sufficient financial resources to keep a besieging army in the field for long, especially in hostile territory, as they reported Wales was now very evidently becoming. Hotspur wrote to the king saying that the common folk of Conwy and the surrounding area were now '*rebellious*'.

[5] May 1401

Documentation tells us of outbreaks of rebel action in Abergavenny and the surrounding district. Brecon suffered the same, including a rash of selected murders and robberies. There were skirmishes between English forces and Welsh rebels throughout Powys. Rebels challenged the civilian administration, refusing to pay fines or debts, and rents were not collected out of fear. The civilian infrastructure was showing the first symptoms of breakdown, though nothing more at this stage.

The North, Powys and Ceredigion declared themselves rebel. Defections to the rebel cause spread through Carmarthenshire, Builth and the Middle March. Throughout April and May, Owain Glyn Dŵr was said to be particularly active in the west.

[6] 4th and 17th May, and 4th June 1401

Hotspur appealed in writing to Henry IV for money to pay the troops in north Wales, especially at Conwy. The money was not forthcoming and tensions rose between the two, as Hotspur was footing the bill for a war of

Henry IV's making, for a cause that was not directly threatening England, whilst simultaneously distracting Hotspur from his Scottish duties. He wrote:

"I see much pillage and mischief in the country, that good and hasty measures ought to be immediately adopted by sea as well as by land. All the country is without doubt in great peril of being destroyed by the rebels if I should leave before the arrival of my successor, the which will be an affair of necessity; for I cannot bear the cost I am put to without ordered from you..."

[7] 26th May 1401
Henry IV arrayed, or summoned, the troops and constables from fourteen shires to meet him in Worcester. He planned to strike at Owain Glyn Dŵr in Carmarthenshire, who, it was claimed was threatening to *'invade our realm'* and *'destroy our English tongue'*.

[8] Late May 1401
Owain Glyn Dŵr sent a personal appeal to the formidable Henry Don. An invasion of the south by Glyn Dŵr's forces was imminent and he sought the support of the strongmen of the local Welsh nobility, Henry Don chief among them. Glyn Dŵr's letter to Don read:

"We inform you that we hope to be able, by God's help and yours, to deliver the Welsh people from the captivity of our English enemies who, for a long time now elapsed, have oppressed us and our ancestors. And you may know from your own perception, that now their time draws to a close and because, according to God's ordinance from the beginning success turns towards us, no one need doubt that a good issue will result, unless it be lost through sloth or strife."

This letter is explicit. The desire to free Wales is clear, showing Glyn Dŵr's belief in himself and in the cause of Welsh independence.

[9] 31st May 1401   Owain the Magician
Owain Glyn Dŵr was engaged in fighting at two places at once. Hotspur claims to have been ambushed by him at Cadair Idris on 31st May, (one source names both encounters as taking place on 13th May however) while John Charlton, Lord of Powys, claimed to have surprised Glyn Dŵr at his encampment at the same time, although Charlton and Hotspur were scores of miles from each other. Charlton said in dispatches that he charged the rebels at 'M.', which some sources claim to mean Machynlleth, in the light of what Glyn Dŵr was to do there in early June, but we cannot be sure. 'M.' could be so many places in Wales. Charlton claimed that due to his sudden attack, the rebels fled carrying what they could. The long pursuit and occasional skirmishing lasted well after nightfall, which was exceptional for the era. Charlton is said to have taken a few lances, a handful of horses and *"a drape of cloth, painted with maidens with red hands."* What this signified we do not

know, but it added to the growing mystery of Owain Glyn Dŵr.

There were a plethora of simultaneous sightings of Glyn Dŵr from this period onwards. Although disproving this phenomenon is impossible, it can be explained in a number of ways, assuming that we do not believe that he was a magician, as some writers, including Shakespeare, would have us believe.

One reason was that English commanders, eager to prove that they were doing their bit to staunch the rebellion, inflated the size of any enemy engaged, and claimed that the rebel leaders were present even when they were not. They did this to prove their worth to the Crown, impressing the necessity of retaining their services, and to build their military reputations. English commanders were to consistently overestimate not only enemy numbers, but their own performances in contact with the enemy, and even invented encounters in order to claim a victory to cheer those at home, as we shall see later.

Another reason for Glyn Dŵr's simultaneous sightings might be that his brother, Tudor, was said to closely resemble him. The two could easily be confused, we are told, especially at a distance by people not familiar with them. Tudor was as experienced in the arts of war as his elder brother, though not so renowned, and we know that he led rebel troops on combat missions. It is quite possible that royal forces in combat with Tudor may have genuinely believed they were fighting Owain Glyn Dŵr, Prince of Wales.

[10] Early June 1401   The Battle of Hyddgen

Glyn Dŵr had raided, pillaged and burnt his way across Ceredigion, Pembrokeshire and Rhos throughout the spring, confounding local and overall English commanders alike. Again, normally reliable sources put him in several places at once. We know that English forces in Ceredigion and Pembrokeshire believed he was in the area at the end of May, and moved against him, intending to decisively end the rebel threat. An Anglo-Flemish force of one thousand five hundred men was raised and Flemish mercenaries hired to accompany them. They went after him at the beginning of June, heading for an area where English steadings had recently been razed, " *fully confident*" that they could "*kill or take him*".

Surviving evidence tells us that Glyn Dŵr was "*with a hundred and twenty reckless men ... riding in a warlike fashion.*" Only a madman or a tactical genius would lead a hundred and twenty men against such an army. This figure has led to debate as to the true size of Glyn Dŵr's force. Some writers take a later French meaning of '*gendarme*'; being three archers and a swordsman, to explain the numbers given, making the force four hundred and eighty strong. That this relies on a later French interpretation of this term seems too tenuous a supposition on which to advance a plausible theory. The evidence available says "*a hundred and twenty men*", who appear to have been mounted, and thus may have formed a mobile nucleus to a force which grew as it met success. In short, we cannot be certain of the exact number of men with Glyn Dŵr, but all sources agree that it was dwarfed in size by the Anglo-Flemish army. Glyn Dŵr, respected warrior of several campaigns, did lead his men against the English and their *"Flemish dogs"*, and won a spectacular victory against them on a lonely heath at Hyddgen, near Machynlleth, in the Plynlimon hills.

The most recent work on this subject tends to conclude that this conflict was a phased encounter, taking place on a number of sites, over a longer period of time than previously suggested. The evidence is sketchy and confusing, but two seemingly different engagements are mentioned, although the casualties quoted are the same for each, leading some to speculate that there was one pitched battle. However, descriptions of the fighting vary enough to allow us to suggest that there were at least two engagements. It would also be more credible to suggest that, though gifted, Glyn Dŵr and his men cannot be expected to defeat such an enemy in one straight fight, and so more than one conflict area is probable. Through the mayhem of battle, we cannot say precisely how the events unfolded, but can be drawn to certain conclusions by piecing together that which we know about the event and the period.

The English slogged their way in good order up Hyddgen valley, some twelve miles from one of their strongholds at Aberystwyth. One source says that it had rained heavily for days beforehand, making the going slow in boggy conditions. The misty uplands which culminate at Hyddgen Mountain are made up of open valleys, covered in peat bogs, tough marsh grasses, the odd rocky outcrop and a permanent blanket of cloud and rain. The Welsh were reportedly heavily armed with an irregular but fearsome range of weapons of all shapes, sizes and descriptions. An accurate contemporary account of the conflict is unavailable, so the action must be pieced together by the modern historian with the surviving evidence, working out plausible theories for the unclear sections of the event.

The traditional theory of there being one straight fight should be revised. While a huge battle, with the rebels overcoming their enemies all at once, is appealing, it is not practical. Recent work by Ian Fleming forwards the idea that the rebels used the whole of the Hyddgen area at this time and that the combat was a multi-phased affair. This seems far more realistic than the 'one battle' theory. However, to date, this multi-phase theory also has inaccuracies and improbabilities. The claim that the English were all carrying longbows, crossbows and pikes must be incorrect. If an army so equipped met another with fewer missile weapons, tactics of the time show us that they would have held back and killed their enemies with their bows, fending off any charges with their pikes before entering melee. A hundred and twenty men, or even a few hundred more, would be quickly cut down by such opposition, especially if they were surrounded, as the evidence suggests happened to Glyn Dŵr's men. One thousand, five hundred bows and pikes would not need to move to close quarters in order to kill Glyn Dŵr's force. It is more plausible that Glyn Dŵr's troops, mounted to facilitate their lightning guerilla raids, were the ones carrying bows of some kind, whereas the English were not.

In this scenario, the rebels could harry, strike and withdraw from their numerically superior enemy, struggling over this rough terrain on foot. We know that Glyn Dŵr's men were mounted, we are told of Glyn Dŵr being accompanied by *"...with one hundred and twenty reckless men ... riding in a warlike fashion."* Welsh soldiers were renowned for their battlefield capabilities with bows, as they were at swift hard-hitting raids. How else could such a tiny force evade, soften, resist and finally confront the Anglo-Flemish army of one thousand, five hundred men? A number of attacks on the slow moving Flemish by Welsh on horseback seems to be the soundest way of envisaging this conflict taking place and concluding in its known end.

One account tells us, *"and no sooner did the English troops turn their backs than two hundred of them were slain"*. This part of the account may well indicate an ambush with arrows in order to fell so many men so quickly. It is entirely possible that this ambush procedure was repeated a number of times by the mobile rebels before the final melee took place. Eventually, the large pursuing force succeeded in catching up with the rebels onto a wide open heath where they encircled them, effectively herding them onto the top of one of the low hills or a hillock for one last stand. The English closed for a close-quarter fight, and *"in a sharp dispute"* the Welsh are recorded as *"falling on [the English] furiously, with courage whetted by dispair"* then *" they put the enemy ... to confusion ... and made them give ground."* The English were forced to break and run, and *" fly outright, leaving two hundred of their men dead on the spot of engagement"*. The other quoted source may suggest that two hundred men were killed as they turned to run, but does not give a figure for those killed in combat before the English the rout took place.

In this period especially, casualties of the actual fighting were often less than those sustained by an army in rout. We do not know how many were killed while fleeing, but a high death toll could be expected. The mass graves of those killed have been discovered in the Hyddgen area at Bryn y Beddau (Hill of Graves), Mynydd Bychan and Nant y Moch. Much of this widespread battle area is now submerged by the Nant y Moch dam, preventing further investigation. A number of stones known as *'Owain Glyn Dŵr's Covenant Stones'* are said to mark the scene of this fight. They are still there today, and are well known to locals and walkers, but it is impossible to know if Glyn Dŵr had any hand in their arrangement.

We know the Welsh won an impressive victory at Hyddgen, but a clear picture of the battle remains difficult to establish. One source claims that two hundred was the final tally of English dead, and that the Welsh, having pushed back and broken the enemy, then left the battlefield victorious, without further ado. This is unlikely for a number of reasons. A force of more than one thousand five hundred well-equipped soldiers would be extremely unlikely to flee from a hundred and twenty surrounded men. Even sustaining two hundred casualties in one encounter would still leave them by far the superior force in the field, and if anything, more likely to press home their advantage and avenge their dead comrades. Therefore, it is probable that either more casualties than stated were sustained in one or both attacks, or

that there were several such initial hit-and-run attacks. The English and
Flemish, being mostly on foot, would only have fled as an absolute last resort,
aware that they risked sustaining heavy casualties while being pursued by the
Welsh rebels on mountain ponies. The figure 'two hundred' is probably a
rushed estimation, and is quoted a number of times throughout the conflict
to give a general casualty estimation. It would have been difficult to
accurately count the casualties, given the style of combat and mobility of the
guerillas, especially if the combat was spread over several sites.

[11] June 1401   The Appeal to the West

After Hyddgen, perhaps from the famed 'Covenant Stones', Glyn Dŵr
appealed to the men of the west and their leaders to join him. He is reputed
to have said:

> *"After many years of captivity, the hour of freedom has now struck,
> and only cowardice and sloth can deprive the nation of the victory
> which is in sight."*

There is some debate as to whether those are in fact his words or not. Some
of these words come from the letter to Henry Don and may thus have been
confused with the speech Glyn Dŵr gave after the battle. Irrespective, in the
wake of his stunning victory at Hyddgen, there were massive defections to his
cause, especially in the west.

[12] 14th June 1401

From Chester, Prince Hal issued more harsh financial and judicial ordinances
against the Welsh. Huge fines were issued and orders to confiscate rebel land
given. Orders for the reinforcement of garrisons across north, mid and south-
west Wales were also sent, to be acted upon as soon as the Exchequer released
funds to pay for the troops.

Henry IV disbanded the army arrayed on 26th May, not having ventured
beyond Worcester. This tells us that either the Battle of Hyddgen had not
occurred by 14th June, which would explain Henry IV's actions, that news
from the west had not yet arrived or that there had been a total
communications breakdown amongst English forces.

[13] June 1401

Harlech and Aberystwyth, the two Edwardian fortresses, are said to have
come under attack from Welsh forces. It is unlikely to have constituted a
proper or effective siege, given the dearth of weapons in rebel hands, and may
have taken the form of several days of attacks by the swelling rebel ranks in
the summer war season. Welsh tactics, particularly at this stage, were finely
tuned to their guerilla needs and equipment, and they still lacked the
resources and probably the know-how to conduct a prolonged technical
siege.

[14] June 1401
The Scots

Scots troops landed on Bardsey Island off the Llyn peninsula, taking and holding it, they said, for the Welsh. A number of their warships patrolled the Celtic Sea and harried shipping, seeking to benefit from the unstable situation in Wales. The arrival of the Scots in Wales, though in small numbers, was significant. It drew both Glyn Dŵr's and Henry IV's attention to certain political and military possibilities in the event of this furious rebellion maturing into a war.

Montgomery Castle coutesy Lise Hull

[15] 24th June 1401 — The Tudors leave Conwy

After months of siege and negotiations, the Tudors finally handed back Conwy to Prince Hal and Hotspur. To overcome their shame at having lost and then failed to retake the fortress, the English demanded the delivery of nine prisoners to be executed in exchange for the pardoning of the others. The affair tainted the reputations of all of those involved. English chroniclers, while scornful of their own leaders, also accused the Tudors of cowardice by betraying nine of their men and delivering them into English hands. Welsh sources claim that those surrendered were men who either volunteered on promises that their comrades and leaders would take care of their families, or were siege casualties, unlikely to survive, and chose execution so that their fellows, almost certainly kinsmen, could escape. However they were selected, nine rebels were executed, the remainder pardoned and went free. Royal forces once again installed themselves in Conwy castle.

[16] July and August 1401

Using monies allocated to him by his father on 10th July, Prince Hal raised an army at Chester and rode *"at great haste"* for Harlech, via Bala. The whole rescue mission must have ridden through the rebel heartland at some speed, as he arrived with a sizeable relieving force in a matter of a few days. Alarm bells that had been ringing for months were now being heard by the authorities. The situation was beginning to look serious. Although Wales was not plunging headlong into an all-out war, it was certainly in the grip of a fierce revolt.

[17] August 1401 — The Slaughter at Radnor

Glyn Dŵr gathered his forces and led them on a summer campaign in the east. They settled scores with a number of people who opposed them, including the monks at Cwm Hir Abbey, because of their patronage by the Mortimers, and for figuring among the few who had railed against the rebels. East Radnorshire was invaded and fell in a massive raid, during which Radnor castle was stormed and the town burnt. If we are to believe what we are told, the survivors of the assault on the castle, " *some three score men and more*", were taken outside and ceremonially beheaded, their bodies hung from the walls with their entrails dangling as a grisly warning to Glyn Dŵr's enemies.

[18] August and September 1401

Montgomery and the surrounding area was overrun by Glyn Dŵr in late summer. The town and castle were taken, plundered and burnt. The defenders and inhabitants experienced an equally ruthless fate in Welsh hands. One contemporary source wrote that Glyn Dŵr had *"deflowered Montgomery"*. Welshpool was also attacked and devastated, but the castle, with the Lords of Powys - the Charlton brothers - within, grimly held the rebels out. English records show Hay, Abergavenny, Grosmont, Usk, Bishop's Castle and others fell prey to this thrust by Glyn Dŵr's forces.

[19] 1st October 1401   Henry IV's second Royal Expedition to Wales

Henry IV again arrayed the army at Worcester and ventured into Wales on a second expedition on 1st October. Before embarking on the Expedition, Henry IV wrote to Prince Hal, his son.

"... Owen Glendower and other rebels of our land of Wales, now recently risen against us and our majesty have assembled in great numbers and from one day to the next commit many grievances and destructive deeds against our faithful subjects there who do not wish to concur with their evil purpose.

And by such coercion a large part of our aforesaid country has been given over to the rebels and, according to our reports, all the remaining parts of our said country and the marches will surrender to the same rebels if we are not there in person to resist their evil."

They passed from Worcester to Brecon, down the Tywi valley to Llandovery and on to Carmarthen. From there they turned north-west and went on to Cardigan and Aberystwyth before returning to England through Builth and Painscastle. Large garrisons were left at these castles and others along the way. English troops occupied the Cistercian abbey at Strata Florida, having first ransacked it. Built in 1164 by Rhys of Deheubarth and burial ground for eleven Welsh princes, Strata Florida was one of the holiest sites in Wales. Monks were killed and taken captive, relics taken, buildings smashed and burnt. Some sources say that hundreds of children were also rounded up by Henry IV's troops and marched off in chains. An English monk travelling with Henry IV wrote :

> *"... the English ravaging these parts and ravaging them with fire, hunger and sword, left them a desert, not even sparing children or churches, nor the Monastery of Strata Florida, wherin the King*

himself was a guest, the church of which and its choir, even up to the High Altar, they used as a stable and pilleged even the patens (silver plate)."

Most of the religious institutions in Wales were fervent in their loyal support of the Welsh cause. Owain Glyn Dŵr's ancestors, as recent as his grandfather, had been generous patrons of Wales' ecclesiastical institutions for quite some time.

During the Expedition, huge communal fines were levied, and local community leaders were bound over to vouch for the good behaviour of their countrymen. As previous rents and fines had not been paid, Henry IV 'gathered' the revenue himself by laying his hands on as much livestock and plunder as he could. Some of the commons of Carmarthenshire and Cardiganshire submitted to the king's mercy and denounced the rebels, at least, while Henry was there with thousands of troops. Another feature of the Expedition was the numerous executions carried out on Henry IV's orders. Many of those executed were known not to be rebels, we are told by English sources, which go on to lament the king's hastiness in executing loyal subjects simply because they were Welsh, and therefore already judged and condemned as potential rebels in English eyes. Even those rebels who were killed seem to have been more honourable than their royal foe. One of them was offered a pardon on the scaffold if he would simply give information on Glyn Dŵr. An English observer wrote how the rebel chose death before betrayal, and knelt in silence, putting his own head on the block to await the executioner's axe. Impressed by this, the English monk commented,

"We Englishmen should follow this example, and depart this life faithfully unto death, keeping our counsel and secrets."

One man executed on this expedition was the local noble Llewelyn ap Gruffudd Fychan, Lord of Caeo. On October 6th 2001, a magnificent statue in his honour was unveiled in Llandovery, his place of execution. He had led Henry's army away from Glyndŵr's men, on the pretext of being a traitor. When Henry discovered after several days of wandering aimlessly, that two of the Lord of Caeo's sons were serving with Glyn Dŵr, he personally supervised his hanging, drawing and quartering outside the gates of Castell Llanymddyfri (Llandovery Castle).

Welsh settlements near the border are said to have suffered heavily from the Expedition's predations. Stories of looting and raping were noted, with the finger of blame mainly pointed at the ranks of the Herefordshire levies. Thomas Percy, Earl of Worcester, was appointed commander of royal forces in south Wales and given troops to relieve and regarrison castles throughout south and mid Wales and along the border with England.

[20] 19th October 1401

The loyal and capable Marcher lord John Charlton, Lord Powys, died. There is a suggestion that he was killed in combat with rebels, probably in an ambush or skirmish, though we cannot be sure. Shortly afterwards, his duties and title were transferred to his brother, Edward.

[21] Late October 1401
Prince Hal's personal baggage train was ambushed and plundered by rebels in the north. They escaped with a small fortune as well as a number of useful items, including weapons belonging to the prince.

[22] 2nd November 1401   The Battle of Tuthill
Glyn Dŵr unfurled his new personal warbanner for this skirmish outside Caernarfon. He flew a golden dragon on a white field, previously the colours of Uther Pendragon, who had passed them on to his son, Arthur. This gesture, taken from well-known mythology, was charged with meaning to the tradition-loving Welsh. With it, Glyn Dŵr was claiming Arthur's inheritance, the leadership of the Welsh, effectively proclaiming himself *'King of the Britons'*. The battle was almost a sideshow in comparison to this heraldic statement. Both sides failed to achieve their objectives. The English wanted Glyn Dŵr's head. They claimed to have met the enemy manfully in battle and inflicted heavy losses upon them before retiring back to their castle. The Welsh wanted Caernarfon. They claimed to have come to this mighty foreign fortress, shown their colours, fought the enemy and forced him to flee the field, back to the protection of his castle. After the battle, Glyn Dŵr is said to have prowled menacingly around the castle walls. It is difficult to judge the final result, several hundred men from both sides lay dead and, as the night closed in, the English still held the castle and the Welsh the battlefield.

[23] November 1401   Negotiations and Planning
Throughout November 1401 Glyn Dŵr is said to have sought a negotiated settlement to the issue. Despite the events of the year, it seems this was still a distinct possibility. Negotiations took place between Glyn Dŵr, Thomas Percy, Earl of Worcester, whom he is said to have held in high regard, and Worcester's nephew, Hotspur, with whom he seems to have enjoyed a mutually respectful relationship. The Shakespearean image of these two at loggerheads is historically inaccurate. Glyn Dŵr refused to come to the border to parley, fearing English treachery and capture. We do not know if he had a mole at court or was simply shrewd, but records show that the English advocated his capture at parley and execution as a traitor, or simply his assassination at parley. Hotspur, offended at the suggestion that he should turn against his code of honour and break his word to *'an honourable and noble opponent'*, came under criticism from certain quarters for not trying to kill Glyn Dŵr while he had the chance. This marked another rise in tensions between Hotspur and those at court.

Hotspur reported that Glyn Dŵr denied responsibility for all that had been attributed to him, and that he was not planning *'the genocide of the English'*, of which he had earlier been accused. He would agree to come to peace if the safety of his family were guaranteed along with his own, and his possessions and rights of inheritance secured. The Percys argued that Glyn Dŵr's restoration was a small price to pay to avert further rebellion. In letters, Prince Hal seemed to agree with them. The Crown agreed that Hotspur should continue negotiations while they planned a three-pronged assault on Wales. The situation was probably still retrievable at this point.

Meanwhile, the Welsh were planning more negotiations, but this time with foreign powers. Glyn Dŵr sent representation to the chieftains of Ireland, also suffering under English occupation and war. He sent emissaries to King Robert III of Scotland and King Charles VI of France, to whom he described himself as 'Prince of Wales'. In his appeal to the Scots he evoked a common ancestry and the benefits of crushing the common enemy. He reminded the French that their oldest overseas alliance was with the Welsh, and dated back to 1212, the reigns of Llewelyn I and Philip VII. He also reminded them that in 1378, his forebear Owain Lawgoch, 'Yvain de Galles', led bands of Welshmen in their armies, fought brilliantly for them and had died in their service before they honoured their promises to him concerning an invasion of Wales launched from France.

The French wished to know more, and also to involve the Scots. They sent a famous Welsh crusader, *"Dafydd ap Jevan Goz"*, or Dafydd ap Ieuan (Yvain or Owain ?) Coch, *'Killer of Saracens'*, to negotiate with Robert III on behalf of the Welsh cause. His ship was intercepted by the English and Dafydd ap Ieuan Coch was taken to the Tower of London. Writers in Scotland such as Walter Bower were warming to the Welsh cause, and reminded the Scots of the legends of Britain, whereby the Welsh and their cousins, the Scots, united, would sweep the Saxon enemy back into the sea and rule in peace over their ancestral lands across the whole island. However, due to a recent English twisting of this ancient prophecy to prove their superiority over the Scots, other Scots writers were investigating the possibility that their origins were other than that stated in the legend of Brutus, progenitor of the British. At this stage, Scots reaction towards Glyn Dŵr was positive on the whole, if slightly distracted by English thrusts at their borders.

We do not know the details of Welsh contact with Brittany, but they were undoubtedly communicating. Although often allied to the English, Brittany's linguistic and cultural links to Wales were much stronger than this recent political alliance. It was probably at this time that the Welsh called upon their other cousins, the Bretons.

1402

GLYN DŴR RAMPANT ON THE BATTLEFIELD

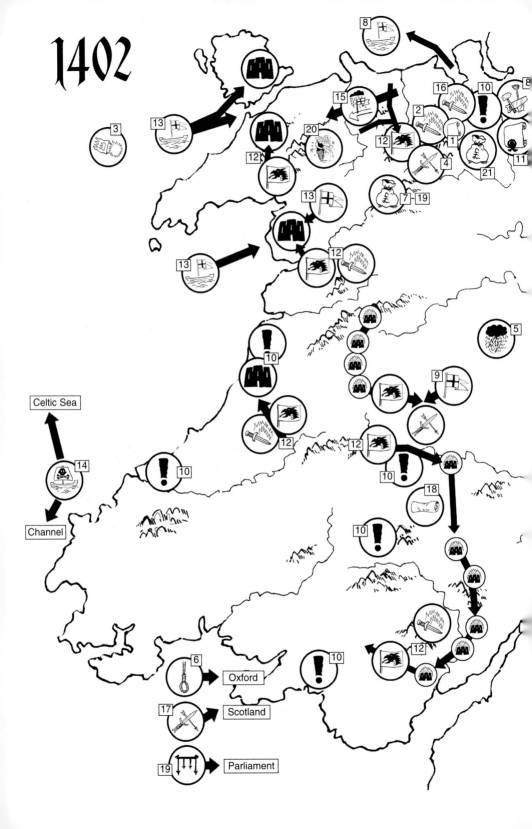

1402

[1] January 1402

Lord Reginald de Grey petitioned Henry IV in an attempt to block any reconciliation between Henry IV and Owain Glyn Dŵr, whose lands he wanted. The former governor of Ireland and current Royal Advisor, Lord de Grey, wealthy, experienced Marcher Lord and Bolingbroke-supporter at the crucial period when Richard II was deposed, reminded Henry IV of the extent to which he disliked the Welsh and their '*malice*'. Grey also used his influence with other nobles to ensure that anti-Welsh rumours and stories circulated in the corridors of power. He was authorised to seize all of Owain Glyn Dŵr's lands, though title of those lands would, in time, be passed to the Earl of Somerset, Henry IV's half-brother.

[2] 30th January 1402

Glyn Dŵr retaliated against Grey on 30th January. He *"cruelly harried"* Grey's lordship of Ruthin, carrying off all the spoil and cattle he could, as well as killing those who stood against him and burning their property. Surrounding lordships under under the control of Mortimer or Hotspur were unharmed by the raid. The message was again clear, Grey had victimised Glyn Dŵr at court where he could not answer for himself, so, in Wales, with sword in hand, Glyn Dŵr had returned the compliment.

[3] The Great Comet 1402

In spring 1402 a large fiery comet, named '*The Great Comet*', was seen in the sky, day and night. All across Europe people foretold events both great and terrible. To the superstitious Welsh it was the third '*Great Star of History*'. The first was the Star of Bethlehem, the second the comet that was seen when Uthr Pendragon and Arthur prepared to do battle with the enemy, and, as it burned brightly overhead, they crushed the Saxons. To the superstitious Welsh, it could mean only one thing, victory. Glyn Dŵr's poet Iolo Goch wrote the poem '*Cwydd y Deren*' to celebrate the comet, some lines of which have been translated as:

'*See ye that blazing star*
The heavens look down on Freedom's war
And light her torch on high,
Bright upon the dragon's crest
It tells that glory's wings shall rest, when warriors meet to die.

Let earth's pale tyrants read despair
And vengeance in its flame
Hail! Hail! Ye Bards, the omen fair
Of conquest and fame,
And swell the rushing mountain air
With songs of Glyn Dŵr's name.'

[4] April 1402   The Battle of Ruthin
The first signs of this victory came in April. Lord Grey, with his large private
army and royal troops, repulsed an attack on his stronghold at Ruthin castle.
The Welsh raiders seemed reluctant to flee and massed for another attack.
Seizing the initiative, Grey rode out at the head of his troops to finish the issue
there and then. A brief skirmish ensued and the rebels made for the hills with
Grey and the English in hot pursuit. They rode headlong into the jaws of a
massive ambush, closed very firmly by Glyn Dŵr and his men. After a
merciless fight in which *"very many"* or *"almost all"* of Grey's men were
killed, Grey was taken prisoner by Glyn Dŵr. The final acts were carried out
at a place called Bryn Saith Marchog, the Hill of the Seven Knights, allegedly
so-called because Grey had just seven men left standing with him on the
hillock where he was captured. We cannot be sure if Glyn Dŵr captured Grey
in person, but Lord Ruthin was certainly a prisoner of the Prince of Wales by
the end of the battle. There is strong, but unsubstantiated, evidence that
Welshmen serving in Grey's household had a hand in the rash decisions that
led to his foolhardy rush at the rebels, subsequent defeat and capture. They
had little difficulty, it seems, in deciding whether their allegiances lay with
their employer or their nation. Stories abound of a ruse involving gleaming
helmets on poles cloaked in robes to fool the English force that a large Welsh
force lay waiting for them, persuading them to ride in a different direction
and into Glyn Dŵr's ambush. A ransom note for Lord Grey's release was
delivered to Parliament. If four weeks elapsed without major payment, de
Grey would be executed.

[5] April 1402
Huge, unseasonal storms and other unusual weather phenomena struck the
whole island, from north to south and east to west. In the east of England,
the Devil is said to have materialised in a church amidst flashes of lightning,
attacked the congregation and smashed up the building. These were powerful
portents indeed and people everywhere were frightened. In Wales though,
they were expectant. Henry IV saw the confusion as a good opportunity to
execute several vocal opponents of his regime, mostly monks.

[6] Spring 1402
Thirteen Welshmen and one Welshwoman were indicted for treason at
Oxford and put on trial. Among those accused of inciting rebellion was a
certain Hywel Gethin, dean of Saint Asaph and Glyn Dŵr's chancellor. One
man called *"Owen Conwaye"* demanded a 'judicial duel', or trial by combat,
as was his right. When his accuser, Wilfred Taylor, backed down, he was
accused of *'making false accusations'*, a very serious offence. Unwilling to
face trial by combat with Owen Conwaye, Taylor was taken to Tyburn and
hanged for his troubles. The trial collapsed and the prisoners were released.

[7] The 'False Gold' Incident? 1402
We have a number of versions of the 'False Gold' incident. Lord Grey's

agents, in league with the Crown, are said to have tried to pay Grey's ransom with false coins. They believed Glyn Dŵr to be a poor Welshman, unfamiliar with money and thus easy to bamboozle. Obviously, the plan failed, as one account has it, some of Grey's agents were put to death, those left alive bound and whipped from the meeting place and the ransom immediately doubled. Seductive though the story might be, it was transmitted only orally for a century before being committed to parchment. It can probably be accounted more fiction than fact.

[8] 31st March - June 1402
The early summer period from the beginning of April until the end of June saw intense reconstruction and strengthening of defences and royal forces in north-east Wales. Two naval patrols were sent out from Chester. Hotspur was persuaded to return to north Wales for this period and oversee operations. He probably left the area in early June, once he had given orders and toured the area to see that they were being carried out.

[9] 22nd June 1402   The Battle of Bryn Glas, or the Battle of Pilleth
There were several events in late May and early June which led to this brutal confrontation. There has been a great deal written about the Battle of Bryn Glas, much of which has been cut through in this brief account. For once, we have a good deal of information from the period, arguably too much, as the picture is distorted by some of the wilder claims and by those writing in order to support a political slant. There are a number of complicated and contested issues to address. We have a reasonable picture of what happened, but, as with most events of this period, the full picture remains somewhat obscured by the murky shadows of history.

In the early summer, the Welsh swept through Maelienydd and the adjacent border areas. They took a number of castles belonging to the Mortimers. The head of this proud Marcher dynasty was Edmund Mortimer, acting Earl of March. Those castles devastated included Bleddfa, Cwm-Aran, Knucklas and Cefnllys. Riches were plundered and ghastly things done to the fallen garrisons. The Welsh also robbed and then destroyed any churches in the area known to be paying tithes to the English. Bearers of a proud military tradition, the Mortimers had to retaliate.

The English gathered an army at Ludlow and prepared to launch a summer campaign against Glyn Dŵr. The Earl of March and his sizeable retinue were joined by a number of other powerful Marcher nobles. Sir Robert Whitney, Knight-Marshal to the king, turned up with his retinue. He also brought his brother and almost all of their male relations old enough, or young enough, to bear arms, along with their own retinues and followers. Lord Kinnersley or Kinnardsley, the given title of Sir Kinard de la Bere, came with a large troop of retainers, as did Sir Walter Devereux from Weobley and Lyonshall castles, situated on the south-eastern border. The holder of four small estates, a knight of partly Welsh decent, Sir Thomas Clanvowe (or Clanowe or Clavenogh), also went on the mission with his men.

The Great Seal of Owain Glyn Dŵr

These men, the Knights of March, all rode with personal retainers and companies of fighting men. The knights, esquires - the same rank as Glyn Dŵr - and sergeants made up the heavy cavalry of the army, while their armed companies, local regulars and hired swords made up the well-armed heavy infantry. As light infantry, they also brought " *almost all the militia of Herefordshire*", who had proven so effective against the monks, women and non-combatant villagers during the Royal Expedition of October 1401. They were led by the Sheriff of Herefordshire.

The estimates of the size of the English army vary from one to eight thousand men, but given the time and resources available to Edmund Mortimer, the figure is probably closer to two and a half thousand men. We do not know if their recruitment went to plan or whether it was disrupted by a Welsh attack on the nearby town of Knighton, forcing them to set out prematurely. We cannot be sure that the attack on Knighton took place at this time, as it is not universally mentioned by contemporary sources.

The Earl of March also took a contingent of archers. This is one of the key issues of the battle and is highly contentious. As with other infantry companies, the bowmen were recruited at Ludlow, where the army was mustered. It seems that a proliferation of Welshmen were available for service, in the right place at the right time. It is possible that they were alerted or recruited initially by Glyn Dŵr's agents who had infiltrated the area the year before. No one wondered at the fact that the general flow of Welshmen had been westwards, " *going home to make war*", yet suddenly, Ludlow was awash with able-bodied Welshmen available for service. They said that they were from the Mortimer lands and Maelienydd, obediently answering their master's call to arms or fleeing the ravages of the marauding rebels. A good number of them probably were from Maelienydd, but there is little doubt that many were from Yale, Maelor, Elfael, Gwynedd, Merioneth and Ceredigion, rebel heartlands. There was nothing unusual in the hiring of Welshmen for wars. The Welsh had served with zeal for almost everyone, against everyone, in Europe and the Middle East since the first Crusade. Frenchmen, Spaniards, Scotsmen and Irishmen had fought for the English against their own brethren, there was no reason to assume this would be any different.

This time however, it was different. The Welsh had always fought anyone and everyone, including each other, and on both sides in a number of battles, particularly in the Hundred Years War. Much to their credit however, the Welsh have never shown much appetite for siding with foreign powers intent on the destruction of their fellow Welshmen. At Ludlow, the English recruited a regiment of Welsh bowmen, and were heading for a fight with the Welsh. Perhaps Glyn Dŵr had just succeeded in what must count as one of the most successful infiltrations in military history. His men had been hired, armed, fed and paid by the enemy.

West of the border, Owain Glyn Dŵr reportedly halted his sweep through Maelienydd and went 'on pilgrimage' to the Church of the Blessed Virgin at Pilleth, on a small plateau half way up the south-eastern side of a hill called Bryn Glas, a well-known holy place. He is also said to have gone to a nearby sacred pagan site, a well, to evoke the native spirits. While there, he may have decided it made a good place to stand and fight the English, and sent men to swell their ranks. We cannot say with any certainty. One source neglects to mention his presence at the battle, but the weight of evidence suggests that he fought there. He probably did not duel the Earl of March, as some of the more fanciful stories, including Shakespeare's, will have us believe.

We do not know the size of the Welsh army at Bryn Glas. We are told that Welsh raiding parties often comprised up to four hundred or so men. It is possible that a force equal to two or perhaps three of these raiding parties had come together for the summer campaign. Some sources claim that Glyn Dŵr led a force of several thousand men, but this seems unlikely for the following reasons. English chroniclers noted that the English were " *clearly the superior force in the field, so rushed towards the enemy.*" Considering that they were also ceding the advantage of the higher ground to the Welsh, and made no attempt to draw them onto a terrain which favoured neither side, they must have considerably outnumbered the Welsh force opposing them. It would be reasonable to estimate the Welsh army at a thousand men or fewer, for reasons given later. Although other famed Welsh warriors were there, a man named 'Rhys Gethin' featured prominently in the battle and its immediate aftermath. He has been attributed with the accolade of being Glyn Dŵr's general, although such a guerilla force probably lacked regimented ranks and titles. Rhys Gethin or *'Rhys the Fierce'* is said to have come from Cwm Llanerch in the Conwy Valley. He was noted for his leadership, stoutness in battle and for atrocities he is said to have committed or ordered. Although some warriors must have been on foot, the Welsh were typically mounted on light, mountain - horses, perfectly suited to the terrain. They were described as wearing light armour, if any at all, and having a fearsome range of weapons; not just the bows, spears and swords for which the Welsh were famous, but also captured and makeshift weapons, such as billhooks, which had proved their worth to gruesome effect at Hyddgen, the year before.

Much has been made of the direction of Mortimer's approach, but it is of little consequence to the battle. The English either went to Knighton a few miles to the north to fight off a raid and were then lured to Pilleth, or came directly across the border, slightly to the south of the valley entrance. Either way, they entered the valley at the same place and marched up the valley to meet the Welsh on Bryn Glas. They may or may not have camped nearby the night before the battle, though this evokes an interesting image of possible clandestine night-time communication between Welsh soldiers both inside and outside the English camp. Opinion is divided on the matter.

Another problem with accurately assessing and describing this battle, apart from the size of the forces involved and their direction of travel, is the all important question of the state of the battlefield on 22nd June 1402. Whether the hill was wooded or not, is important in consideration of troop movement and deployment. If it were as bare then as it is today, Glyn Dŵr would have had difficulty in concealing his men and executing his tactics. Since much of the surrounding area is densely wooded, and the tactics employed required the covert movement or concealment of troops, it would be reasonable to assume that the hill was at least partly wooded, even though the lower part and perhaps a higher field or meadow were cleared. The name of the hill, Bryn Glas, literally 'Hill Blue', does not help us either. 'Glas' can represent a number of different hues, but most commonly registers as 'blue'. One modern - day source speculates that it must have been devoid of trees, due to the fact that 'glas' can mean blueish-green, and that therefore it was grassy and open. This assumes that the whole hill was named because of the features on that face. Unfortunately, we do not know when or why the hill was named Bryn Glas.

On 22nd June, the English marched the short distance up the valley, along the north bank of the river Lugg. We are told that a number of the Welsh were spotted on the valley floor. They immediately shot at the English who moved to engage them. As the English came on, the rebels withdrew uphill, shooting as they went. As they did so, a great roaring mass of Welshmen, clashing their weapons and taunting the enemy below, was seen and heard on the hill. The English hurried across the valley floor and mounted a charge up the punishingly steep slope, in armour, eager to get to grips with the enemy. The rebels must have moved rapidly or unseen or both, as the charge petered out in exhaustion without making contact with the Welsh. Whether they were lured or goaded into it, the Army of March charged a second time, uphill, in armour, and again failed to make contact with the enemy, who must surely have had some form of concealment for the English to misjudge their charge twice.

As the Army of the March were catching their breath and regrouping after the second charge, Glyn Dŵr attacked. Evidence suggests that the Welsh cavalry, probably shooting arrows and hurling spears as it came, charged directly at the head or centre of the English, where the Knights of March were positioned. As they came thundering down on the enemy, the Welsh contingent in the English army drew their bowstrings taut and aimed at their onrushing brethren. At the last minute, just before impact, probably with the English commanders screaming at them to shoot, they lowered their aim and unleashed volley after murderous volley into the English soldiers behind, alongside and in front of them. Whether the bowmen under English colours were in one massed regiment behind the English heavy cavalry, or as common military practice of the age dictated, divided into archer's wedges and dispersed throughout the army, determines how we envisage the action.

However they were organised, the infiltrators succeeded spectacularly, as Glyn Dŵr's men crashed into the shocked English. Hundreds of Englishmen fell in that first savage assault. After what was probably a brief, ferocious fight, the English either lurched back and to the right under the weight of the attack, or a rear section of the army, quite possibly the Herefordshire Militia, was hit by another cavalry charge, probably from their right, and almost certainly having first been raked with arrows. It is possible that the second, lower battle site saw a third charge by Welsh fighting companies on foot who closed in for the final kill. Irrespective of the finer details, the result remained the same, the rampaging Welsh massacred the English on the hillside that day. The wolves from the surrounding forests ate well that night.

There are two mass graves at Bryn Glas. One is over half-way up and marked in remembrance with Wellingtonia trees; the other, below it and to the right, is on a small plateau or shoulder where a church stands. Those who died would almost certainly have been buried where they fell, carrying hundreds of men off the hill would have been too laborious a task in midsummer. We know that only a small number were removed later by their relatives and neighbours who came for their corpses. The English army was completely destroyed, no recognisable component or unit escaped. Even in a time used to the habitual nastiness of medieval warfare, the Battle of Bryn Glas stunned and appalled observers. The words that come down to us from most, if not all sources, are " *horrific carnage*". English civilian and military reporters emphasised in gory technicolour the details and extent of the massacre. It was not, and could not, be brushed under the carpet, as was case with the Battle of Hyddgen, to name but one occasion when English forces have been beaten by enemies for whom they have no respect. This can be substantiated by how little is known of French victories in the Hundred Years War, which, after all, history records as a successful campaign for the French. Stunning French victories over the English in any war, such as at Fontenoy, go unknown in Britain, yet are common knowledge in France. Similarly, few of Robert the Bruce's battles are common knowledge in Britain, despite his successful liberation of Scotland. History is littered with many such examples, from all nations' histories.

We know very little of Welsh losses at Bryn Glas. They are not mentioned and thus were probably light. Most armies have a tendency to overestimate their successes, and the English are no exception to this. However, there is no mention of Welshmen lying dead on the ground, nor even of the English giving as good as they got, in time-honoured 'I took one with me' fashion. The fact is that at Bryn Glas, many hundreds of Englishmen were slaughtered by a smaller Welsh force. English losses are easier to quantify than those of the Welsh, but are still not an accurate figure. A variety of estimates are given, though we can disregard the ubiquitous '*two hundred*', which appears again, just as we can disregard the almost hysterical '*eight thousand*' by a distant English monk. Eight hundred is another figure offered, but a more sober contemporary English source tells us that "*most of the English host were slain ... on that field, more than one thousand one hundred of our people were killed.*" The use of the word 'most' is very interesting as logically it implies 'more than half', but usually a good deal more than half. Other sources support this amount, or settle for a figure of around one thousand five hundred Englishmen killed, all of which helps us to make an educated estimation of the size of the original army.

Given that the casualties accounted for over half of the army's strength - and they were probably upwards of a thousand, and probably a few hundred more – indicates an approximate figure of two thousand cavalry and infantry. Adding the Welsh bow contingent to this should give a figure of around two and a half thousand, assuming of course that the casualty estimations are reliable. The Welsh forces therefore could not have numbered anything approaching this figure, or the Army of March, with its experienced commanders, would not have thrown caution to the wind and gone after them so recklessly.

Sir Kinard de la Bere, Sir Walter Devereux, Sir Robert Whitney and all of his relations who accompanied him were killed on the battlefield. Their retainers, cavalry and infantry companies and militia were cut to shreds. Edmund Mortimer and Sir Thomas Clanvowe were taken prisoner on the battlefield, the only ones taken that day.

The tale of this battle is not finished though. As the English lay dead or dying on the battlefield, Welshwomen, camp followers of Glyn Dŵr's army, are said to have taken to the battlefield and mutilated them. The tale is a particularly gruesome one. They are said to have cut off the English soldiers' genitals and rammed them into their owners' mouths, and cut off English noses then shoved them into the soldiers' backsides. Certain rumours justified it as payback for the abuses of the Royal Expedition of October 1401. Shakespeare recorded the impact and horror in Act 1, Scene i of King Henry IV part II thus:

The Earl of Westmoreland:
> '*But yesternight : when all athwart there came*
> *A post from Wales loaden with heavy news;*
> *Whose worst was, that the noble Mortimer,*
> *Leading the men of Herefordshire to fight*
> *Against the irregular and wild Glendower,*
> *Was by the rude hands of that Welshman taken,*
> *A thousand of his people butchered;*
> *Upon whose corpse there was such misuse,*
> *Such beastly shameless transformation,*
> *By those Welshwomen done, as may not be*
> *Without much shame retold or spoken of.*'

We do not know if this really happened. It was certainly a nightmare engraved in English minds, common enough to be easily recalled to Shakespeare's audience when he wrote about it some two centuries later. Thomas Capgrave, chronicler writing at the time of the battle, wrote;

> "*After the batayle ful schamefully the Walsch women cutte of mennes membris and put hem in here mouthis.*"

Rhys Gethin is blamed for ordering and carrying out the first mutilations. He is also said to have killed "*those who resisted or ran*". It is an interesting account, but the description of the mutilations arguably relegates the story to a fictional, symbolic castration, that of English power in Wales. The mathematics and practicalities of doing such acts to so many dead or dying men, covered in their own blood and defecation, seem to distance it from literal truth.

The reaction along the English border, the March, was one of hysteria. The entire border sent out distress messages, from Chester to Monmouth communities claimed they were under attack and at Glyn Dŵr's mercy, adding to his mysterious ability of being in numerous places

Usk Castle courtesy Lise Hull

at the same time. Popular myth has Leominster razed after the battle, though documentation requesting ordnance from the town neglects to mention its own destruction at Welsh hands. It can be counted as simply another statistic in the wave of panic which swept through England in the aftermath of total defeat at Bryn Glas. It is most probable that Glyn Dŵr and the Welsh army retired to the hills to celebrate their victory and the midsummer solstice, taking their two prisoners of note and their enormous new stash of weapons and armour with them. They must have wondered if this was the victory foretold by The Great Comet, or was the ultimate victory still to come?

Mortimer's enemies and others who sought to profit from his downfall started rumours that he had collaborated with Glyn Dŵr and had surrendered too easily on the battlefield. It is preposterous to maintain that anyone would suffer the plundering of their own estates, the killing of peers, friends and supporters and endure the humiliation of bloody defeat, simply for a percentage of a ransom. Mortimer had everything to lose by siding with the rebels. The rumours may have spawned from the king himself, who certainly manipulated them to his own ends.

[10] Late June/ Early July 1402

Henry IV cancelled his intended invasion of Scotland because of the war in Wales. Castle garrisons across Wales were in a state of high alert, especially Aberystwyth, Cardigan, Swansea, Brecon and Radnor, fearing a large attack in the south. Huge fines were levied on border areas, particularly in the north-east, even though they were clearly not the rebels involved at Bryn Glas, or even rebels at all. The Crown ordered a judicial session to be held in north Wales in May, and in south Wales in June. They were to be the last held in Wales for some time. Fines could only be demanded in areas close to centres of English military power on the border because English control of Wales was collapsing rapidly. Across Wales, fines and rents went unpaid and the courts were ignored, and the king's writ ran only where his soldiers were physically present in sufficient numbers to impose his will. Throughout Wales, especially along the border, men defected in droves to Glyn Dŵr's cause. Even Flint, ringed by English strongpoints, began to show the first signs of rebellion.

[11] 31st July 1402
Prince Hal was appointed commander-in-chief of the army being assembled for the impending royal chevauchée, that being a massive raid by a mostly mounted army, in south Wales.

[12] August 1402
Owain Glyn Dŵr led his swollen army south on a grand chevauchee of his own. The rebels beseiged Brecon, while Glyn Dŵr is reported to have stormed Abergavenny, Usk, Caerleon, Newport, Cardiff and others in some style. We are told that *"he overthrew the castles ... and fired the towns."* The castle of Whitney-on-Wye, which belonged to Sir Robert Whitney, slain at Bryn Glas, was utterly destroyed by the rebels, the walls pulled down, and the ruins lost beneath the river Wye when it changed course many years later. One legend of the conflict tells of the capture of mighty Caerffili castle, just north of Cardiff, as Welsh forces rampaged through the area at this time. Lacking the complicated seige technology necessary to assault such an immense fortification, the rebels are reputed to have flung themselves at the walls and formed a human pyramid, up which the second wave of warriors scrambled, took control of the parapet and fought their way to the gatehouse, from where they were lowered the drawbridge and opened the gates, allowing Glyn Dŵr's men to pour into the castle.

Some sources suggest that not all of these targets were achieved, again, we cannot be sure. We can be sure that Glyn Dŵr was striking the fear of God into the English populace and observers alike. After he rode south, and the men of Gwent and Glamorgan rose with him, one English chronicler wrote this of him:

"In short, like a second Assyrian, the rod of God's anger,
he did deeds of unheard of cruelty with fire and sword."

No revenue was collected for the authorities in the south-east, or anywhere else, thereafter. The English civilian administration in Wales collapsed in this late summer period. In many respects, Wales was free of the English yoke. Outright independence had not yet been obtained, but the enemy state which dominated Wales had been defeated on the battlefield and the apparatus of civilian control had been brought down. It is certainly true that there were still English military installations on Welsh soil, but their role changed from one of dominating and punishing the native population, to one of withstanding its attacks, cowering within the well-built castle walls.

Before returning to his strongholds in the mountains of the north, Glyn Dŵr and his men briefly attacked Aberystwyth, Harlech and Caernarfon, and then inflicted another raid on Ruthin and Dyffryn Clwyd. Glyn Dŵr's summer campaign took him and his army all around Wales.

[13] August/September 1402

The English navy sent relief forces to Beaumaris, Caernarfon and Harlech. The latter two castles also had to be rescued by hurriedly despatched land forces, who rode hell-for-leather across the north to help the besieged garrisons and those troops landed by the navy. They held on, this time.

[14] Summer 1402   Pirates

The first tangible signs of foreign aid come from the summer of 1402. Welsh and Breton pirates plagued shipping in the Celtic Sea and the Channel. Some fell to the English navy in the Channel, who found the fighting companies and boarding parties contained a number of heavily-armed Welshmen aboard Breton vessels. This type of Welsh-Breton action was to be a lasting feature of the rebellion, which was steadily maturing into a war. The Bretons were the first outsiders to become noticeably involved, though clearly, pirates carried no official sanction or recognition.

Another story worthy of retelling suggests that a party of Welsh and Bretons bearing Owain Lawgoch's colours landed near Llandybie, guided by the English navigator, David Perrot of Tenby. The party is said to have contained a number of men who had served under Owain Lawgoch before his murder by an English agent in France. Lawgoch's second-in-command, Ieuan Wyn, is said to have buried Lawgoch's heart, which they had brought in a casket, in the church at Llandybie. Other veterans of Lawgoch's continental adventures are believed to have returned to Wales to fight alongside Glyn Dŵr following this event.

[15] Early September 1402   Henry IV's third Royal Expedition
to Wales

In August, Henry IV summoned and massed the men of eighteen counties and other troops, and prepared to tour north Wales. He intended to crush the seemingly invincible rebels. In order to tempt the comparatively meagre Welsh forces out into battle with his enormous, armoured monster of an army, the English torched the rebel town of Llanrwst and massacred whoever they could find there.

Henry's Welsh enemy was nowhere to be seen, again. The weather once again vented its anger on foreign forces in Wales. Massive storms, torrential rain, even summertime snow, nearly killed the king by sweeping him away while crossing a river in spate. During another storm one night, the king was reportedly struck and pinned by a large falling timber, the central pole of his royal tent. He was saved by the fact that, fearing rebel attack, he had decided to sleep in his armour, somewhat uncomfortably, and so was not crushed. A flash flood then raced through the camp carrying various items away.

Henry IV returned home with a certain amount of stolen livestock and looted goods yet again, but with no victories to his name. The third expedition had also been a failure and the elements had almost killed him. If it had not been clear before, it was now dawning on the English that holding on to the castles, the only remaining bastions of Englishness in Wales, would be crucial.

In the aftermath of Henry's campaign, as the villagers of the north buried those killed by Henry's army, Owain Glyn Dŵr is known to have attended the funerals of at least two common squires and bestowed gifts upon their families.

[16] September 1402
Once Henry IV and his army had passed by, on the outward part of their expedition, fast-moving raiders attacked and mercilessly plundered the Grey lordship of Dyffryn Clwyd.

[17] 13th September 1402   The Battle of Homildon Hill
The Percys, led by Hotspur, scored a crushing victory over the Scots at Homildon Hill. Not only was this revenge for the Battle of Otterburn some years earlier, but it was so comprehensive a victory that the Scots were not even in a position to sue for peace terms. Regardless of the final casualty toll, more than seventy Scots nobles were captured, breaking the back of the Scots' capacity to make war. Also some thirty French nobles on the Scots' side were taken. All captured nobles were later ransomed or executed.

For Hotspur, it was another stunning victory in a career characterised by battlefield success. Having broken the Scots, he was probably looking forward to significant remuneration from the ransom money and a reward from Henry IV. For the Welsh, this was a disaster. The Scots had shown an interest in Glyn Dŵr's war from the first negotiations, or even before. The closest foreign nation able to bestow large-scale military support for Wales was effectively dead in the water.

[18] 24th September 1402
Letters sent to Henry IV from the panicking garrison at Radnor Castle urgently appealed for help. They had heard of renewed rebel activity in the area and feared another attack. Bearing in mind the events of August the year before, their alarm is understandable. Also adding to their worries, was the fact that the town and castles walls, damaged by the rebels in 1401, had not been fully repaired and were only *"partly defencible"*.

[19] Negotiations and Ransoms 1402
By 1st November, Sir Thomas Clanvowe was free and was promoted by Henry IV. We do not know how long he remained a prisoner after Bryn Glas, or how much was paid to free him.

Parliament was again petitioned to pay the ransom for Lord Grey of Ruthin. There seem to have been cynical motives in this. Those calling for his release were Bolingbroke supporters. In a contrite move to be seen to be bowing to the pressure of so many noble voices, a ransom of ten thousand marks was paid in two instalments, the second of which was paid in November. The first instalment of six thousand marks bought Grey's release, with his eldest son and heir handed over as a hostage to ensure the arrival of the second payment. Grey was bound over not to recommence hostilities against the Welsh, which he honoured. There is reason to believe that this ransom impoverished the de Grey dynasty. They clung on to their diminishing estates until 1508 when they sold them to Henry Tudor, grandson of one of Glyn Dŵr's captains. We can only ponder the delights that captivity with Glyn Dŵr held for Reginald de Grey. Later accounts claim that he was held at Dolbadarn Castle, at the foot of Snowdon.

Hotspur petitioned Parliament for Mortimer's release. He and a few others sought to scotch rumours that his brother-in-law, Mortimer, was in league with Glyn Dŵr. Appeals on Mortimer's behalf were flatly refused. Henry IV, in most insistent mood, would hear nothing of it, and did nothing but impede efforts to secure Mortimer's release. Moreover, Henry IV added cryptically ; " [I] *would not use royal revenues to strengthen my enemies against us"*. We can only guess at what that meant, though he obviously recognised this as a perfect opportunity to annul any Mortimer threat to the throne, by tainting him with the charge of conniving with the Welsh, or by actually causing Mortimer to rebel. Henry IV then astounded everyone with his treatment of Hotspur. Having returned from Scotland, the conquering hero, with an unprecedented number of noble prisoners, Hotspur was obliged to hand over the captives to Henry IV, who then also kept the ransom money. This must have severely riled the Percys. On top of this they were ordered to undertake further negotiations with Owain Glyn Dŵr on Henry IV's behalf. Having brought the Scots to their knees, they might have expected a fitting reward. They did not get one, nor were they allowed to take a break from campaigning, as Henry IV despatched them to Wales immediately to bolster royal forces and carry out negotiations with the enemy.

They did negotiate with Glyn Dŵr, though quite possibly on a subject of which the king would not approve, as later events would illustrate. Parliament passed yet more of its anti-Welsh ordinances, some of which were mentioned in an earlier section, 'The Welsh in Battle'. Those laws relating to 'racial intermarriage' were enforced, and those which disqualified Welshmen from official positions were reaffirmed on the statute books. Those Welshmen removed from their posts were also obliged to raise the money required to hire the Englishmen replacing them.

[20] 30th November 1402   Edmund and Catrin

Edmund Mortimer, defeated and captured at Bryn Glas, married Glyn Dŵr's daughter, Catrin, on 30th November. He then became a rebel against the Crown. There are many reasons for this. There is a strong possibility that in their negotiations with Glyn Dŵr, the Percys informed Mortimer of the king's opposition to any attempt to aid his release. Henry IV's ingratitude, betrayal and contempt for his cousin, Mortimer, after he had faced the enemies of the Crown in battle, must have been a factor.

Another reason was that a hostage who cannot raise his ransom is of no use to his captors. As his erstwhile master no longer required his services, he needed a new master, and who better than the man who held the power of life or death over him? There is another, more romantic factor, Catrin and Edmund. Shakespeare has the two falling madly in love, with the Chieftain's beautiful daughter doting on the recuperating gentleman, so helpless in his chains. Other sources also suggest there was genuine affection between them, though we shall never know for sure.

Mortimer's first tangible act of rebellion was to write to the gentry and knights of the border, some of whom had Welsh connections and sympathies. In his letter he outlined his case and asked them to join him and the rebel cause. He wrote to men he must have known would never support him and would warn others against so doing. Little came of this attempt to lure support for the rebels, though he did have the support of the Mortimer household, of which he was acting head. The Mortimers were in decline though, the death of the fourth Earl of March in 1398 and the defeat at Bryn Glas, dealt the family a severe blow. The heir to the fourth earl's title was still just a child, and under the 'protection' of Henry IV.

In the eyes of many at court, Mortimer's letter simply justified his condemnation as a traitor. They failed to make the simple leap of logic of realising that if he had not been abandoned in captivity and labelled a traitor for his efforts, he would not have then turned against the Crown he had so loyally served. It read:

"My very dear and well-beloved John Greyndor, Howel Vaughan, and all the gentles of Radnor and Prestremde [Presteigne]. I greet you very much and make known to you that Oweyn GlenDŵr has raised a quarrel of the which the object is, if King Richard be alive to restore his Crown: and if not, that my honoured nephew, who is the right heir to the said crown shall be king of England, and that the said Oweyn will assert his right in Wales. And I, seeing and considering it good and reasonable, have consented to join in it, and to aid and maintain it, and by the grace of God to a good end, Amen. I ardently hope and from my heart that you will support and enable me to bring this struggle of mine to a successful issue.
Written at Melenyth [Maelienydd] the 13th day of December."

[21] November/ December 1402
The government enacted its statutory right to demand 'war loans' to finance the war against Glyn Dŵr. They plundered money and things of value throughout north-east Wales, mainly in Flint. This must have helped convince anyone left undecided in the area exactly who was the dangerous, aggressive thief and who acted in the people's best interests.

1403

WALES ABLAZE

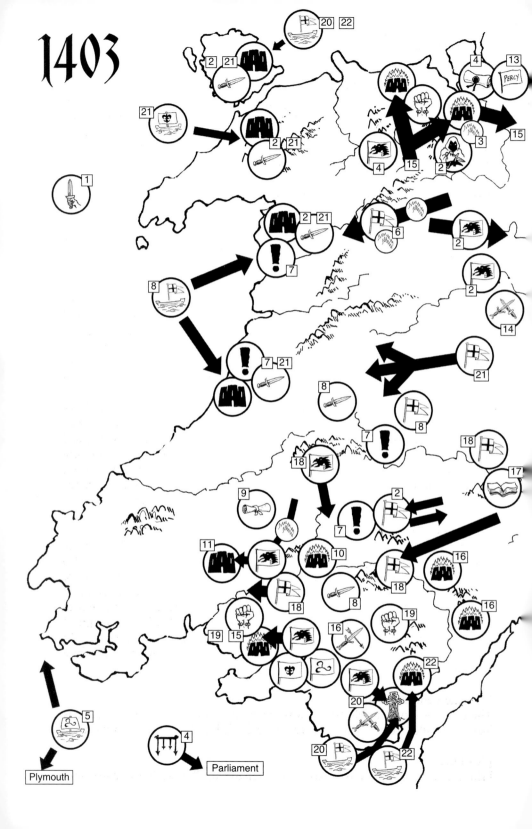

1403

Percy

Plymouth

Parliament

[1] Constant Warfare - 1403

The latter part of the previous year saw a continuation of military campaigning beyond the traditional war season of the summer months into autumn and winter. The Welsh had been in action in winter months before this point, but their efforts had been more sporadic in nature. From 1403 we can identify a transition from the early rebellion in Wales, characterised by fitful action involving planned military objectives and violent opportunism alike, to a state of war. The campaigning intensified to such an extent that before this time, moments of planning and action were noted and in between these moments were lulls; from this point on there was constant warfare. Hereafter, only the large attacks or moments of planning or parley are noteworthy, above an undercurrent of continuous fighting where there had previously been peace.

Arguably, the seeds of this constant warfare were planted in the summer of 1402 with the early summer raids which culminated at Bryn Glas, the collapse of any hold the English civilian administration may have had, and the August chevauchée which tore through the south before turning west and then north. Yet it is from the beginning of 1403 and thereafter we see their fruition. English castles and towns in Wales and nearby England were under the constant threat of lightning raids by Welsh forces, or under the very real scenario of incessant harrying, frequent assault or siege.

Other significant aspects are the duration and timing of military campaigning. War was accepted as being a summer affair, the Welsh ignored these standard rules of war and rewrote their own. The rebels campaigned throughout the year, through the unseasonal period of deep winter and the traditional time of summer alike. On such a scale, this was perhaps without precedent in western Europe and thus, Glyn Dŵr and his men deserve a place in military history among the founding fathers of guerilla warfare.

[2] January 1403

Heavy fighting broke out across Wales and beyond. Beaumaris, Caernarfon, Harlech and Aberystwyth came under determined attack. There were also raids deep into Shropshire, just a few days after excessive 'war loans' were extorted from Welsh communities on the border. The Welsh plundered and laid waste a wide area east of the border, recovering what these communities had lost in taxation and more. Ferocious raids into England were a sign of Welsh military dominance not only over the area, but over the whole war. In January, rebel agitators from Llŷn were known to have infiltrated Flintshire and began inciting insurrection.

[3] 22nd February 1403

The town of Hope, in Flintshire, was taken and burnt by the rebels. Hope is just a few miles from Chester, the centre of English military power in the area.

[4] March 1403

Prince Hal was appointed Royal Lieutenant in Wales. This made him

Commander-in-Chief of royal forces. He immediately sent out more garrisons to north, mid and south Wales, hoping to stem the tide of war, flowing very much in favour of the rebels. He also began planning and raising English armies for their summer campaign and was appointed his very own personal army of four barons, twenty knights, five hundred men at arms and two thousand five hundred archers. Meanwhile, his adversary, Glyn Dŵr, appeared in person in the north-east, where his spies and agitators had most recently been at work. There were widespread defections to his colours by the men of the area, who had previously remained uncommitted.

Parliament met in spring, where Hotspur was removed from his military commands in Wales. Lands granted to him *'for life'* were reallocated by Henry IV, despite the fact that he had no right to do so. Hotspur was again criticised for not attempting to capture or kill Glyn Dŵr at parley, or draw him onto the battlefield and then defeat him. Hotspur reacted angrily at these unexpected attacks upon him and his fine reputation. He gave Parliament a piece of his mind, snarling:

> *"You courtier knights say great things, and promise to do even greater ones.*
> *In the ease and comfort of court nothing seems difficult."*

He strode angrily from the assembly and left Court without Henry IV's permission.

[5] March ? 1403   The Bretons

We cannot be certain of the time, numbers or leaders, but evidence suggests that the Bretons again came to help. They were not just attacking English shipping, both military and mercantile, but bringing in supplies and provisions for the rebels. It is also conceivable that they were recruiting Welsh fighting companies for seaborne warfare, as they had done previously.

There is a report of the Bretons sacking a number of southern English ports, including the naval base at Plymouth. There is a question mark over the date and year. It was in spring, but if they attacked it in 1403, then their colours were well and truly nailed to the mast of the Welsh cause, for we know with a degree of certainty that they plundered Plymouth the following spring. It is also possible that the Bretons carried out these attacks in both years, 1403 and 1404. Although the Bretons were raiding and plundering for their own benefit and enrichment, they were openly assisting their Welsh cousins against England, Brittany's ally against their traditional mutual enemy, France.

[6] Early May 1403

Prince Hal, fifteen years old but no ordinary teenager, was showing signs of becoming the warrior king that his father was not. Inventive, daring, energetic and esteemed by his men and peers, he was already a respected figure among English nobles. It was in Wales that he learnt the arts of war that he would later use to great effect in France.

In early May, he led a five thousand-strong army on a raid into north-east Wales. His objectives were Owain Glyn Dŵr's long abandoned manors at Sycharth and Glyndyfrdwy, which he burnt and then he pillaged the surrounding area. When he wrote to his father telling him the good news on 15th May, he bragged of his deeds, as a precocious teenager with too much wealth and power could perhaps be expected to do. It would not be the last occasion he would do so, as we shall see later, but interestingly, he wrote in admiration of Glyn Dŵr's *'fine houses and lodge'*. He also wrote asking about payment for his soldiers and included the following warning:

"... *they* [the rebels] *strive to raise all the forces of North Wales and South Wales to over-ride and destroy the March and the counties adjoining thereto; and there is no resistance here, so that they can well accomplish their malice; and when our men shall have retreated from us, it is necessary that we should by all means retreat into England, there to be disgraced forever.*

... for too our castles of Aberystwyth and Harlech are besieged ... and we must rescue and provision them within ten days and besides defend the March around us with our third body against the entry of the rebels."

[7] May and June 1403
Harlech, Aberystwyth, Brecon and Radnor garrisons sent numerous requests imploring help. The tone of these repeated requests was often one of panic, and a good number of those messages sent out refer to previous correspondence which never reached English hands.

Letters sent on 30th May reveal that there were rumblings of discontent among the English soldiers and garrisons in Wales. They wanted to be paid and many wanted to be relieved or posted elsewhere. The menace of constant attack and a hostile populace meant they were safest in their castles, and even then still in grave danger. These rumours, in tones of desertion and mutiny, spelt trouble for the authorities.

[8] More Rescue Missions and Reinforcements 1403
Radnor was reinforced just in time. Fighting broke out along the border and the areas surrounding Brecon and Builth fell to the rebels who then assaulted nearby castles. Harlech and Aberystwyth received massive reinforcement from naval rescue missions. Harlech, for example, received one thousand three hundred men as reinforcements in June 1403 alone, such was their need. The Archdeacon of Hereford, Richard Kingeston, addressed the King in the following letter :

" *The Welsh rebels in great numbers have entered Archenfield, and there they have killed the inhabitants, and ravaged the country to the great dishonour of our king and the unsupportable damage of the country. We implore you to consider this very perilous and pitiable case and to pray to our sovereign Lord that he will come in his royal person or perhaps send some person with sufficient power to rescue us from the invasion of the rebels. Otherwise we will be utterly destroyed, which God forbid: whoever comes*

will as we are led to believe
have to engage in battle, or
will have a very severe
struggle with the rebels. And
for God's sake remember that
honourable and valiant man,
the Lord of Abergavenny,
who is on the very point of
destruction if he is not
rescued."

Carreg Cennen courtesy Lise Hull

[9] 15th June 1403

On 15th June hurriedly
despatched letters warned the
English authorities and
military not only of the tremors of a new campaign felt throughout the south,
but of an advancing Welsh army. They chose to ignore the warnings. In late
June, the people of the Tywi valley rose in revolt en masse.

[10] 2nd July 1403

Letters from Dinefwr Castle's commander, Jenkin Havard, dated 2nd July,
revealed that Henry Don of Kidwelly, his large, powerful family and their
supporters had raised the standard of revolt and were leading a rebel force
assaulting Dinefwr Castle.

This was a significant defection to Glyn Dŵr's cause. It marked a
dangerous rise in Glyn Dŵr's power. Henry Don was the most powerful
noble in the south and a well-connected war veteran of long experience. It
was a situation of the government's own making: anti-Welsh legislation
passed in the 1401 and 1402 parliaments drove Welshmen working for the
Crown out of their posts, homes and towns, all Welshmen were considered
potential rebels and treated thus. This was particularly inappropriate in
south-west Wales, where generations of Welshmen had served the authorities
in administrative and military roles as a means of social advancement. Across
Wales, disgruntled soldiers and administrators with practical experience of
the functions of state and detailed knowledge of the English towns, military
capabilities and methods were forced out, and into the welcoming arms of the
rebels.

[11] The July Campaign 1403   The Tywi Valley March.

More panicked dispatches confirm that Glyn Dŵr arrived in the mid-Wales
area on 3rd July, not only with his own battle-hardened personal retinue,
numbering hundreds of men, but with a Welsh army several thousand-strong.
This was possibly the largest independent Welsh army ever raised,
contemporary English forces had certainly never seen anything of the like and
it terrified them. They claimed to have counted eight thousand, two hundred

and forty men mostly armed with spears and swords. This would not have included the advance strike-force of three hundred men Glyn Dŵr had sent to deal with Llandovery.

They started at Newtown, which they took and burnt. Llandeilo followed, then they swept south, crushing everything in their path. The Chamberlain of Carmarthen went out to meet the Welsh with his own army, saw them and fled back to Carmarthen in panic. A number of his men were killed in a skirmish with one of Glyn Dŵr's pathfinding parties. Glyn Dŵr's vanguard took Newcastle Emlyn next as the advance gathered momentum. Carreg Cennen also fell, quite how we are not sure. One story tells of starvation, another of threats as happened later at Dinefwr, but the two most plausible are of a sum of money changing hands and a door being opened from the inside to let the rebels flood in at night. One of the English commanders captured in the campaign was Sir John Scudamore or Skidmore, of Dryslwyn Castle, who would not only marry one of Glyn Dŵr's daughters later, but would play a significant role in Glyn Dŵr's future.

The Welsh marched on Carmarthen, the English capital of south Wales. The fortress there was one of the mightiest in the land, built to remind the natives that a foreign power reigned over their homeland by means of stifling oppression. We do not know the precise series of events, but by sometime on 5th July, or possibly early on 6th July, Carmarthen had been stormed and was in Glyn Dŵr's hands. Jenkin Havard wrote:

"...Oweyn Glyndour, Henry Don, Rhys Ddu, Rhys ap Griffiths ap Llewellyn, Rhys Gethin have won the town of Carmarthen and Wygmor, Constable of the Castle, has yielded up the castle to Oweyn who has burned the town and slain the men of the town ... and a siege has been ordered of the castle that I keep and that is a great peril for me and all that are here with me, for they have made a vow that they will kill us all ...Written in haste and dread"

There are a number of contrasting claims about the attack and the aftermath, but factors common to all accounts are that the town was thoroughly plundered and burnt over a number of days, people were killed both during and after the assault, and that buildings, sections of the town and fortress walls were razed to the ground. Nearby Saint Clears and Laugharne are also reputed to have fallen prey to the rampaging rebels.

Other castles fell, including Dynefwr and the impressive Carreg Cennen. Safe passage was refused to all garrisons and their families, as Jenkin Havard, Crown Commander at Dinefwr had sent out an English messenger, a soldier dressed as a woman who passed safely through Welsh lines. The ploy did not work a second time however, Dinefwr was cut off and fell without being attacked, but only after being taunted and threatened into submission by the enormous Welsh army outside, which called out all day and night the imaginative punishments they planned to carry out on the garrison once it fell into their hands, as it inevitably would. The garrison sought terms the next morning.

On 11th July, a local marcher noble, Lord Carew, and his forces met and defeated one of Glyn Dŵr's scouting parties. Carew claimed it as a major military victory, boasting they had seen off or killed seven hundred men. It is possible, but one must again question the numbers involved and wonder why Carew returned home without taking any more action against the rebels, who continued to maraud the area unopposed for several weeks before heading north.

No English administrative records relating to Wales were made after July 1403. It had taken some time to stumble and then fall, but the evidence shows that English civilian control of Wales was no more. By summer 1403 at the latest, Wales had been recaptured by the Welsh.

[12] Early July 1403
On 7th July, troops led by John Bodenham, the sheriff of Herefordshire, broke the siege of Brecon, apparently leaving a death toll of two hundred and forty men. While there, Bodenham heard reports of the size of the Welsh army at the other end of the Tywi valley at Carmarthen. They hastily withdrew to Hereford's fortifications and appealed to Henry IV for immediate aid, saying that should Owain Glyn Dŵr decide to overrun Hereford, as previous raids had threatened to do, then they did not have enough men in the county to resist him. The commander at Brecon, John Faireford, wrote similar appeals to Henry IV:

"Ordain a remedy for the resistance and destruction of the traitors which are daily reinforced and from time to time cause great evil and destruction to your faithful subjects without any resistance; considering my most gracious lord that if assistance come not speedily, all the castles and towns and your loyal subjects within them are in great peril and on the point of being utterly ruined for default of succour and good government."

The Archdeacon of Hereford, Richard Kingeston also sent advice to the King:

"Letters are arriving from Wales containing intelligence by which you may learn that the whole country is lost if you do not go there as quickly as possible. For which reason it may please you to prepare to set out with all the power you can muster and march night and day for the salvation of these parts. And it may please you to reflect that it will be a great disgrace as well as a loss, to lose or suffer to be lost in the beginning of your reign a country which your noble ancestors have won and for so long a time peaceably possessed. For people talk very unfavourably."

[13] 10th July 1403   Hotspur Raises the Standard of Revolt.
On this day, Hotspur declared himself a rebel against the king at Chester. He laid charges of perjury against Bolingbroke, that he had usurped the throne after claiming he only wished to be restored to his inheritance, following his return from exile. Hotspur also accused him of murdering Richard II, failing

to call free parliamentary elections, failing to raise Mortimer's ransom and raising taxation against the clergy without the consent of Parliament.

He called the men of Chester and Shropshire to his banner in revolt. His uncle, Thomas Percy, Earl of Worcester, joined him, with all his military experience and might. Hotspur's father, the Earl of Northumberland was campaigning in Scotland and so was not involved, while Henry IV was leading an army northward to join Northumberland. A troop of Scots, led by the Earl of Douglas, captured by Percy at Homildon Hill, took to the field under Percy colours.

There are plausible theories regarding Percy collusion with Glyn Dŵr, decided upon during earlier negotiations, supposedly for Glyn Dŵr's submission. The speed and timing of Hotspur's move seems to have surprised everyone. Had he waited a few more weeks, probably as arranged, he would have been joined by his uncle and his father, who would have been able to amass and unite their sizeable forces. They might have combined with Glyn Dŵr and his fearsome force at Chester as they returned from the south-west, and marched on the king with a truly formidable army. There is no clear reason why Hotspur did not rebel in the north of England, the traditional Percy powerbase. Three Percy armies advancing on Henry IV with the Scots at his back would surely have sealed the king's fate. However, Henry IV heard of this on 12th July, while at Nottingham, where he was leading a fresh army to Scotland. He immediately left for Shrewsbury to prepare to battle Hotspur and Worcester before they could gather larger forces.

[14] 21st July 1403   The Battle of Shrewsbury

For once, Henry IV acted quickly and decisively. Having force-marched his army to Shrewsbury, he reached the town before the Percys, who were only a few miles away at Chester. Once there, Henry IV consolidated his power and joined forces with his son and his army, and other loyal nobles and their contingents.

On 21st July, the two sides met in battle. The Percy army of 15,000 men held the higher ground, but Henry's Lancastrian army was far larger, at least 25,000 strong and following a reportedly bitter parley, advanced upon the Percy rebels without delay. The Percy army and a small number of Welsh rebels, fought with their usual courage. Another mid-battle troop defection against royal forces took place, this time, the knights of Worcester defected to their rebel earl's banner. Prince Hal was severely wounded by an arrow which struck him in the face. Evidence suggests that the arrow, apparently in a downward trajectory towards its target, struck Prince Hal on his right cheekbone. It is supposed to have pierced his face, some say damaging his right eye, and penetrated for *"fully six inches"*, taking the bodkin through the roof of his mouth, possibly pinning or at least slicing his tongue, and possibly lodging in his head with the bodkin protruding through the soft tissue between the chin and the Adam's apple. This must surely have left a scar, perhaps even affected his speech, changing forever the image of a picture-perfect boyish king leading his troops some years later at Agincourt, where, as a soldier of almost fifteen years hard campaigning experience, he was more of a grizzled veteran than an exuberant youth.

In spite of all this, Henry IV's weight of numbers told over Percy talent. The Percy army, with Hotspur and the Earl of Douglas to the fore, repeatedly drove into the royal army seeking to kill the king, who had dressed a number of men in his livery in order to confuse the enemy. Hotspur was killed on the field in a mass of men and Worcester was taken prisoner. The battle raged all day and after nightfall, the merciless pursuit went on well into the night. This caused a stir at the time, as it was extremely unforgiving, even for the era. The casualties on both sides were very high indeed.

Prince Hal survived, but his heavy wound forced him to take time out of campaigning to recuperate, and enforced an absence from duty of a year and a half. Worcester and other 'traitors' were executed on 23rd July. On the same day as the executions, Prince Hal's military posts in Wales were divided amongst the Earl of Arundel, Lords Berkeley, Audely and Powys, and Hugh Burnell. The new commanders were given orders to defend the English border *"against the invasion of the Welsh rebels"*, not to mount offensive actions against Glyn Dŵr. Hotspur's corpse was quartered on the same spot as Prince Dafydd, brother of Llewelyn II, had been in 1283, and his body parts sent to Chester, Bristol, London and Newcastle-upon-Tyne to be displayed. Hotspur's father, the earl of Northumberland was pardoned from his son's revolt, as he had been making war on the Scots on behalf of the Crown and had not been involved.

[15] July and early August 1403
There was no respite in Wales. One of Glyn Dŵr's stalwarts, Hywel Gwynedd, led rebels into Flintshire as the men of the area rose in rebellion. They burnt Flint, Howarden, Hope, Overton and Rhuddlan before taking on local forces in Shropshire, with the king and his forces still in the vicinity. At Flint, the townsfolk managed to save themselves by taking shelter within the castle walls and the rebels rushed the town.

On 13th August, the men of Cydweli, Carnwyllon and Iscennen assaulted Kidwelly. A large flood prevented them from executing their planned surprise raid. The troops and English townsfolk with time to organise themselves, managed to hang on grimly to Kidwelly Castle but the town was lost to the rebels. The English survivors of the attack wrote to the king detailing the attack, the damage, how Henry Don's men had taken all the town's victuals (corn) and that English men and women had already left Wales for the safety of England and that others were also preparing to do so. The rebels, led by Henry Don, comprised a large number of men of the area formerly employed by the authorities, who had fallen victim to recent anti-Welsh legislation, losing their positions and homes.

[16] August 1403
It was at this time that Crickhowell supposedly fell to rebel forces and the castle was rendered inoperable for future use by its partial destruction in the

assault. The rebels are also supposed to have made a sustained attack on Abergavenny, taking and burning the town, and harrying the surrounding area. Nearby garrisons went on full defensive alert, thinking Glyn Dŵr was about to overrun the area with the army raised for the July campaign which took and damaged Carmarthen. Fighting raged across Glamorgan, notably at a place called Stalling Down outside Cowbridge, where a huge pitched battle was fought, allegedly lasting eighteen hours, and a large English force was routed by Glyn Dŵr's army. During the battle a man named Cadwgan, from Aberochwy, near modern-day Treorchy in the Rhondda, was described as playing a key role in defeating the English that day, repeatedly charging into their ranks on horseback, making savagely efficient use of his axe. He was known thereafter as *'Cadwgan Fwyall'*, 'Cadogan the Axe'.

[17] Early September 1403   The Archbishop's Diaries.
Archbishop Kingston's diaries, compiled in Herefordshire during Glyn Dŵr's war corroborate evidence to which other sources allude. The entry dated 3rd September 1403 is most interesting. Having earlier sent off despatches, cries for help, to the king for protection from their highly destructive Welsh enemies, he recorded a recent raid well into Herefordshire. Kingston wrote *"four hundred and more rebels came violently* [into the area]*"* and that they *"took men and beasts, our truce notwithstanding."*

This is an invaluable first-hand account. It tells us three very important things. Firstly, that the Welsh were embarking on plundering raids into England and attacking targets with impunity. Secondly, that they were abducting men as well as taking trinkets and comestibles. Other evidence tells us that they were not only kidnapping men for financial recompense, but to put them into Welsh combat units. Once placed into a warband, the prisoner would have little option but to fight. If they did not, they risked death at their captor's hands and bringing down their wrath upon the communities from where they were taken. If caught by the English authorities, they faced execution as traitors.

Thirdly, the phrase *"our truce notwithstanding"* is a clear indication that communities were making truces with the Welsh, surrendering to their dominance and buying peace with lump sums and with troop levies. This infuriated Henry IV, faced with the maddening reality that the Welsh were dominant throughout Wales and the borders, and that the scope of their power even ran into England, except when he could be there in person with an immense army. Added to this blow to his martial prestige was the implication that he had lost control and, to a degree, sovereignty over these parts of England. It seemed Henry IV was unable to protect his subjects who consequently sought and agreed terms offered in treaty by another power in a time of war. Community leaders said that if royal armies protected them they would not be obliged to surrender to the Welsh. This showed pragmatism on their part, not treason. Henry IV knew this, which is why he did not act against them.

[18] Mid to Late September 1403   Henry IV's fourth Royal Expedition to Wales

Henry IV summoned soldiers from thirty-five shires for the next campaign against Wales. He ordered the reinforcing, restocking and repairing of twenty-two castles in Wales and the Marches. He gathered the army at Hereford in a calculated show of strength in the area, before going on a two-week tour of south Wales. He went to Brecon and then on to the undefended, smouldering ramparts of Carmarthen. He arrived there on 24th September and regarrisoned it, ordering its rebuilding at the same time. He needed to stamp his authority on English troops in Wales who were again threatening to desert. This was a highly punitive expedition, and a significant amount of cattle was rustled by His Majesty, the King of England. In a time of theft and lawlessness, the English monarch proved to be the biggest thief of all. The expedition was yet again a failure. Henry IV made no contact with enemy forces regrouping in the interior, who moved to repossess everything Henry IV and his massive army had believed they had retaken, except Carmarthen, which remained in English hands for the time being.

[19] Late September and October 1403

Gwent and Monmouth rebelled again in a show of loyalty to Glyn Dŵr and the fighting continued as Henry and his army had returned to England. On 29th September, Kidwelly came under attack again. With the Welsh attacking forces this time were Breton land forces with French contingents. Their numbers were small but none the less significant, showing that the Welsh had achieved a growing measure of foreign recognition and aid. Foreign troops were involved for the first time. Kidwelly's reinforcements were immediately in the thick of the action, and after a desperate struggle, they held on to the castle, but again lost the town. This period also shows that the rebels, although outnumbered and, therefore, unwilling to engage Henry IV and his huge army, were nonetheless prepared to conduct operations virtually under his nose, bearing in mind that Henry was in Carmarthen on 24th September and was still in the area when the rebels took Kidwelly town, some seven or so miles from Carmarthen.

Sources recorded that Glyn Dŵr attended the funerals of common men killed by English forces following the 1403 royal expedition, just as he had after Henry IV's previous missions.

[20] October 1403

Naval vessels brought massive reinforcements to Beaumaris on Anglesey which, like the rest of Wales and the borders, had seen almost constant warfare throughout the year. The relief mission to Cardiff, which some sources believe took place in August, went badly. The relief mission from Somerset and north Devon turned into a plundering raid, seeking to profit from the misfortune of those Englishmen in the area who had been attacked by the Welsh. The rescuers plundered Llandaf Cathedral before they were *"driven off with heavy loss"* by the Welsh rebels who swarmed to meet them.

[21] November and December 1403   Winter Campaigning

The Welsh stepped up their attacks on Aberyswyth, Harlech, Caernarfon and Beaumaris. In fact, a French force led by Jean D'Espagne (John of Spain), carried out the assault on Caernarfon. He landed in the Menai Strait, and constructed and used siege engines in the attack, supported by warships offshore. This sort of winter campaigning showed the hardiness and determination of the guerillas, who would continue through the winter into 1404. Relief columns were hurriedly sent out again, stopping first at Radnor, Montgomery and Builth, before spreading across Wales to other castles. It is a noteworthy point that Welsh siege technology improved markedly following the advent of French involvement, albeit still of an unofficial nature.

[22] December 1403

Beaumaris and Cardiff again needed to be rescued. In December, royal naval forces relieved them. Glyn Dŵr himself is reputed to have led those who stormed Cardiff, torched the town, took and burnt the castle, damaging the walls and putting the garrison to the sword before sweeping westwards. This time, English rescue forces in the south maintained their discipline, and did come to the aid of those in the charred remnants of the town, and set to work repairing and reinforcing the town and castle.

1404

FREE WALES AND GLYN DŴR'S PARLIAMENT

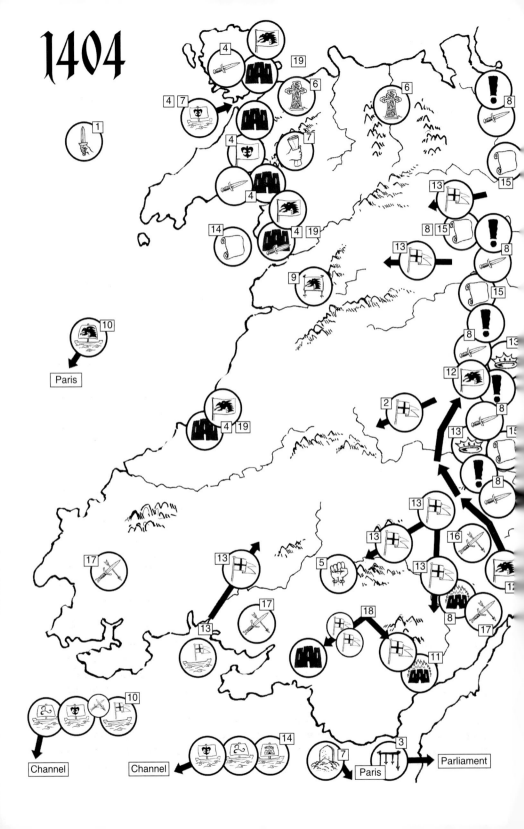

1404

Paris

Paris

Channel

Channel

Paris

Parliament

[1] Constant Warfare 1404

As in 1403, warfare was constant throughout 1404. The military campaigning continued virtually unabated from January to December. As before, there were more specific attacks during the traditional war season, summer, but the following points and the following entries detail notable objectives, negotiations or movements. The course of events through 1404 is somewhat confusing however. There is a certain amount of first-hand evidence and a wealth of more distant secondary supporting evidence from a range of different sources. From all these, we can discern a picture of the year's events, though some sources offer contradictions to commonly accepted evidence.

[2] 24th January 1404

On that day another relief column reached and reinforced the embattled castle at Radnor. Being so close to the frontier made it much easier to rescue than most other castles.

[3] January 1404   Parliament

While once more railing against the Welsh, parliament reallocated Prince Hal's duties. The Earl of Arundel was appointed as overall commander of English troops in north Wales and the Duke of York was given the southern command due to Prince Hal's enforced absence from duty. Other commanders appointed in July 1403 kept their posts, but now deferred to their respective northern or southern commanders instead of to Prince Hal.

[4] January and February 1404

The French force under Jean D'Espagne constructed siege artillery and pounded Caernarfon. The heavy attacks on Harlech and Beaumaris were maintained or even stepped up. The chroniclers of the war are strangely quiet about Aberystwyth, which may well have fallen to the rebels by storm at this time. Other sources believe it was taken by Glyn Dŵr's men later in the year, but we cannot be sure when. Those writing about these events, safely ensconced in England, may not have mentioned it for some time as it was so far away, deep in hostile territory, and suffering the medieval equivalent of a news blackout, as the Welsh pressed home their attack.

Richard Massy, the constable, or commander, of Harlech fell into Welsh hands. Several versions of his capture involve him leaving probably the most formidable fortress in the land to parley with besieging Welsh forces. It seems he forgot to arrange the usual exchange of hostages to ensure his survival at parley, and only became aware of this tiny oversight when he walked directly into Welsh hands and an unpleasant spell in captivity. Other versions have him being taken in an ambush, but these might be confused with the deputy sheriff of Anglesey, who was ambushed as he set out from Beaumaris to tour the island. Showing the English flag, he rode with a military escort of *"over two hundred men"*. While out riding, they were ambushed, the deputy sheriff was taken prisoner and *"over two hundred"* of his escort were slaughtered.

It may have been during these successes, or shortly afterwards, that Glyn Dŵr took possession of the fortresses of Harlech and Beaumaris. Much of the evidence indicates that it happened later in the year, as is discussed below, but there is every chance that they fell to the rampant Welsh in the winter, or more likely, the spring of 1404. Criccieth Castle, near Harlech, also fell to the rebels, probably in this period of sustained sieges and repeated assaults. The rebels successfully destroyed the walls and allegedly massacred the garrison. Criccieth was never rebuilt or used again.

[5] February 1404
The inhabitants of upland Brecon refused to submit to Henry IV, little matter that he was titular sovereign. If he could not bring the rebels in Gwent and Glamorgan to heel, they said, then they would not recognise him as Lord or Sovereign, pay taxes and so on. Henry's forces failed to defeat the rebels in adjacent areas, and Brecon remained defiant of the king. It is also worth remembering that Henry Bolingbroke had been Lord of Brecon since 1384.

[6] April 1404   High Level Defections to the Cause.
The bishops John Trefor of Saint Asaph Cathedral and the recently appointed Lewis Byford of Bangor Cathedral, also known as Lewis ap Ieuan, went to Glyn Dŵr and joined his cause. This tremendous coup not only gave him two high level ecclesiastical supporters, but also presented Glyn Dŵr with two experienced diplomats and opened up a network of possibilities and connections that were previously closed to him. As well as their potential influence abroad, he now had prime candidates to lead an independent church in Wales, should he decide to pursue that plan. He already had enough experienced men to organise, and run, civilian and military authorities in Wales, but now he had the other important branch of statehood within his grasp, a national church. Other ecclesiastical defections followed in their wake.

[7] 23rd April (Saint George's Day) & 27th April 1404
Letters from this date implored parliament to raise a naval force to drive away the French who were led by Jean D'Espagne and his warships. They were bombarding Caernarfon and involved in the attack on Harlech. A letter warned that Harlech was in imminent danger and would fall, if it had not already done so by the time the letter arrived. This was the last that was heard from the English at Harlech.

The Duke of Burgundy, Philip the Bold, the aged peacemaker in the French court, died on 27th April. This led to more factional manoeuvrings around the troubled Charles VI. The hawks took control, led by Louis, Duke of Orleans, the king's brother, who bayed for war with the English. This was good news for the Welsh. Philip the Bold's son, Jean Sans Peur (literally, John Without Fear), took over his father's title. The Duke of Orleans opened correspondence with Henry Bolingbroke, King of England, asking him for a fight. The exchanges are a highly interesting verbal encounter, with Bolingbroke repeatedly declining, though always adding some pointed comment or another to rile Orleans. The French duke persisted in offering to meet him in single or multiple combat, and:

"We will not employ any incantations that are forbidden by Holy Church but make use of the bodily strength granted to us by God, having armour as may be the most agreeable of his person and with the usual arms; that is to say, lance, battle axe, sword and dagger and each to employ there as he shall think most to his advantage, without aiding himself of any bodkins, hooks, bearded darts, poisoned needles or razors ..."

The King of England declined time after time, when Bolingbroke sent Richard II's child bride home, without her sizeable dowry, it provoked the following response from Louis, Duke of Orleans, her brother:

"As I am so nearly related to her I will cheerfully meet you in single combat or with any number you please."

Henry Bolingbroke never took up the Duke of Orleans on his numerous challenges.

[8] Spring and Summer 1404
Letters from panicking English towns, the first of which was dated in April, tell of a prolonged campaign of heavy Welsh attacks throughout Cheshire, Shropshire, Archenfield and Herefordshire. One such letter read:

"Most excellent and mighty Lord, we humbly beseech your highness that you may hear how your loyal lieges of your county of Salop [Shropshire] are in great doubt and despair from day to day at the malice (and mischief) which your Welsh rebels and their adherents are purposing to do and sooner or later will do with all their might in your said county, threatening your good lieges with the destruction of their goods and chattels ... Most excellent lord, may it please you to show grace and favour to your said lieges, and to send them some men-at-arms and archers who have come into these parts with our most redoubted lord the Prince. Your said rebels and the French, knowing that this county is less well quartered than your other counties adjoining your marches of Wales, were intent on a chevauchée into your said county before the coming of our lord the Prince... Most mighty lord, a third of your said county has been destroyed and devastated by your said rebels, and your lieges formerly living there have left to gain their meat and sustenance elsewhere in your realm."

Abergavenny, an English town on the Welsh side of the border, was not spared, and was again taken and burnt. In May, western Shropshire made a truce with the Welsh in an effort to stave off their rampaging attacks, giving large sums of silver and gold for Glyn Dŵr's war chest.

This campaign, involving large-scale Welsh attacks in England, may give us a strong indication that fighting in the west had wound down or even ceased, the western fortresses now in Welsh hands. Rather significant meetings, discussed below, took place in areas close to Aberystwyth and Harlech, which would surely have drawn English attack had they been in control of the fortresses in that area.

[9] May and June 1404
Breton and French warships fought against their English counterparts in the Channel in a series of skirmishes which flared throughout the summer. More ships captured in the fighting showed clear proof of French, Welsh and Breton seaborne collusion, with men of these nations found freely serving on each others' warships. Gruffudd Yonge and the Hanmers led Glyn Dŵr's high-powered diplomatic mission to Charles VI of France, leaving Dolgellau on, or very soon after, 10th May. In early June, the Bretons scored a stunning victory at sea over the English off the south coast of Brittany. The Bretons then launched an attack on the English coast, but failed to take their target, Dartmouth in England.

[10] May? June? July? 1404   The First Rebel Parliament.
We know that Owain Glyn Dŵr convened his first parliament at Machynlleth during the summer of 1404. Possible dates given range through May, June and July. We cannot be sure of when it was held, but there are a few clues. In light of the fact that diplomatic missions were sent to France on 10th May 1404 at Glyn Dŵr's behest, it is possible that this Welsh Parliament first met beforehand to discuss the matter and/or after to discuss the results of the initiative. Another date given is 30th July, however this is almost certainly confused with a later year and a later parliament. However that date, 30th July, may indicate a return date for the diplomatic mission which sailed in May. Several sources state that Glyn Dŵr's Parliament met to ratify the treaty with France negotiated in Paris during the diplomatic mission in May. This would indicate that the session took place in June or July 1404.

Parliament was held in the presence of ambassadors from France, Scotland and Castile, who witnessed Glyn Dŵr's formal coronation as Prince of Wales. Glyn Dŵr's Great Seal was struck, with him bearing an orb, sceptre and crown, Wales' own crown jewels. He was presented to assembled foreign ambassadors as " *Owynus Dei Gratia Princeps Wallie*" or Owain, by the grace of God, Prince of Wales. The foreign ambassadors also witnessed the rebirth of an independent state, Wales, complete with its own legitimate native monarch, legal system, treasury, civil servants, military, clergy and diplomats. This Welsh Parliament consisted of *"the nobles of our race"*, church and other religious leaders, and four men from each commote, or cantref, in Wales came to represent the commons on an equal footing. Glyn Dŵr's first rebel Parliament raised funds for the hiring of a French military mission consisting of sixty ships, later known as 'The de Bourbon Mission'.

The ratification of the Treaty between Owain Glyn Dŵr and Charles VI

One story, written a hundred and fifty years after Glyn Dŵr's first parliament met, claimed that Dafydd Gam, loyal to Henry IV went in disguise and tried to assassinate Glyn Dŵr. Thwarted as he moved in for the kill, Gam's life was allegedly spared by Glyn Dŵr's closest captains who argued for Gam's imprisonment instead of

Caerffili Castle courtesy Lise Hull

execution. Gam is then supposed to have escaped confinement by climbing through a small window and then fleeing to Hereford.

We can discount it as a later fabrication to embellish Glyn Dŵr's mythic status. Gam would not have gone to Glyn Dŵr's parliament, not by invite nor guile, and it is a nonsense to say that any would-be assassin would have been spared, least of all by Glyn Dŵr's captains and guards, who were never reticent about killing. There was an assassination attempt made on Glyn Dŵr later, as we shall see. The would-be assassin's grisly end would surely have been a warning and a typical example of what traitors could expect.

[11] June 1404

Evidence suggests that Cardiff town and castle again fell to the rebels. There was no attempt to recover Cardiff until December that year, but evidence clearly placed it in Welsh hands *"by midsummer"*, therefore by the 21st of June. (June 21st is Midsummer Day, the longest day, but Midsummer Quarterday is June 24th, so this date could be three days later). Reports tell us that the Friars at Cardiff, members of sects sympathetic, loyal or active supporters of Glyn Dŵr, allegedly asked if they could have their books and silver returned from the ransacked castle. On top form, Glyn Dŵr allegedly replied *"why did you leave it in the castle? If you had left it at home it would have been safe!"* This may go some way to scotch the myth that the rebels were church-burning pagans. They did loot and burn those churches not loyal to Glyn Dŵr, but none that were. He took the Bishop's of Llandaf's fortified palace and again battered the few enemy strongholds still manned in the Vale of Glamorgan. Local folklore also says that Glyn Dŵr went on from Cardiff and took a number of other castles in the area, including mighty Caerffili.

[12] June 1404

Another well-documented flurry of hysterical cries for help from the border communities dates from June. The Welsh tore through Herefordshire at lightning speed, hitting the county hard and allegedly attacking the nunnery at Aconbury. There is no evidence to corroborate the source which makes that particular claim. Indeed, the report concerning Aconbury is rather dubious and can probably be put down to government-inspired propaganda.

[13] Late June and July 1404

Radnor, Hay, Abergavenny, Brecon, Welshpool, Oswestry, Bishopscastle and Carmarthen received massive royal reinforcements again in late June. In July, Prince Hal moved his base to Hereford and Leominster, between which he alternated. He still played no military role, but supervised and gave orders. It was a full year since his injury at Shrewsbury, and would be another eight months before he would make his return to the war.

[14] July and August 1404   The Treaty of Alliance and the de Bourbon Mission.

The diplomatic mission to France was a great success. A formal treaty of alliance between Wales and France was signed on 14th July 1404. It was signed by Gruffydd Yonge and John Hanmer for Glyn Dŵr, and by Le Compte de la Marche, Louis, Compte de Vendome, Arnaud de Corbie, Chancellor of France and by the Bishops of Arras, Meaux and Noyon on behalf of Charles VI. This would remain an interesting date in French history, though it is somewhat better remembered for another, entirely unrelated, event on the same date several centuries later. Glyn Dŵr's ambassadors returned with the glad tidings. They brought the Treaty document, which began *In the first place that the said lords, the King and the Prince shall be mutually joined, confederated, united and leagued by the bond of a true covenant and real friendship ...* It promised that the two countries were now allies and all that that entailed. When it was read to Glyn Dŵr's Parliament, it must have met a rapturous reception. The Welsh could expect arms and military support, and were guaranteed representation or inclusion in any future negotations held between France and England. The ambassadors brought home French arms for the war effort and personal gifts from Charles VI of trinkets along with fine weapons and armour for the Prince of Wales.

The count of La Marche, Jacques de Bourbon, was ordered to recruit men and launch a mission to Wales that summer. He was to have overall command of the fleet being assembled at Harfleur, and a Breton fleet being assembled at Brest. Before sailing, they were also joined by twenty warships from Castile. They put to sea in mid-August, attacked and sacked Plymouth with their land force of some eight hundred knights and esquires, before returning to Saint Malo, apparently fearing an English counter-attack which never materialised. They put to sea again, but La Marche led them up and down the Channel going after plunder instead of heading to Wales as ordered. This led to annoyance and disaffection among the Bretons and Spanish in particular, especially when de Bourbon once again attacked Plymouth. The English fended off the second attack and another on Falmouth a few weeks later.

The fleet dispersed and La Marche returned with little booty for his efforts. French chroniclers were critical to the point of scorn at the ignominy and shame of La Marche's mission, which had undeniably tarnished the name and colours of France and wasted an entire summer.

[15] July and August 1404

Throughout July and August, border communities, towns and villages made peace treaties with Glyn Dŵr's men. The precise terms of the treaties have been lost, but probably involved cash payments, provisions and, in some cases, troops levied or hostages taken. This, of course, was deeply embarrassing to the Crown, and an admission of continuing rebel supremacy.

[16] July 1404?

Forces led by Richard Beauchamp, the Earl of Warwick, one of Prince Hal's favourite commanders, are supposed to have engaged local Welsh raiders near the border in the south-east at a place called Campstone Hill. Warwick is supposed to have inflicted " *a bloody defeat*" on the enemy and personally snatched the enemy warbanner from its bearer, one Richard ap Elis. The moment was glorified in the form of sketches and paintings done especially for the earl. Strangely though, when later writers emphasized English victories, they fail to mention Campstone Hill. There are a number of possible reasons for this. Firstly, it is possible that it never happened, the sources are not always reliable. Secondly, it is possible that he won a small skirmish and exaggerated it for his master's benefit, bearing in mind the English had gone without a victory of note since the beginning of the war. Lastly, and most likely, is that the source that placed the event in July 1404 confused the date with March 1405 and the Battle of Grosmont on virtually the same spot, in which Warwick participated and performed well.

[17] 20th August 1404

Letters, reports and other evidence tell of three simultaneous Welsh attacks in the south. In the south-west, the rebels took and held Haverford, making good use of its port. Henry Don led a successful attack on Kidwelly town, taking and burning it again. Accompanying Don was the nobleman, William Gwyn ap Rhys Llwyd, formerly one of the Crown of England's favourite and most trusted servants in the area. English parliamentary legislation had dispossessed and branded as a traitor William Gwyn, and others like him, earning the Crown his undying enmity.

While in the south-east, Welsh forces attacked (or counter-attacked if there was the alleged earlier fight at Campstone Hill) at a site mid-way between Monmouth and Abergavenny, at Craig-y-Dorth. In the encounter at Craig-y-Dorth, English sources recorded a *"horrific massacre"* being visited on their troops. The few survivors are said to have scrambled to safety, being chased to the gates of Monmouth *"with the Welsh snapping at their heels."*

[18] November and December 1404

Two huge English armies were sent to break the long siege of Coity in Glamorgan. The defenders held onto the castle, the rescue columns apparently arriving in the nick of time. As two armies rode to the rescue at Coity, another went to Cardiff to recover the abandoned, blackened remains of the town and castle in December. It is difficult to say whether these immense operations constitute a fifth Royal Expedition to Wales, rather than being the largest of rescue missons.

Coity Castle courtesy Lise Hull

[19] Winter 1404
Aberystwyth, Harlech and Beaumaris.

By the end of the year, the mighty fortresses of Aberystwyth and Harlech were definitely in Glyn Dŵr's hands. He made Harlech his capital. Reports that the fall of Harlech, battered by Glyn Dŵr's experienced assault troops, was facilitated by the changing of hands for an undisclosed sum of gold are unsubstantiated, but worthy of mention. We have no reason to doubt that these castles fell by storm to the Welsh. We do not know when they fell exactly, Aberystwyth was probably first and Harlech sometime around 23rd April. The only solid confirmation comes in November and December, which tells us that they had already fallen, but does not state when. The fact that Glyn Dŵr's summer parliament was held at Machynlleth, near Aberystwyth and within striking range for troops at Harlech, probably tells us that the area was securely in rebel hands by that time. The English would hardly pass up an opportunity to attack such a gathering of Welsh nobles, clergy and community leaders if it was in their power to do so. They clearly knew it was taking place, yet did not, or could not, move against it.

Furthermore, English strategy in the west was characterised by naval rescue missions and relief columns racing across the land to break the sieges. In 1404, there were no such missions to Aberystwyth or Harlech, their key installations in west Wales. This would suggest that they had fallen by the start of the summer war season. The capture of these castles added a new dimension to Glyn Dŵr's war capabilities, for we know that these castles, especially Harlech, boasted a small number of guns in their inventory. Those Welshmen who had served abroad were experienced in the handling and operation of gunpowder weapons, especially those of Owain Lawgoch's forces, who had used them in a number of conflicts.

Like much of the west, Beaumaris Castle fell silent during 1404. We do not know for sure if, or when, it too was taken by the rebels, but one crucial piece of evidence cuts through the speculation to say that it indeed fell to Glyn Dŵr. In the summer of the following year, 1405, stated and recorded English

Aberystwyth Castle courtesy Lise Hull

military objectives include a campaign *"to go to Anglesey and recover the castle of Beaumaris."* This implies that it was in Welsh hands, or at the very least had been taken, cleared and then abandoned as had happened at so many other much smaller castles. If the trio of great Edwardian fortresses had fallen to Glyn Dŵr during 1404, that would mark a year of extremely significant successes for the Welsh. If the capture of Conwy in 1401 had Edward I turning in his grave, he would have been spinning wildly at the very real prospect that the Welsh held Aberystwyth, Harlech and Beaumaris. Glyn Dŵr's poet, Iolo Goch wrote a verse to mark the event, translated as follows:

> *'Here's the life I've sighed for long*
> *Abashed is now the Saxon throng*
> *And Britons have a British Lord*
> *Whose emblem is a conquering sword.*
> *There's none I know that knows him well*
> *The hero of the watery dell*
> *Owain of bloody spear in field*
> *Owain his country's strongest shield'.*

1405

INTERNATIONAL ACCLAIM, INTERNATIONAL ARMIES

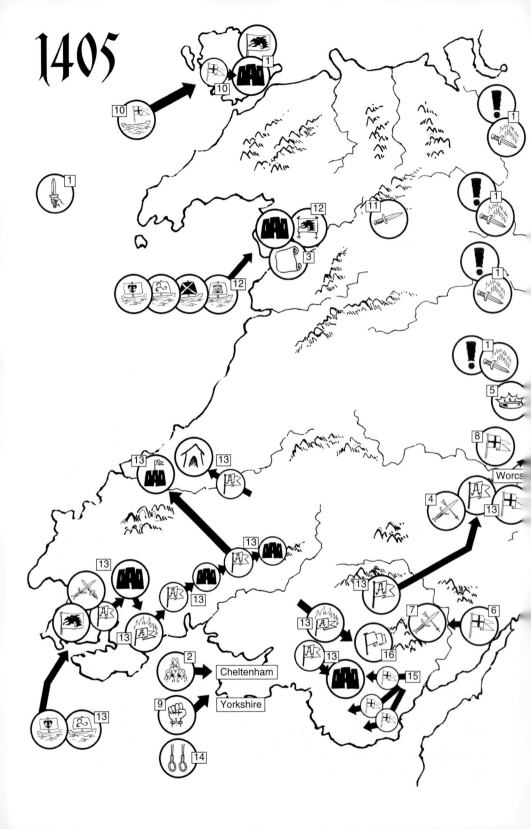

1405

[1] Winter 1404-1405   Beaumaris ?
Beaumaris may well have already fallen into rebel hands. If it had not, then its capture may date to early 1405. The rebels did not seem too determined to hold on to it, but it remained out of English control. Correspondence from the few English commanders left in Wales, and those along the border reported constant Welsh attacks and that the rebels were in *"high and haughty"* spirits, meeting success after success against English troops.

[2] February 1405 and thereafter   English Plotting.
In 1405 there were a number of plots of English design against Henry IV, originating from feuding elements at court. The first came to light in February, when the Countess of Gloucester, Lady Despenser freed the two young Mortimer heirs from imprisonment in Windsor castle, smuggled them out and spirited them away. She was caught with the two boys at Cheltenham, just a few miles from the Welsh border, on 15th February. She was seeking to link up with their uncle, Edmund Mortimer, now commander of the rebel garrison at Harlech. Had she succeeded, Glyn Dŵr would have had a genuine claimant to the English throne under his wing. Glyn Dŵr could then have sought English and foreign support to topple the incumbent from his precarious tenureship and install a new regime, friendly to the powers which placed Mortimer dynasty on the throne. The possibilities of such an opportunity make interesting speculation.

   Manipulated by courtiers and rumour, Henry IV, enraged by the incident, briefly imprisoned the portly Duke of York for his role in the affair. Prince Hal protested at this, York being one of his trusted comanders, in spite of the duke's poor performances and dubious reputation. All others involved in the affair escaped with little or no punishment, except the locksmith responsible for the door into the boy's quarters, who felt the sharp end of the king's wrath. His hands were cut off and then he was executed.

[3] 24th February 1405   The Tripartite Indenture.
Only one copy of this 'three-way treaty' bears a date, being 24th February. It was a negotiated agreement between Glyn Dŵr, Edmund Mortimer, and Henry Percy senior, the earl of Northumberland. The latter was accompanied in the venture by Lord Bardolf, the disaffected royal counsel. It had quite probably been negotiated by Henry Percy junior, Hotspur, before his hasty and ill-timed revolt in July 1403. The three powers involved, or their representatives - Bishops Byford and Lewis on Glyn Dŵr's behalf, signed this alliance which agreed to partition England and Wales between the factions. An enlarged Wales including much of the Marches would go to Glyn Dŵr and his heirs, the north of England roughly down to the border with north Wales to the Percys, and the south to the Mortimer dynasty.

   If Hotspur had bided his time and amassed the Percy forces for the right moment, and Lady Despenser had succeeded and rallied Mortimer support in the south, the possibilities are again, very interesting to ponder. It is highly questionable whether Henry IV's unsteady regime could have withstood a co-ordinated, determined enemy.

The language of the treaty gives a fascinating insight into everyday beliefs and common knowledge of the time. When demarcating the boundaries of the three territories, Northumberland listed the names of the shires within his intended land north of the Trent, whereas Glyn Dŵr referred to boundaries and sites which, to a modern reader at least, are drawn from distant history and mythology. Glyn Dŵr referred to one border marker as being 'Onnenau Meigiawn'. Roughly translated as 'the ash trees at Meigen', this refers to a spot on the field at the Battle of Meigen, where Cadwallon led the Welsh to a famous victory over the Saxons in 632 or 633. The Britons were called there, legend has it, by 'The Great Eagle', a Celtic battle spirit of sorts, who, according to the Prophecy of Merlin, would reappear in time, and lead the Britons to another battlefield where they would again be victorious over the Saxons or their descendants. The fact that this was sufficiently well known about to be spoken of casually and instantly recognisable to people of the time, tells us of the role played by myth and legend in everyday fifteenth century life. On modern maps 'Onnenau Meigiawn' is near the village of Six Ashes, a few miles south-west of modern-day Wolverhampton.

[4] 11th March 1405   The Battle of Grosmont.
Prince Hal told his father of this battle in a letter, which saw his return to active service for the first time since being wounded on 21st July, 1403. He gave the date as 11th March, and we have no reason to doubt its validity. However, we have good reason to doubt him on other points, and it is noteworthy that very few other sources mention this encounter at all, and only those that quote from his letter speak of it in such glorified terms.

Prince Hal claimed that the English *"were but a small force"*, and then went on to name those commanders who accompanied the prince as the Earl of Warwick, Lord Talbot, Sir John Greyndour and Sir William Newport. The prince and Warwick were well known for having huge, heavily armed retinues - as has been shown in previous entries - the others were the English crown's commanders in the field in south Wales and led substantial forces. Sir John Greyndour had commanded Prince Hal's troops at Radnor from August 1402 to March 1404, from where he left for Aberystwyth, and was allegedly present at its capture by Glyn Dŵr. Some evidence suggests that Edward, Duke of York, was also at Grosmont, but the reports are somewhat contradictory. It is not clear whether he had yet been imprisoned, released or not yet been tried for his part in the Mortimer heirs affair, from February that year. The likelihood of such men, and the heir to the throne, going into battle with meagre forces can be dismissed as fanciful boasting by the teenage prince, in an attempt to exaggerate the scale and importance of the encounter, and thus the victory won. In fact, so unrealistic are his claims, that any chance of gleaning an accurate picture of the battle is effectively spoiled.

Prince Hal's letter claimed a stunning victory, saying that the rebels *" from the districts of Glamorgan, Morgannwg, Usk, lower and upper Gwent assembled to the number of eight thousand men, by their own account."* They apparently burnt part of the village of Grosmont before being met and defeated in a battle during which, and in the ensuing pursuit, the rebels supposedly suffered around a thousand casualties. The hard facts of the history of military engagements between Welsh and English forces show us that smaller Welsh forces regularly and convincingly defeated much larger and better equipped English forces, therefore, we can dismiss Prince Hal's claims regarding the size of the force he faced and the number of casualties inflicted. Otherwise, why would this Welsh army, equal in size to that of the glorious sweep of July 1403 which took numerous castles and the fortress of Carmarthen, fail to take a mere village, Grosmont, and flee such *"a small force"*? Why did the rebel force have no known, or stated, or captured, or killed leaders? Where did this Welsh army come from and why did it not attack any other targets in its path? Are we to believe that the rebels mustered *inside* the English border on the hills above Grosmont? Surely an army this large would have been noticed by someone else? Why are there no mass graves, as at Bryn Glas? Why did the English not squeeze as much capital as they could gain from such a stunning victory? The facts simply do not tally with Prince Hal's account. It is not recorded by Welsh sources, nor by any sources prior to Prince Hal's letter.

Moreover, Prince Hal clearly lists places twice, presumably to give credence to his claim that he faced a large enemy force; Morgannwg is the Welsh name for Glamorgan, and Usk is in Gwent. We cannot be sure if he faced men from Gwent and Glamorgan, this is not supported by any existing records. Equally, by adding the phrase *"by their own account"* he could pass any charge of dishonesty onto any captured raider.

What we are looking at is an English victory of some kind. Anything more than this, we cannot be sure, but can offer a more logical possiblity than Prince Hal's wild boasts. A force with no leaders probably indicates a small local initiative bent on raiding. English chroniclers, such as the Archbishop of Hereford in September 1403, mention that Welsh raiding parties often consisted of a few hundred men, perhaps four hundred. A large raiding party might have twice that at best, giving a figure which is at least feasible, unlike Prince Hal's ludicrous *"eight thousand"* . If he had overestimated by a factor of ten or more, then the situation is at least credible. A local initiative of border rebels, perhaps numbering eight hundred, intending to sneak across the border and set light to Grosmont, alerted the royal forces in the area who rushed them, putting them to flight with the advantage of surprise and, in all probability, numbers. If rebel losses were around one hundred, it would have been a small enough skirmish not to make an impact on other contemporary writers. We do not know for sure and can only speculate as to what actually happened.

The place of the victory is noteworthy. Is this the real date of the rarely mentioned skirmish on adjacent Campstone Hill, a mile away, later identified to have taken place in August 1404? Grosmont was the birthplace of Henry, the first Duke of Lancaster, Henry IV's grandfather. Where better for a titular Prince of Wales to claim a victory to bolster morale or kickstart a campaign to recapture the lost country of Wales for his father's, and eventually his own, crown? The English had suffered defeat after defeat since the outbreak of Glyn Dŵr's revolt, which by 1405 had been a war for quite some time. Crown forces badly needed a victory. Being constantly humiliated by those *"bare-footed clowns"*, as parliament described the Welsh in 1401, can only have harmed national morale and the prestige of the King. All the evidence points to invention and exaggeration to rectify this in the account of their victory at Grosmont.

[5] April 1405

Prince Hal raised a personal army of three thousand five hundred men, and a further two thousand were raised and sent to Wales. They were to relieve beleaguered garrisons in Wales and the borders or to re-establish a garrison in castles plundered, burnt and damaged by the Welsh, who, with the exceptions of Aberystwyth and Harlech, never tried to hold castles as part of their guerilla strategy.

[6] 27th April 1405

Prince Hal's forces and other royal forces from England moved up to Usk en masse, to prepare for the English summer campaign. This massive force was to link up with the remnants of English troops in the eastern border area and prepare for an even larger force led by Henry IV.

[7] 5th May? 1405   The Battle of Pwll Melyn Mountain.

We learn something more of Welsh forces of the time from this defeat. Only one source gives a date for this battle, 5th May 1405. We do not know where Pwll Melyn Mountain is, except that it is near Usk, probably somewhere to the north or west, nor do we know why it is so named. As some of the fighting took place on the banks of the River Usk, Pwll Melyn (literally 'Pool Yellow'), could be a pool in a meander of the river or a small lake on the hills near the town.

Unknown to the Welsh, the English were planning a large summer campaign in the south. Henry IV was already moving towards Hereford where he planned to assemble an army for the campaign. Existing forces in the area were banded into what was described as *"a very large army."* This makes Prince Hal's claim from Grosmont that he, along with the earl of Warwick, Lord Talbot, the knights Greyndour and Newport and possibly the Duke of York led a *"small force"* at Grosmont all the more unreliable. Leading this army in May were Lord Codnor, Sir John Greyndour and Sir John Oldcastle, who later became Lord Cobham. They had moved their large army up to Usk to secure the town and castle, and ensure an ambush-free entry into Wales for the planned Royal Expedition. They were apparently accompanied by the Welsh esquire, seen as the arch-traitor to his people, Dafydd ap Llewelyn, or Dafydd Gam. A Welsh raiding party with very well-known leaders rode out of the woods and raced towards Usk, looking to burn the town and, if an opportunity presented itself, take the castle too, burn it and damage the walls before riding off again, hopefully laden with booty. A classic hit-and-run attack, they were not equipped or numerous enough for a large assault or a protracted struggle. The usually efficient scouts were either not deployed this time or did not do their job properly.

The Welsh rode in quickly and immediately attacked everything and everyone they could find, including discharging several volleys of arrows at Usk castle. The English, seeing that they had the Welsh hopelessly outnumbered, responded by shooting back, while English forces in and around the town mounted and rushed out to meet the raiders. The rebels fled immediately on seeing the *"very large army"* emerging from Usk, without engaging them. English troops pursued them, and, during the chaotic flight, fighting broke out as royal troops caught up with knots of dispersing rebels. The general direction of their flight was towards the north or northwest. Some went across the river Usk, or a tributary, and onto low hills nearby. The highest ranking leaders of this raid were killed in the race to escape.

One warrior of renown called Hopcyn ap Tomos died, along with a man called John ap Hywel, the Cistercian abbot of Llantarnam Abbey. John ap Hywel cuts a fascinating figure in the history of the war. It was he who, earlier in the campaign, rebuked Glyn Dŵr for the timing of his revolt. Aware of the prophecies which told that the hero who would save Wales would come in the year 1500, he reminded Glyn Dŵr of this one morning. When Glyn Dŵr remarked " *You are up early this morning, Father Abbot!*", he replied " *No, it is you who is early ... a hundred years too early!*" Certain sources attribute these words to the abbot of Aberconwy Abbey. John ap Hywel was hated by the English, who rejoiced in his death. He was one of Glyn Dŵr's military chaplains, and was exemplary as a soldier and as an influential priest. The perfect warrior-monk, he was famed for his rabble-rousing speeches, drawing men to the cause and firing up those about to go into battle. He was a fine propagandist and believer in the cause.

He is known to have called upon his men to *"bring death to the Saxons"* and to be prepared to pay the ultimate price for the liberty of the nation. Although not all priests were as dedicated, John ap Hywel led by example, even in the face of certain death. His final moments in this world are worthy of retelling. He was killed making a stand with some seventy others, possibly on a river bank, probably trying to buy time for comrades in a bid to escape. When gathering men to make the final stand, although conscious that their sacrifice might enable others to escape, his men faultered, realising that they were all about to die. John ap Hywel is said to have spoken warmly and reassuringly to them, one recorded fragment of what he is purported to have said was a promise that he would join them *that very evening, to supper at Christ's table in your company, where the toast will be to you men."* Another version of the account puts those words in the mouth of another priest, who expressed that he regretted that he would not be joining them at the said supper, and fled.

The Welsh were to suffer more serious blows that day at, or around, Pwll Melyn. In a place identified as 'Monk's Wood', one of Glyn Dŵr's sons, Gruffydd, was captured after a fight. When checking the bodies of the slain, the English began rejoicing, thinking they had found the corpse of Owain Glyn Dŵr. They established that it was in fact his brother, Tudor. The two were almost identical save for a wart above an eyebrow, which Owain had and Tudor did not. A source tells us that the English returned to Usk castle with the prisoners they had rounded up. They then took them out to a place they named as 'Ponfald', where they beheaded them. The source tells us that three hundred Welshmen met their deaths that day. It is possible, though again we cannot be sure. There is some doubt to the final rebel death toll, whether it was the figure mentioned, three hundred, or whether that was solely the number of prisoners executed. Again, there is no known mass grave, as there was at Radnor and Bryn Glas. Given the lack of certainty surrounding the location of the various actions on that day, it is possible that one lies undiscovered, though this is unlikely due to the area's constant habitation.

Although Welsh losses probably numbered in the low hundreds, the rebels lost three important figures, Tudor Glyn Dŵr, Owain's son Gruffydd and John ap Hywel. This was not a local initiative gone wrong, as probably happened at Grosmont in March. This was an organised raid with distinguished, high-ranking leaders, who rode right into the English, who, by chance, had moved into the area, unaware of the impending raid. It was at Pwll Melyn that the authorities scored their first large success in this the sixth year of the war. This was a small, but significant blow. Gruffydd was taken to the Tower of London, where he was held prisoner until his death six years later. He died in suspicious circumstances, the recorded cause of his death in prison was *"pestilence"*.

[8] 14th May 1405
Henry IV arrived at Hereford to prepare for an attack on south Wales.

[9] May and June 1405   Scrope's Rebellion.
More English plotting against Henry IV came to fruition in early summer. The archbishop of York, Richard Scrope, precipitated a rebellion in the north of England, protesting about the tax burden incurred by the clergy. It was Richard Scrope who, in 1399, read Richard II's enforced renunciation of the throne on Bolingbroke's behalf. This act enabled Bolingbroke to claim the throne by right of descent from Henry II and that he was obliged to do so in order to ensure the installation of *"good government"*. Pulling the strings of the rebellion were the Earl of Northumberland and Lord Bardolf. The king acted with the same speed and determination as when faced by Hotspur's revolt in July 1403. He abandoned the proposed attack on south Wales, raced north and crushed Archbishop Scrope and his supporters. The rebellious Earl Marshal, Thomas Mowbray, and Scrope were executed. The clergy accused him of sacrilege over Scrope's execution and noted pointedly that, after this event, Henry IV's health deteriorated rapidly. Divine retribution, they intoned. Northumberland and Bardolf fled to Scotland, accompanied by Bishops Byford and Lewis, present on behalf of Glyn Dŵr. Could this indicate

an intended dual initiative between Welsh and English rebels, led by Tudor Glyn Dŵr in Gwent and the Earl of Northumberland in Yorkshire?

[10] From June 1405 onwards.   The Pacification of Anglesey

English forces, launched from bases in Ireland, raided Anglesey in June and began a campaign to recapture the island. Being an island, Anglesey was always a likely target and vulnerable to attack. One of the prime objectives for the English troops was *"to go to Anglesey and recover the castle of Beaumaris."* They apparently beat local opposition at Rhos-y-Meirch and went on to reoccupy the seemingly undefended fortress at Beaumaris. From their bridgehead and retaken stronghold, the pacification campaign continued. Their commander, Stephen Scrope, King's Lieutenant in Ireland, looted a number of church relics important to the Welsh, and took them back to Dublin, where they became Irish church relics, and have remained ever since.

[11] June 1405

Glyn Dŵr lost another close personal friend and extended family member when his advisor John Hanmer was captured by English troops and imprisoned.

[12] July 1405   Glyn Dŵr's Second Parliament.

Letters reveal that Glyn Dŵr held his second Parliament in the majestic setting of Harlech. We know that it was concluded on or by 30th July. Ambassadors from Scotland, France, Brittany and Castile attended and, apart from standard parliamentary business, were treated to an impressive international tourney with jousting and duelling. Funds were again raised to hire foreign troops to fight for Glyn Dŵr's cause; a force of two thousand men was to be hired from France, which came to fruition in August 1405, and a force of ten thousand troops in the north of England or Scotland, to be raised at an unspecified time. This tells us that Glyn Dŵr's Parliament was well able to govern not only its own affairs, but act beyond Welsh borders as well.

[13] August 1405 onwards.   The French Expedition.

There had been petitions and protestations at Charles VI's court that something urgently needed to be done to redeem the French reputation after the *"shameful exploits"* of the de Bourbon mission of 1404. In order to be seen to be honouring the treaty of 1404, and to make amends for de Bourbon, a successful military expedition was required.

An expeditionary force embarked on the fleet assembled for the mission at Brest, in Brittany. The army was mostly composed of *"auxiliary troops"* raised in Normandy and Brittany, which clearly implies Franco-Breton co-operation and collusion, and was paid for, at least in part, by Glyn Dŵr's parliament. They were apparently commanded by Marshal de Rieux on land and by Admiral Renaud de Tries at sea. There is some debate about who went altogether, but other named captains were Seigneur or Lord des Ventes, Robert de la Heuse, known as 'Le Borgue' or 'One-Eye', and Sieur or Sir de Hugueville, Jean de Hangest, the much respected 'Grand Master of the Crossbows of France'. They took eight hundred heavy cavalry, six hundred crossbowmen and one thousand, two hundred levies.

They put to sea in a fleet, estimates of which range from thirty-two to one hundred and forty ships in July. They were becalmed for two weeks, during which, all of their warhorses died of thirst. Instead of turning back and re-equipping, they pressed on and sailed into Milford Haven, in rebel-held Pembrokeshire, probably on 4th August. French chroniclers incorrectly claimed to have landed at the walled harbour town of Tenby, and were met by Owain Glyn Dŵr, Prince of Wales, and *"ten thousand men"*. We can be sure that they were incorrect about the place at which they landed because after the French disembarked at Milford Haven, they marched to Tenby and attacked it. The figures quoted concerning the number of Welsh soldiers seem somewhat questionable also. Notwithstanding, it was a highly significant and exciting development. Not only did Glyn Dŵr have recognition as the rightful Prince of his people, he also had military support from England's major rival, France. If this were just the start of French co-operation, the vanguard of permanent aid, it could herald great things.

There were a number of problems with the French force which landed in Wales. Firstly, it had been shorn of its main punching power; heavy cavalry without heavy warhorses simply become slow-moving heavy infantry with long, mostly inadequate, weaponry. The Welsh could resupply them with the same fast, mobile mountain horses they used, but not the 'destrier' warhorses, of which the French nobles deemed themselves worthy. Secondly, crossbows were powerful, but unwieldy, and had a very slow rate of fire, and so, were completely unsuited to the guerilla style warfare and shock assaults typical of Welsh tactics in the war, where the enemy is quickly overrun and killed. Thirdly, they found campaigning in Wales very hard, with much harsher terrain and conditions to which they were accustomed. They were used to grand chevauchees across flat, open countryside and long, grindingly slow sieges of castles with engaging parley, debate and prisoner-taking with English nobles. In Wales they found an unforgiving climate, punishing terrain, hard, uncompromising combat in upland woods and streams, and a military environment in which prisoners were not taken. They were constantly on the move, eating on the march and the fighting ranged from rocky beaches to steep hills to the streets of English-held towns. It was quick and merciless, and the French were not adequately prepared for it.

However, they were in Wales to mend the honourable reputation of France, and they were men of war. The Welsh and French allies immediately set about local enemy forces. They defeated the English in a skirmish near Haverford West and then laid siege to the town. The French pounded the town with siege artillery and repeatedly assaulted it. They inflicted many casualties on the defenders, who held firm. The French however, also took casualties. One noted fatality in the attack was Patrouillart de Tries, brother of the Admiral of the fleet.

As it looked set to fall, they abandoned the siege of the battered town, buried their dead, and moved on. A French scouting company rushed Picton castle on the first assault, to much celebration. The allies moved on to Tenby, ravaging any resources they could find. At Tenby, according to their sources, the French were accompanied by *"two thousand Welsh knights"*. The French built siege engines in preparation for the attack. As they began the attack, rumours swept through the French army that an English fleet, full of armoured knights, had been sighted heading their way. The French fled in terror, abandoning the Welsh attacking the town and their own siege equipment.

When the Welsh eventually caught up with the French, having awaited the phantom fleet which never materialised, they were engaged in parley with the garrison of Saint Clears instead of laying siege to the town. Saint Clears agreed to surrender if the reinforced, rebuilt capital of the south, Carmarthen, did so first. The allies surrounded Carmarthen and the French engineers set to work. In an excellent display of siege engineering, the French engineers undermined and breached the walls. Fearing the Welsh were about to pour in and massacre everyone, the defenders immediately sought terms with the French. Glyn Dŵr bestowed his most magnanimous gesture on these captured enemies under the gaze of his French allies. He allowed them, and any of their English comrades in Wales, leave to go unmolested to any other 'Englishrie' outside the area, or to England itself, on condition that they left their arms and goods. Then, over several days, the Welsh again took possession of Carmarthen, sacked it, burnt it and pulled down as much of the walls as they could, before leaving it a smouldering ruin once more.

Although the French were shocked at the mercilessness and brutality of their Welsh allies, they were intrigued by them and the Medieval revision of the gentlemanly chivalry which lionised and gave revered status to Arthur, one of the fathers of the Welsh nation. To have captured Carmarthen, fabled city of Merlin, reportedly delighted them. According to the French chroniclers Froissart, de Monstrelet and the monk of Saint Denis, the French believed they were the natural inheritors of Arthur's chivalric mantle, and congratulated themselves for being the bravest and most noble people of the age. They were later equally enthralled by the amphitheatre at Caerleon and Llantarnam Abbey, the original church of John ap Hywel, which were respectively believed to be the site of the Round Table and Arthur's own cathedral. They also believed that by visiting and participating in the capture of such temples of chivalry, that they were somehow touched by Arthur's knightly virtue.

The allies left Carmarthen and marched to Cardigan, which they took with little opposition. The whole of Cardigan Bay, from north Pembroke to Llyn was very firmly in Welsh control and a perfect point of entry for a larger French invasion force. At Cardigan, it is quite probable that the French somehow came into possession of a large number of horses or settled for Welsh mountain horses as acceptable replacement steeds for those lost at sea. The Welsh and French allies then launched the sort of attack for which the French were trained. From Cardigan, they went on a chevauchee across the south, blazing a trail, literally, through Glamorgan, where they attacked but failed to take Coity, and then swept on through Gwent to the English border. The truth concerning the next part of the French Expedition is lost under a deluge of folk tales, far too numerous to recount or refer to all versions of events. Indeed, some later sources claim it never happened.

On 7th August, Henry IV heard about the French landing while at his castle in Pontefract and immediately called the men of eighteen shires to arms. He arrived at Worcester on 19th August. Some sources say that this was just after the Welsh and French had burnt it, or part of it, with Smock Alley, Anger Lane and Black Friars' cemetery named as places where the Allies killed locals *en masse*. Henry IV went out to meet this enemy army, which showed no fear, being of roughly comparable strength to his army, being between five and eight thousand men. Allegedly, the Allies camped on Woodbury Hill, just a few miles north of the town, while Henry IV and his army set up on, or around, Abberly Hill. Sources suggest that the two armies seemed equally matched, unwilling to risk everything in a fight to the death on the mile-long field which separated the two hills. They vied for supremacy and probed each other for weak points. After an interesting parley they fought *"eight days of chivalric combat."* Losses were recorded as upwards of two hundred men on each side for this eight day period, equating an average of twenty five fatalities on each side for every day of jousting and duelling. Although the French lost the knights Sieur de Martelonne and Sieur de la Valle in the fighting, they wrote that they were delighted to have taken part in such a glorious *"adventure"*.

An all-out battle did not take place. English nerve broke, French chroniclers tell us, Henry IV ran for Worcester having decided the enemy was about to overwhelm him. He withdrew in secret at night, the Allies realised too late, and attacked his rearguard and sacked his baggage train. Once safely ensconced behind Worcester's fortifications, there would be little point in attacking him with a similar sized force, such was the advantage of being within solid defences.

The Allies went north, then turned west and burnt and pillaged their way over the horizon. They almost certainly did not do the damage that was later attributed to them. English communities saw the sense in buying them off with huge amounts of food, instead of provoking attack. The Allies probably went back to Cardigan, where the English in Pembroke made generous, panicking truces with them for wagonloads of provisions and large sums of silver. This they did without Henry IV's consent and much to his impotent annoyance. On 1st November 1405 de Trie, Jean de Hangest and the other French nobles left for France in six warships, leaving their troops abandoned in Wales. This met a wave of virulent criticism in France when they returned to a heroes' welcome from their peers and indulged in a period of prolonged, sumptuous feasting. Only one minor noble, known as 'Le Borgue de Bellay' or 'One-Eye de Bellay', sometimes confused with 'Le Borgue de la Heuse' volunteered to stay the winter in Wales with the French and Breton troops.

If the French made it to Worcester as the evidence suggests, then it was a highly significant historic event. It marked the deepest penetration into England by

Dryslwyn Castle courtesy Lise Hull

French forces since the Norman invasion, during the Hundred Years war, or thereafter. This Expedition had taught the French the hard realities of warfare in Wales, and they had hardly given a good account of themselves. They fell well short of covering themselves in the glory that they felt was their due. Perhaps of greater importance to the French was that they were then sure that there would be no anti-Lancastrian rising in England by Richard II's supporters or by Henry IV's enemies. It was clear that they would not be supported by Englishmen in England, as were the English by Frenchmen in France. This went unknown to the Welsh, though this knowledge did not bode well for supporters of the Welsh cause at Charles VI's court, or for Welsh hopes of future French military involvement.

[14] August 1405   Tales from the Gallows
In two separate, apparently unrelated incidents, two thieves, John Oke and John Veyse independently made the same confession before death. Each claimed that they had nothing to lose by revealing that they had collected donations for Glyn Dŵr's cause from all over England. East Anglia was, apparently, particularly generous and supportive. Each gave a detailed account of the affair and pointed the finger at a number of high ranking donors, mostly clergymen. They also named Sir John Scudamore, who, they alleged, collected funds for Glyn Dŵr. We know that one of Scudamore's relatives, Philip Scudamore was an infamous rebel, and that Sir John, captured at the fall of Dryslwyn in 1403, married Glyn Dŵr's daughter, Alys, later in the revolt. It was a very serious offence to marry anyone Welsh and he risked forfeiting his lands. We have no solid proof that Sir John was involved. Both Oke and Veyse were proven liars and convicted thieves whose word counted for little, even less against priests and knights of the realm. They were both executed for their crimes and nothing more was said on the matter.

[15] September 1405
Henry IV led three enormous armies to break the renewed siege of Coity.

Once the siege was broken, he relieved and replaced the garrison and left south Wales in a hurry. Why did he not relieve other garrisons further west or go after the enemy and force the issue with the combined Franco-Welsh army? We do not know for sure, but he knew where they were, had he chosen that option. Instead, he returned to England in a huge armoured convoy as quickly as he could. Did this mission constitute another Royal Expedition ? Probably not, as other Expeditions had been tours, showing the flag in a processional raid of looting and executing civilians. This time, Henry IV planted his flag and scampered home. The weather took its cue nicely again, and brought down more terrifying storms and floods against the invader. The Welsh attacked and plundered the baggage train and made off with " *forty wagons laden with provisions, jewellery etc ...*". Another English source described how the Welsh disappeared into the hills and forests before Henry IV's 1405 mission, and, as with Henry IV's previous military tours into Wales, they repeatedly ambushed the English with apparent impunity:

" *... and there the king could do them no harm at all, but often they stole the kings carriage* [transport] *and every day destroyed his people.*"

Meanwhile, the monks of Saint Albans hung drapes from their abbey walls exclaiming " *God save us from Glyndŵr.*" In the west around Pembroke, more English communities negotiated truces with the Welsh, paying substantial sums of silver for a certain period during which they were not to suffer Welsh attacks. The French are supposed to have camped somewhere near Cardigan for the winter, almost certainly near, or in sight of the sea.

[16] The Submission of Glamorgan ? December 1405?

There are a number of suggestions that Glamorgan had submitted to Henry IV by the end of the year. With three large armies tramping across the land, it is entirely possible, but difficult to prove definitely. If it had submitted, was it simply a tactical submission as had previously been seen elsewhere ? The south-east was the most vulnerable part of the mainland, and would be expected to be the first territory to fall. Whether this was a temporary or a permanent setback, only time would tell.

1406

THE WELSH DECLARATION OF INDEPENDENCE

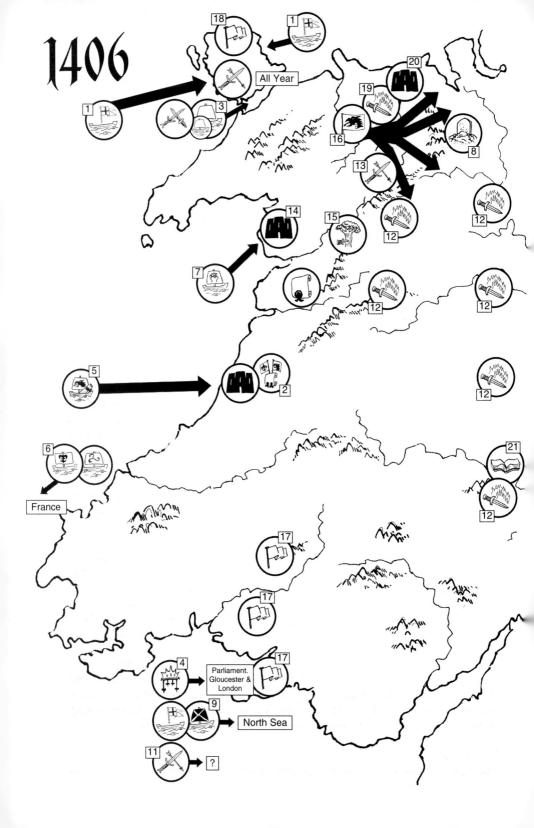

[1] 1406 - An All Year Campaign   The Pacification of Anglesey
During their operation of June 1405, English forces noted that Glyn Dŵr's
men had evacuated a good deal of their cattle, people and equipment off the
island to safety in Gwynedd. In January, the English undertook a two-
pronged naval attack on Anglesey. Ships and troops came from Ireland and
Chester in a move designed to give the remaining rebel forces on the island
neither respite nor room for manoeuvre. Both sides knew Anglesey's
vulnerability to isolation and invasion. Once cut off, it would only be a
matter of time and hard fighting before the island fell.

[2] 12th January 1406   Ratification of the Franco-Welsh Treaty
Glyn Dŵr signed and sealed a French- drafted treaty binding the French and
Welsh together in friendship and mutual aid. This was done at Aberystwyth
Castle on 12th January. Glyn Dŵr then sent his ambassadors to Paris, who
met Charles VI and returned to Wales with his reply before the remnant of
the French and Breton soldiers had left Wales. One can only wonder how they
felt towards their noble leaders, who were being feted as heroes at royal feasts
in Paris, while they wintered near the sea in Ceredigion.

[3] 1st February 1406
Reports of heavy fighting on Anglesey and ship-to-ship warfare in the Menai
Straits, as well as on the mainland around Caernarfon, prompted the
immediate despatch of a large reinforcement column to Caernarfon in
February. These actions were intended to support the campaign on Anglesey
itself.

[4] February 1406
The English Parliament was summoned to Gloucester to address the ongoing
Welsh question. Eventually, it met in London instead, where Prince Hal was
granted an additional five thousand troops to deal with said question.

[5] 8th March 1406   Letter from Charles VI, King of France
Glyn Dŵr's ambassadors, the Dominican, Hugh Eddouyer, and Morris
Kerry, handed their master a letter from the king of France on 8th March.
This letter, apart from the usual profuse greetings, compliments and bluster,
intimated that more French military support may be on the way if Glyn Dŵr
declared his allegiance to the French Pope in Avignon, over the Pope in Rome.

[6] Lent (March) 1406   Departure of the French and Bretons
The French sent troopships so their soldiers could return to France and
Brittany. Eight of the original fleet of twenty-eight ships turned back or were
lost to the English in the Channel. Their journey home, aboard the remaining
twenty vessels, though no doubt cramped, passed without incident.

[7] March 1406
The Earl of Northumberland and Lord Bardolf landed with supporters in

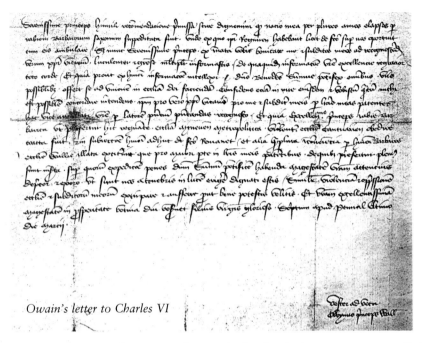

Owain's letter to Charles VI

Wales. Having spent the winter plotting in Scotland, they were eager to link up with Glyn Dŵr, who was reportedly pleased to hear of the safe arrival of his English allies.

[8] 6th March 1406   The Death of Hywel Gwynedd
News spread around Wales that Hywel Gwynedd's stockade on Halkyn Mountain had been breached in heavy night fighting in March. His base had been the launch pad for many terror raids across the English border, and he was a fearsome warrior of renown. Many from both sides died in the bitter struggle in March, including Hywel Gwynedd.

[9] March 1406   The Scots Crippled Again
King Robert III of Scotland, whose health was rapidly failing him, sent his twelve year-old son and heir, James, to France for safety. The English intercepted his ship en route and imprisoned James. Robert III allegedly died upon hearing the news. James was held captive until 1424. With the heir to the throne of Scotland prisoner, the English installed a 'client-ruler' in Scotland, Robert Stewart. This would effectively guarantee Scots neutrality for the meantime, at such a crucial time for the Welsh. The Scots were showing signs of recovering from the disaster of Homildon Hill in 1402, but this dealt them another severe blow, which crippled them again. If this was bad news for Wales, it was worse still for Scotland, as it marked the beginning of a period of minority rulers and decades of instability and fratricidal violence.

[10] 31st March 1406   The Pennal Letter
This remarkable document, still possessed by the French authorities, deserves
more widespread coverage than it has so far received. It was the response to
Charles VI's letter of 8th March, and clearly set out in writing a declaration
of independence from England. It was not just a rallying cry to the banner of
the nation, but a statement of policy and aims, underpinned with a full
diplomatic mission to a large, wealthy, influential power. Glyn Dŵr
summoned his people, especially the new Synod of Welsh Clergy, to debate
this policy before sending his response to France. It is therefore highly
probable that Glyn Dŵr summoned a third Welsh Parliament in March 1406,
and reconvened it later that year.

The letter, signed by Glyn Dŵr and dated 31st March was written at
Pennal, near Machynlleth, and sent to Paris with a number of ambassadors
shortly after. It pledged full support for Pope Bendict XIII of Avignon. It
requested support and recognition for a fully independent church in Wales,
with its seat at Saint Davids. The highly respected Dr. Gruffudd Yonge was
to be its head. The letter spoke of the enemy, led by *the usurper, Henry of
Lancaster*", and, in recognition of many crimes and heresies perpetrated by
him, condemned *"the madness of the Saxon barbarian"*. It called for a
crusade against Charles VI's and Glyn Dŵr's English enemy, it read:

*" that the Lord Benedict shall brand as heretics and cause to be tortured in
the usual manner, Henry of Lancaster, the intruder from the kingdom of
England, ... and his adherents ... and that the same Lord Benedict shall grant
to us, our heirs, subjects, and adherents, of whatsoever nation they may may
be, who wage war* [against the English], *full remission of our sins ..."*

Moreover, apart from the international scope of the document, and the
establishment of a Welsh church authority, Glyn Dŵr set out his plan for two
Welsh universities, one in the north and one in the south. It is a sure sign that
the Welsh under Glyn Dŵr had created and installed the apparatus of modern
statehood, and were making bold plans towards an independent future. This
had been made possible by notable defections to the cause, and the ousting of
administrators from their posts by the English. Those anti-Welsh laws passed
by Parliament had, for once, been a blessing in disguise for Wales. They
compelled the Welsh, as one people, to revive their nation from its century-
long slumber, liberate their ancestral territory with the sword, hold their own
Parliaments, and achieve foreign recognition and support. In the Pennal
Letter, that revived nation set out its aims for its own future.

[11] 23rd April 1406   Propaganda?
One English source claimed a stunning English victory in battle. By sheer
coincidence it took place on Saint George's day. The report scoffingly claimed
that a thousand Welshmen had been slain, including one of Glyn Dŵr's sons.
The report neglects to mention where this battle took place, who led,
organised or paid the English troops involved, who they were or where they

came from, who they fought against and which of Glyn Dŵr's sons was killed. No other sources mention this fictitious encounter, propaganda for the English public.

The English were still hungover from the brutal battering they received at Bryn Glas, a devastating victory which they could not match. They had scored victories, such as at Pwll Melyn, and were making progress on Anglesey, but had achieved nothing approaching the carnage of Bryn Glas. The Welsh were dominant still, but the weight of English power, leaning on the border and the two most accessible areas, the south-east and Anglesey, was beginning to bring the results they wanted. There was no monumental victory, but a gradual, piecemeal advance creeping forward in one area, checked or turned back in another. At this time, Wales was most definitely still ruled by its own people.

[12] May - August 406
The familiar flux of panic letters and reports from the border tells of the furious extent of the Welsh summer campaign. The Welsh war machine vented its force upon English border counties to devastating effect. There was much killing and burning in Powys, Shropshire, Worcestershire and Herefordshire, all of which again bore the brunt of the attack and suffered accordingly

[13] June 1406
Northumberland and Lord Bardolf and their retinue were convincingly beaten and put to flight by Edward Charlton and his by then seasoned troops. This is said to have happened in north-western Powys. The English rebel leaders all escaped unharmed.

[14] The July Session 1406   Glyn Dŵr's Third Welsh Parliament?
Sources suggest that Glyn Dŵr held another Parliament at Harlech. It is supposed to have been attended by foreign ambassadors, as was the 1405 Parliament. The lack of official documentation makes it difficult to be certain, there is a possibility that some sources confuse the year, be it 1405 or 1406. It is probable that Parliament met twice in 1406. Firstly in March, to discuss the policy framed in The Pennal Letter, and later in July, perhaps because this was the appointed month of the previous parliament in 1405 and thus a trend was being established. A second session would presumably have discussed the state of the campaign and the diplomatic initiatives with France, as well as other, more regular parliamentary business.

[15] Late Summer 1406?   The Assassination Attempt on Glyn Dŵr
The evidence available very strongly suggests that this event did take place, but again may well have undergone transformation on the lips of bards over the years. Assuming that this event occurred in the first place, it is difficult to say exactly when it happened. It has been placed in 1401 by one source, although by late summer 1406, the first signs that the war may not continue to go well for the rebels may have been discernible to some. This might have

provided an opportune moment to strike at the native Prince of Wales, and enhance the fortune of any would-be assassin in the eyes of a grateful, rewarding enemy.

There are two principal versions of the event, both with the same gruesome outcome. It was a commonly recounted tale as late as the nineteenth century. The attempt on Glyn Dŵr's life took place near Dolgellau, the would-be assassin was Hywel Sele ap Meurig of Nannau. He was Glyn Dŵr's contemporary, and the two certainly knew each other. It is possible that they were distantly related, or simply from the same peer group who had hunted together since they were young men, we do not know for sure. The slight differences in the stories come in how Hywel Sele tried to kill Glyn Dŵr and how he met his death.One version placed the two men and others out on a hunt, during which Hywel Sele took a pot-shot at the Prince with an arrow. The other says that Glyn Dŵr was aware of Hywel Sele's hostility towards him, but had agreed to meet at Hywel Sele's request, so he could ask Owain's forgiveness and be welcomed back into the fold of the rebel brotherhood. Fearing for his safety, Hywel asked if they could meet at a neutral venue they both knew well, having hunted there together as young men. Once there, Hywel Sele plunged a concealed dagger into Glyn Dŵr.

Both versions say that Glyn Dŵr, possibly acting on advice from Crach Ffinant, wore armour under several layers of clothing which saved him. His revenge was terrible, Hywel Sele ap Meurig's home, and everything inside it, was torched. One version says Sele was killed immediately after his assassination attempt, and his body hidden inside a hollow oak tree. The other says he was made to watch the burning of his home, then taken back to the meeting place and immured alive inside a hollow oak tree, from where he screamed for several days before dying. The place is known as 'Ceubren yr Ellyll' or 'The Hollow Tree of the Devils'. When part of the tree collapsed in 1813 and was measured by English travellers, who accorded it a circumference of 27 feet, they reported that a skeleton holding a rusty sword was visible in the decaying core of the tree.

[16] August - September - October 1406

A letter from Kidwelly recorded that Henry Don and his men attacked the town and castle again on 1st August, causing much damage. They campaigned throughout the south-west, meeting little effective opposition. Welsh attacks into English border counties were widespread throughout this period. Glyn Dŵr rode into battle in the north-east and swept all before him. His troops pillaged Clwyd before riding west with their spoils. Earlier in the year the French had opened up two fronts against the English in France, by launching their own offensives in Picardy and Gascony. By the end of autumn, the French had suffered heavy defeats against the English on both fronts.

[17] September- October 1406

A number of submissions or defections from the cause through war weariness were recorded in Gower, Ystrad Tywi and south Ceredigion in autumn of that year. The rebels of Gower rose again soon after, led by Morgan Gethin from his base at Llangennith.

[18] 9th November 1406   The Submission of Anglesey

The battle for Anglesey was almost over. Just over two thousand men of the island were named and pardoned on that day, provided they submitted and paid a 'fine' to secure their pardon. Many others were not to be pardoned though, and the affair was not yet finished on the island.

[19] 18th November 1406   The Devastation of the North-East

A massive raid by Glyn Dŵr devastated north-east Wales, shocking those already used to seeing the rebels at their worst. They had attacked the area in October, and now rampaged through the area again with notable vigour.

[20] 1406?   The Spy

The devastation of the north-east may have been provoked by the actions of a spy. A man named Maredydd Ieuan Gwyn had been passing on information regarding rebel movements to the English authorities. He had stayed on his farm west of the river Conwy and passed on what he had seen and heard to his master at Rhuddlan Castle, Sir Henry Conway. At one point, Gwyn slipped away from his farm taking all his goods with him, once the rebels had retired west of the river. The rebels discovered what he had been up to and went after him in fury. Gwyn fled to Rhuddlan Castle with his family. His young son was tending cattle for the English at Rhuddlan when the rebels crept up and killed him. Maredydd Ieuan Gwyn also died mysteriously in the castle, apparently murdered by unseen assailants.

Gwyn's daughter sorrowfully commited the tale to posterity. An accurate date is not identified, but the event did occur and deserved retelling. This is the most obvious occasion that the rebels crossed the Conwy twice and attacked the same area in a short space of time, the second raid seemingly vindictive in its targets, damage and ferocity. It could have happened during another assault of Rhuddlan, July 1405 for example, but the series of events in late 1406 seem to fit the pattern described by contemporary accounts.

[21] December 1406   Bishop Mascall's List

Robert Mascall, the bishop of Hereford since 1404, published a 'list' detailing the extent of the damage inflicted by rebels in the diocese under his ecclesiastical jurisdiction. It was presented to the Exchequer and has survived the passage of the centuries. It described the scale of the damage in an area approximately ten miles across, along the border of Shropshire and Herefordshire. By the end of 1406, not counting the suffering of the towns, villages and other settlements of the area, some fifty-two churches had been plundered and razed by Welsh war parties campaigning in England. This gives us an insight into the scale and effectiveness of the raiders' activities, and helps to explain the plethora of panicked cries for help from western English counties throughout the war.

1407

SIEGES AND
SUBMISSIONS

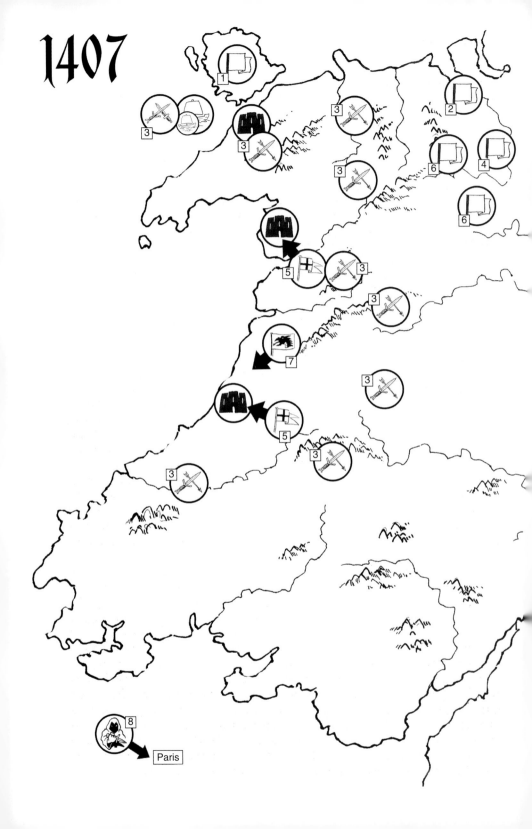

1407

[1] Anglesey Finally Pacified 1407
By the end of January, at the latest February of that year, Anglesey had been pacified. The loss of Anglesey's food producing capacity, and thousands of rebels or sympathisers now brought to peace, was a severe blow to the Welsh cause. From February onwards, Gruffudd Yonge was the Bishop of Bangor.

[2] March and April 1407.
Flint submitted. A thousand men bought pardons and came to peace. The fringes of Wales were seeking peace, but the situation was far from irretrievable.

[3] May 1407
There was heavy fighting in Ceredigion, Merioneth and Gwynedd, particularly at Caernarfon. There was also more naval warfare in the Menai Straits.

[4] May 1407
Maelor submitted and sought peace in this month.

[5] May 1407   The Siege of Aberystwyth
More heavy fighting in southern Powys and especially in Ceredigion, told of repeated rebel ambushes on the slowly advancing English army, finally confident enough to attempt to prise power from Glyn Dŵr's grasp. Prince Hal brought another huge army to Wales, along with siege equipment, cannon and a number of the stars of the English military. Prince Hal was accompanied by the usual suspects of the war in Wales; the Duke of York, the Earl of Warwick, Lord Carew, Lord Audley, Sir John Greyndour, Sir John Oldcastle and a host of others, supported by several thousand soldiers. English forces began the siege of Aberystwyth in May 1407, using all the firepower at their disposal. A few months later, we cannot be sure exactly when, similarly equipped English armies led by Sir Gilbert Talbot, his brother Richard, Lord Furnival and Edward Charlton and a massive army began the siege of Harlech.

It became obvious very quickly to Aberystwyth's commander, Rhys ap Gruffudd ap Llewelyn ap Ieuan, known to history forever as Rhys Ddu, or Rhys the Black, because of his dark deeds, that the end was nigh. Rhys the Black was a gifted soldier however, and was unwilling to submit. The English launched a fierce assault as soon as they were in their positions and had dispensed with the customary parley. The defenders repulsed English attacks and Aberystwyth's walls withstood the pounding they received from English guns, catapults and other siege artillery remarkably well. This was the first time heavy guns had been used against a castle on the British mainland. One gun, weighing over five thousand pounds, named *"messenger"*, meaning 'messenger' in modern English, was lined up and fired at the Welsh. It exploded spectacularly, killing a number of people who gathered around to see the effect it would have on those in the line of fire. The Welsh garrison must have taunted the besiegers in their moment of misfortune.

With the siege entering its fifth month in September, Rhys Ddu negotiated a truce with Richard Courtenay, Chancellor of Oxford University. The truce was to last six weeks until 24th October that year and, thereafter, the Welsh would have until All Saints, 1st November, to surrender themselves, their arms and the castle. During the truce, Welsh movements were unrestricted. Rhys Ddu went directly to Glyn Dŵr in the north and spoke of the intended surrender.

[6] June - July 1407

In June, John, Lord Charlton issued the Charter of Welshpool. It showed that a measure of English control had been re-established in the embattled border town. It stated that no Welshman was to be allowed into the town, nor were they to be allowed to purchase or bear arms within the town's area of influence. The Welsh of the area were not to gather in groups, on suspicion of plotting insurrection and that only French and English could be used in official proceedings in the town. A series of submissions followed throughout the north-eastern border areas of Bromfield and Yale, Chirkland, and Oswestry.

[7] October 1407

Furious at Rhys Ddu's truce with the enemy, Glyn Dŵr amassed his fighting men around him and went south to Aberystwyth. He is then reputed to have made Rhys Ddu an offer he could not refuse: to hand over command of Aberystwyth to Glyn Dŵr, thus nullifying Rhys Ddu's treaty with the English, or to have his head cut off with Owain's own axe. As the new commander, Glyn Dŵr, had not signed or agreed to the truce, he was not bound by its terms.

There are other stories concerning this event, which are almost certainly folk tales embellished over the years, perhaps somewhere containing an element of truth. One version has Owain Glyn Dŵr and his crack troops wading through the English army, along with Rhys the Black and his men, and breaking through to the castle, where Glyn Dŵr then put his famous offer to Rhys.

The English army suffered high desertion rates in this operation, and at the time of Glyn Dŵr's arrival it is probable that most of the English leaders and troops were stood down and retired to more comfortable surroundings. Another tale has the Welsh leaving a large payment of silver in place of hostages exchanged to ensure the truce, arguing that they did not have men to spare, unlike the English who had thousands. Once Glyn Dŵr had taken command, he allegedly ordered the execution of the English prisoners and hostages, then catapulted their severed heads into English lines. A message tied to an arrow was then shot out informing the English they could keep the money they held in place of hostages. When he left with his battle contingent, Glyn Dŵr is said to have carved a swathe through English lines again, before riding north with his men. We can discount these as elaborations at best, fabrications at worst. That Glyn Dŵr went to Aberystwyth and regained control is true. Also, once the truce was broken or had elapsed, the English resumed the siege in earnest as quickly as they could properly reconcentrate their efforts on Aberystwyth. There was to be no Welsh surrender, only a fight to the bitter end.

[8] 23rd November 1407   **The End of French Involvement.**
As long as the Welsh held onto the west, and vital points of entry into Wales, there was still a hope of the French sending a major expeditionary force as promised. English underhand tactics took the French, like the Scots the previous year, out of the equation in no uncertain terms on this day.

The Welsh, outnumbered and poorly armed, had caught Europe's - effectively then the world's - attention with years of stunning, blood-soaked victories against the English. The Duke of Orleans was fiercely in support of sending armies to help the Welsh. He believed in pursuing any means to attack, harry, frustrate, engage and defeat the English in France or elsewhere. His rival at court was the Duke of Burgundy, Jean Sans Peur, leader of the Burgundians, who were often allied to the English, and fought for them against their own countrymen.

On 23rd November, while on his way to visit Queen Isabeau, his brother's wife, the Duke of Orleans was assassinated in a Parisian street by the agents of Jean Sans Peur, allegedly working in collusion with the King of England. France was plunged into an internecine civil war between the factions. Fearing for his own life, as his very capable brother had been killed less than a mile from the palace where Charles VI lay sleeping, the king sought to extend the existing, if fragile, truce with the English. The English agreed, at the price of not including or mentioning the Welsh in any way in the binding terms of the treaty, violating French promises to the Welsh, secured firstly in the 1404 Treaty of Alliance and reaffirmed in numerous subsequent occasions. The French were only too eager to agree, thus ending any realistic hopes of French intervention in Wales. The new truce was signed on 7th December and came into effect on 15th January 1408. The English also treated with Brittany, ensuring a temporary peace and denying the Welsh any hope of foreign support. The death knell was now sounding for the Welsh fighting in Glyn Dŵr's war.

1408

ENGLISH ARMIES IN WALES, FRENCH VACILLATION

& 1409

HARLECH & THE FALL OF LIBERTY

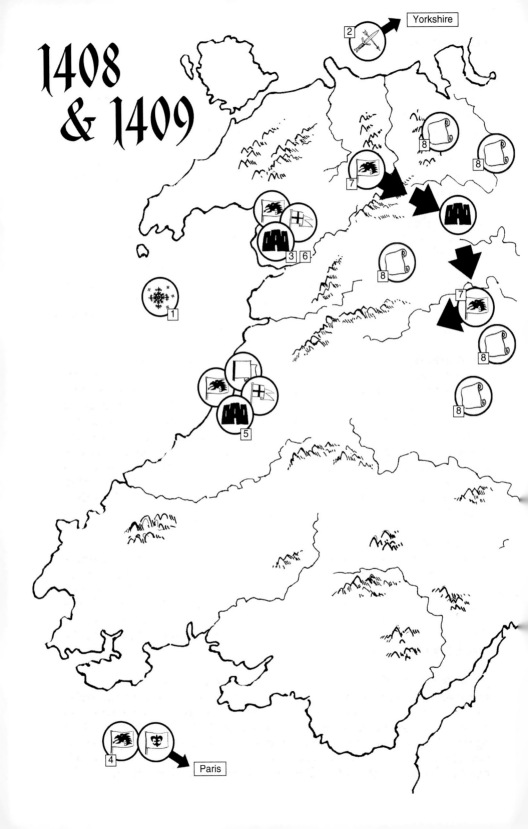

1408
& 1409

Yorkshire

Paris

[1] 1407 - 1408   A Hard Winter
The weather, for such a long time Glyn Dŵr's ally, finally turned against both peoples, and the rest of Europe at the same time. The winter of 1407 - 1408 was exceptionally severe, with snow lying thick on the ground for at least four months. Many animals died, causing starvation. Fighting at the sieges of Aberystwyth and Harlech was decidedly less vigorous than before, some sources suggest that it stopped completely while both forces suffered and died in their frozen camps.

[2] 19th February 1408   The Battle of Bramham Moor
Northumberland led his men and a large contingent of Scots fighting for him in a last-ditch attempt to wrest power from Henry IV. It is likely that monies raised by Glyn Dŵr's 1405 Parliament was used to hire the Scots. Northumberland was defeated and killed at this battle, and support for his faction was finally broken. Interestingly, one man taken prisoner, and then released because he was unarmed, was the erstwhile Bishop of Bangor, Lewis ap Ieuan or Lewis Byford, one of Glyn Dŵr's negotiators and diplomats.

[3] March, April, May 1408   The Siege of Harlech
Though both sides were impressively well led, the battle for Harlech was proving to be a difficult and bloody affair. The Welsh were stubbornly hanging on, and casualties were surprisingly high on both sides. Throughout the spring and early summer of 1408 English forces threw themselves into the assault in an attempt to finish off Harlech. In spite of their sophisticated siege engines, artillery and cannon, they suffered horrific losses in this three-month concentrated attack. The siege continued throughout the year but this period marked the heaviest fighting. From the early summer onwards, the English moved in column after column of reinforcements, not only to bolster their attack but to replace their heavy losses.

[4] May 1408   More Diplomacy
Welsh ambassadors were in Paris asking the French to honour their promises and send troops. The Welsh were still in control of Aberystwyth and Harlech, the major fortified points of entry into Wales. This was the last realistic appeal for French help, the situation was still retrievable; if the French broke the sieges, the commons would surely rise again. The French did not honour their promises and did not send any help, but made vague allusions to the possibility of future support.

[5] September 1408   The Fall of Aberystwyth
Fierce fighting had raged since May 1407. As the siege dragged on, the Welsh sought terms at least once. The English only offered unacceptable terms, so the Welsh fought on. After the events of October 1407, it would clearly be a fight to the end. In spite of all their men, guns and engines the English could not take Aberystwyth. As the siege entered its sixteenth month, the castle's reinstated commander, Rhys Ddu, had held out as long as he would.

Knowing that they would not be offered terms for an honourable surrender, many men refused to do so and escaped, probably up the beach at night, and went north to Glyn Dŵr or to Harlech. The loss of life had been high for both sides, though considerably lighter than at Harlech. One notable Welsh casualty was the nobleman, William Gwyn ap Rhys Llwyd, formerly in the employ of the Crown at Kidwelly. He was killed by a cannonball. The pitiful remnant of the garrison, including the old and the wounded, capitulated in the last week of September. It is unclear whether Rhys Ddu stayed with them as charged. Some sources say he was taken at Aberystwyth, others, identify a later time for his capture, detailed below.

[6] February 1409   The Fall of Harlech

After the fall of Aberystwyth, Prince Hal took his army to Harlech to add yet more men and firepower to increase the pressure of the siege. Some of the evidence suggests that a number of Rhys Ddu's men went to Harlech and fought with the attackers outside, some making it in to the fortress. These claims cannot be substantiated, the latter in particular smacks of embellishment.

Throughout the siege, the English drummed on the walls with cannon and catapult. One cannon called *'The King's Daughter'*, like *'Messenger'* at Aberystwyth, blew up to murderous effect. Although English losses were painfully high, the defenders also sustained numerous casualties. One 'Welsh' casualty was the fortress commander, Edmund Mortimer, Glyn Dŵr's son-in-law. We cannot be sure how he died, some stories identify starvation as the cause, others a cannonball as the cause of death, though one has him felled while repulsing an attack on the walls.

Some stories place Glyn Dŵr at Harlech, and say that he escaped at its fall by walking out with the old men, women and children, paying a fine and then being freed by the authorities who clearly had no use for an elderly peasant. This story is probably a folk tale designed to emphasise his cunning, outwitting the English once again. It does not fit into the picture we have of Glyn Dŵr's character, firstly to surrender at all, but especially not after having endured the war for so long, and secondly, to deliver his family into the hands of his hated enemy. It is most likely that he was in the safety of the mountains in Gwynedd, looking helplessly on with his trusted warband as the last light went out in Harlech. His wife, Margaret, two daughters, one of whom was Catrin, and her children by Edmund Mortimer, a boy and three girls, were captured and taken to the tower of London.

One would expect the fall of Harlech, Glyn Dŵr's capital, to signal a cessation of hostilities, but this was not so. In terms of a general, definable campaign, this was the case. However, wherever and in whichever ways they could, rebel elements resisted and fought for years to come.

[7] August and Early September 1409   'The Last Ride'

Owain Glyn Dŵr must have suffered terribly after the fall of Harlech. His wife, two of his daughters and four grandchildren were imprisoned in the

Tower of London, along with one son taken there in 1405. His brother and a son-in-law had been killed in battle. Other friends and relatives had been killed or captured. His foreign allies had ultimately and totally failed him, his beloved homeland was scorched and scarred and rang with the sound of English boots marching on it.

If the evidence presented is true, and we have no reason to doubt its veracity, then by late summer Glyn Dŵr's grief had turned into beserking fury and he was preparing for one final suicidal charge at the enemy. It seems that many of the nobles, war captains and common soldiery wanted to go with him. We know this because of the resulting casuality list. A group of Scots and French soldiers, loyal to Glyn Dŵr, landed in the north in May, and joined up with the last native Prince of Wales, Owain Glyn Dŵr.

The Welsh embarked on one final, blood-drenched, sword-wielding charge into England, striking into Shropshire in August. This was not a raid for booty, simply vengeance. Whether they were looking for one last, massive fight, or seeing how far they could ride into England before death overtook them, we do not know. Local folklore tells us that they took and burnt Shrewsbury with much bloodletting, but claim and counter-claim make it difficult to know the truth. By this stage in the war, due to their violent history, both Shrewsbury and Oswestry shared the nickname 'Burntown'. As Glyn Dŵr and his men crashed through Shropshire, they inevitably sustained casualties in the fighting. One engagement near Welshpool was said to be particularly merciless.

Among those wounded and captured were the notorious rebel leader from Anglesey, Rhys ap Tudor, famed for the capture of Conwy Castle, and an Englishman from Troy, near Monmouth, Philip Scudamore, a close relative of Sir John Scudamore, the English military commander. Rhys ap Tudor and Philip Scudamore survived their wounds only to be executed later on the gallows. Several sources insist that Rhys Ddu, Rhys the Black of Aberystwyth Castle, the Sheriff of Cardiganshire until the English laws threw him out of a job and into the rebel camp, also rode with them on this last adventure. He too was captured and sent to London. We know that he was tortured for his exploits against the English in Glyn Dŵr's war, and was hung, drawn and quartered late in 1409 on the gallows at the Tower of London. Owain Glyn Dŵr and many of his men survived and returned to prowl the woods and hills of Wales.

[8] September/ October/ November 1409   More Truces
Henry IV was incensed at the news that English commanders, sheriffs and communities were still seeking and making truces with Welsh rebels. On 3rd November 1409, he vehemently reprimanded his Marcher Lords and knights for doing so.

1410 onwards

THE END AND THE AFTERMATH

1410
onwards

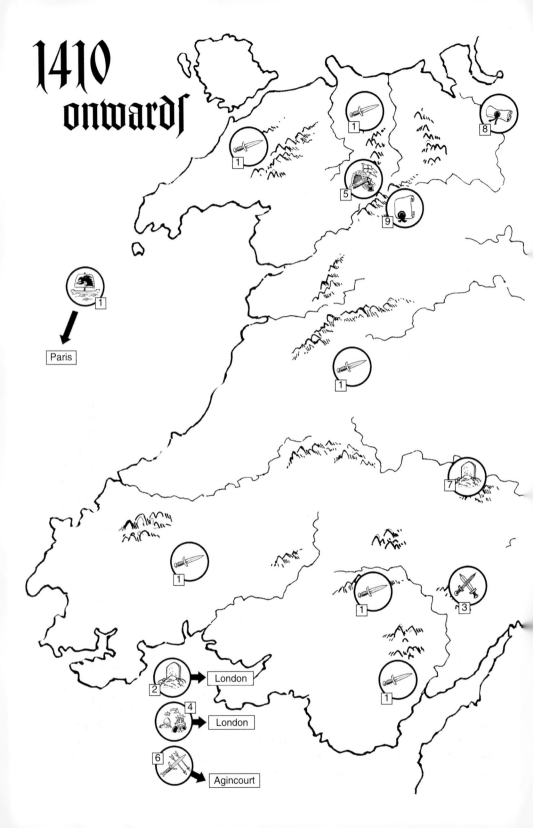

Paris

London

London

Agincourt

[1] From 1410 Onwards

There were no more out-and-out battles between the two sides in this war, and, by and large, the people and the land came to an uneasy peace. It came too late for Henry IV though, the wars left the crown bankrupt and weak. He was unable to rule from this time on, through ill health rather than the stupidity which characterised his reign. Prince Hal and his closest advisors governed in the king's infirmity. The rebels were not done yet though. Two legal systems existed in Wales at this time, and although Welshmen were not entitled to pursue anyone through the English legal system, they were entitled, under Welsh law, to take action against other Welshmen. Those who found legal proceedings started against them included Welshmen who had purchased confiscated or forfeited rebel property, submitted early or without good reason, or simply had not been loyal to Glyn Dŵr. In a Welsh court, under Welsh law, before a Welsh judge, such people were rebels against Wales, and as such, liable to punishment. Where judicial recourse failed, or did not exist, as with the pursuit of Englishmen or very high-ranking Welshmen, the rebels thirstily pursued the old way of satisfying a vendetta, through violence. Ambush, assault and murder took place.

The scale of such action remained relatively small because the Welsh, as a whole, had remained solidly loyal to the cause. They had submitted tactically, when an English army was nearby, and continued as rebels once the enemy had left the vicinity. Welsh spirit was not broken, there was much tension and insecurity. English townsfolk, merchants and soldiers were ambushed, kidnapped and taken hostage from 1410 onwards, to be exchanged for Welsh prisoners held by the English authorities. This strategy met with remarkable success in freeing prisoners of the Crown. Recriminations over war damage began, most controversially concerning Saint Asaph Cathedral. The authorities claimed the rebels had destroyed it out of ungodly malice, but Saint Asaph had been one of Glyn Dŵr's steadfast centres of support throughout the war. It seems improbable that the Welsh would destroy such an institution, especially as it was earmarked as an important northern centre for the new independent Welsh church.

In March, Anglesey was again boiling over into rebellion, naval patrols responded to the alert and a force of nine hundred additional English troops were landed on the island. In 1410, Welsh ambassadors were in Paris, still pressing the French to honour their promises.

[2] 1411

Owain Glyn Dŵr's son, Gruffudd, died in suspicious circumstances in the Tower of London. The cause of death was given as *"pestilence"*.

Fighting broke out again in Ceredigion, notably around Cardigan, and throughout Merioneth. The authorities tried to negotiate with Glyn Dŵr in an attempt to buy off the renewed attacks and bring the land to peace. Glyn Dŵr was unrepentant and would hear nothing of the Crown's offers. The authorities were obliged to negotiate with former rebels who refused to submit. Some rebels demanded, and got, pardons, positions of office and overseas military postings. Taxation in Wales recommenced in 1411, as did the reconstruction of the country's castles, battered and damaged after the heavy fighting of the past decade.

[3] April 1412

Dafydd Gam was the rebels' chosen hate figure. His elderly father was prosecuted in court, relatives and servants were attacked and killed. To cap it all, Dafydd Gam, personal retainer to Henry IV, was ambushed and humiliatingly taken prisoner by Glyn Dŵr's men in April 1412. One can only wonder at the delights months of captivity brought to Gam whilst in Glyn Dŵr's hands. His ransom was raised and paid by Henry IV.

The fighting in Merioneth eventually ended in November 1412. More columns of English troops were regularly sent to Wales in the period 1412 to 1414.

[4] 1413

Henry IV died in March and Prince Hal became Henry V. He appears to have had a more pragmatic approach towards the Welsh than his father and many other English leaders. Although heavy fines for rebellion were imposed throughout Wales, many of which were never paid, there was not the same vindictive insistence on harsh punishment that had always been the central feature of English governance in Wales. This did not mark the advent of a policy of enlightened rule in Wales by any means, and there was one major exception to this easing of past rigidity in 1414.

An entry in English records shows that on, or by, 1st December 1413, Catrin Mortimer and her daughters had also died in suspicious circumstances in the Tower of London and had been buried in the grounds of Saint Swithin's church in London. It is unclear what happened to Margaret Glyn Dŵr and her grandson Lionel Mortimer, a legitimate heir to the English throne, but it is almost certain that they too were murdered in prison by the authorities. On 16th September 2001, at Saint Swithin's church in London, a memorial to Catrin Glyn Dŵr was unveiled, dedicated to her and her children and also to the suffering of all women and children in war.

[5] 10th March 1414   The Submission of Bala

Other submissions had taken place without need of parade or fanfare. The men came, paid, or agreed to pay, fines for rebellion, were bound over before the law and were sent on their way. At Bala, near the place where Glyn Dŵr had been crowned Prince of Wales on 16th September 1400, a very different submission was made. On 10th March 1414, the earl of Arundel, Sir Edward Charlton, judges, scribes, translators and hundreds of troops, organised and presided over a judicial session in the open air in the name of the new king, Henry V.

Six hundred men of the area, the veteran hard core of Glyn Dŵr's fearsome personal retinue, were made to kneel in the mud before the English.

Having congregated in the nearby town of Bala, they were disarmed and obliged to kneel in the lashing rain in a field outside the town and swear an oath to the King of England. Not only that, the terms of the oath were arrogant, haughty and not at all conciliatory. The men of the area were to agree that they deserved death for their actions and that they gave praise to God on bended knee that their king was indeed merciful. They had to swear on the Bible that neither they, nor their heirs would rise in rebellion again, and would be loyal to the king of England. They then had to pay a collective fine before being pardoned. They could then recover their forfeited lands and property, and, importantly, restore property to the widows and families of dead rebels. If the idea had been to humiliate the Welsh into peace, it was a monumental blunder. It guaranteed that the embers of hatred would burn on for years, arguably for centuries to come.

[6] September 1415? February 1416?   The Death of Owain Glyn Dŵr.

There is much debate and speculation concerning the time and place of Glyn Dŵr's death, however the fact remains that we do not know the definite answer. Later chroniclers wrote that his final years were spent on the run, hiding in caves and living the miserable life of a fugitive. Many places in Wales claim, with pride, a connection with Glyn Dŵr. We have no solid evidence to back up the myriad claims from all over Wales that Glyn Dŵr hid in such and such a place. These stories paint an interesting picture of the cunning and unrepentant rebel defying the authorities here, there and everywhere. We do not know which parts of these folk tales are true, whether they were really believed, intended to throw the authorities off his scent once again or simply to embellish the already legendary reputation of a genuinely cherished leader. It seems unlikely that a man of his years, in his mid-fifties at least, could have scaled the cliffs, jumped the chasms and other impressive natural barriers attributed to him in stories of his life on the run. It is far more likely that he lived on or near the south-eastern border estates of Sir John Scudamore and his second wife, Alys Glyn Dŵr, Owain's daughter, lamenting his losses.

Though no longer charging into the enemy with a sword in his hand, Owain Glyn Dŵr must have remained the focus for native affection, and in all probability played a role in the planning of the raids and fighting which took place after 1409. It is quite probable that he held court, protected by his men, who remained loyal until his death.

The story of the unsuccessful hunt for Glyn Dŵr is born of popular folklore. He was never betrayed by his people, despite the huge reward money on offer by the English Crown, and the crushing burden of oppression they bore, then as in other times. In reality it seems that Henry V's regime sought to close the chapter definitively. Pardons were offered to Owain Glyn Dŵr and his son, Maredudd, on 5th July 1415, while, by all accounts, he was still alive, and on 24th February 1416, when he may not have been. It is not clear however, if the later pardon was intended for Owain or Maredudd, or both. If it were only offered to Maredudd, it may indicate that rumour of his death had reached the authorities, who no longer extended the pardon to him as they had previously done.

Much that was written about Glyn Dŵr in the following decades and centuries was prejudiced and claimed things that the various writers could never have known. Some say he starved, some say he froze, some say other ends befell Glyn Dŵr, but they are all consistently unpleasant, keeping faith with the pattern of damning, derisive and patently untrue accusations levelled at the Welsh by certain English writers. There is no way of knowing what actually happened to him. It seems that these writings aim to act as a warning of what would happen to Welshmen who detatch themselves from England's teat; misery, isolation and death. Perhaps they intended to tarnish his fine reputation and decry his impressive achievements as a leader of a small independent nation in the face of the barbaric oppression of a larger neighbour. Those Welsh writers who wrote ill of him may have wished to distance themselves from the patriotic embers still aglow in Wales, perhaps because they believed what they wrote, perhaps because they wanted to 'get on' and needed English approval or patronage. He should not be seen in such a light.

Some sources claimed that he died on the feast of Saint Matthew, being 20th/ 21st September 1415. If true, this would match their incorrect claims as being the date he ended his first attack on the north-east in 1400, and match the traditional date for his birth in 1349. If the first and last of these are true, when he died, he would have been sixty-six years old to the very day. Other sources, mainly ones local to the area in which he was suspected to have passed his last years, say that he died and was buried at night in February 1416. Would this event have prompted the government to reissue the pardon to Maredudd in an attempt to bring the matter to an end ? We cannot say for sure. It is highly questionable that distant writers would know precisely when he died, when other, more able searchers failed to find any trace of him. The fact that his last known appearance in the limelight was in April 1412, when Dafydd Gam was ambushed in Gwent, not too far from the Scudamore properties on the south-eastern border, makes these confident predictions all the more unsound. If we are to believe the seers of the age, then he did not die, but slipped Arthur-like into legend, sleeping, but ready and able to rise again for his people and nation when ultimately needed. Glyn Dŵr's poet, Iolo Goch composed a poem for his master, translated thus:

> 'I saw with aching heart
> The golden dream depart;
> His glorious image in my mind,
> Was all that Owain left behind
> Wild with despair and woebegone
> Thy Faithful bard is left alone,
> To sigh, to weep, to groan.

Thy sweet rememberance ever dear,
Thy name still ushered by a tear
My inward anguish speak;
How could'st thou cruel Owain go
And leave the bitter tears to flow.'

[7] 25th October 1415   The Battle of Agincourt

The Welsh campaigns, as at the time of Edward I, had been the costliest of military operations and left the English crown bankrupt and weakened. By the time he undertook this new campaign against the French, the scarred Henry V was a veteran of Glyn Dŵr's war, which had begun fifteen years earlier. At Agincourt, just after his twenty-eighth birthday, he had known nothing but war since being strong enough to bear arms. Having been blooded in the war in Wales, Henry V had survived his military baptism of fire, and emerged as an energetic and capable commander. Some called him courageous and valiant, but there are no ready examples of his valour, and it is difficult to estimate the courage of a general who deploys thousands and thousands of heavily armed soldiers against a poorly equipped enemy, usually consisting of a few hundred men. Henry V had seen first hand what the Welsh were capable of in combat. The fact that he recruited large numbers of Welshmen for his military campaigns confirmed that he valued and respected them as soldiers.

He took a massive force of Welshmen with him on his campaigns in France, notably at a battle called Agincourt, or Azincourt in French, on 25th October 1415. It is a very interesting battle for a number of reasons. Not only did the mainly Welsh archers win a stunning victory for Henry V and give the famous "We've still got our fingers" two-fingered salute, but there are also suggestions that they settled a few scores that day. We know that Welsh contingents fought, and some of them died, in French colours on the battlefield. In such a scenario, with vengeful Welsh troops on both sides, men like Dafydd Gam might find themselves in trouble in the chaos of battle. Dafydd Gam paid the ultimate price for his allegiance and adherence to the King of England, and died in his colours at Agincourt. Legend has it Henry V knighted him on the battlefield as he lay dying. Edward, the bulbous Duke of York, who campaigned in Wales during Glyn Dŵr's war, also died in the melee at Agincourt. Due to intelligent battlefield preparations and the massed use of bows, English losses at Agincourt were light, the highest estimate puts the total at one thousand five hundred men. The French were, famously, slaughtered, losing at least six thousand men.

Gruffydd Yonge and the Hanmers had been in Paris since February 1415, and were still seeking French intervention in Wales. It did not come, but the Welsh did not stop trying for several more years, ultimately in vain. Gruffydd Yonge led a concerted effort to obtain the promised French support until 1418. He realised the French would not honour the treaties they had signed with the Welsh, and gave up the last vestiges of hope. He also knew he could not return to Wales, for the authorities were still intent on punishing this unrepentant rebel. A man of such talent could not remain inactive though. He went to Scotland and became the bishop of Ross, before taking a bishopric in north Africa.

In Wales, Crown officers in Merioneth refused to leave the security of their castles to gather revenues, for fear of Welsh ambush, and no taxes were paid.

[8] 1417   Government Reports
Government despatches recorded the continuing need to send columns of troops into Wales and provide armed escorts for officials. They noted pointedly that a worrying number of their officials and supporters were murdered in Wales in the period following the official end of the war. This situation continued for years, in 1420, the sheriffs of Merioneth and Caernarfonshire appealed to the rebels to surrender so that they could receive pardons and come to peace. The rebels did not heed the authorities' pleas. In the 1430's, the English were still suffering the occasional ambush, and noted that " *the Welsh bear ancient malice and enmity towards the English.*" As late as 1443 murders of government officials and rebel activity in Wales were still being recorded.

[9] 8th April 1421   The Final Act
Some sources identify Maredudd ab Owain as Glyn Dŵr's last surviving son, yet we can only confirm the death of one of each of the six males and five females reportedly born to Owain and Margaret Glyn Dŵr. They were Gruffydd and Catrin, who both died in the Tower of London. There are no reports of the deaths of Glyn Dŵr's other children, so it is difficult to accept this particular claim as true. Maredudd refused pardons offered by Henry V in 1415, 1416 and 1417, but finally accepted a royal pardon on 8th April 1421, and was no longer labelled a rebel, closing the final chapter on Glyn Dŵr's war.

Epilogue

In the wake of Glyn Dŵr war, Wales was bound even more tightly with punitive legislation. Those prejudiced laws, briefly mentioned in 'The Welsh in Battle', were rigorously enforced and others added. The civilian administration sank its claws into Wales and carved it up, each district carefully parcelled up into taxable, controllable units. The English military re-established itself throughout Wales. The Welsh were again disarmed, taxed into poverty, and subdued by the reimposition of the 'apartheid' laws.

The pervading mood of the nation in the post-Glyn Dŵr era has been described as sullen. Their sense of loss may well have been compounded by cruel climate change. Climatologists believe average temperatures in Britain plunged as this part of Europe was gripped by Canadian-style winters. They estimate this cold cycle began in the early 1400's and continued for several centuries, encouraging events such as London's "Frost Fair", held on the river Thames when it froze solid every winter. The bizarre, unseasonal storms of the first decade of the fifteenth century and the harsh winter of 1407 - 08 may have been the first tangible signs of this climate change. To such a superstitious people as the Welsh, feeling a strong bond to nature, this may have been perceived as a sign, perhaps even punishment.

So what prevented Owain Glyn Dŵr from attaining independence for Wales? Glyn Dŵr was undefeated by the authorities, and, apart from the recapture of Aberystwyth and Harlech castles from the rebels, there had been no major battlefield defeat, no invasion nor any public damning of the leader. In fact, from 1411 to 1414, the authorities tried to negotiate with Glyn Dŵr, asking him to intercede in their attempts to bring unrepentant rebels to peace. There were no mass murders or public executions in Wales after Glyn Dŵr's war, as there had been in the 1280's and 1290's. Neither the King of England nor his troops mounted a grand tour of Wales to show the natives he was their regent. Instead, there was an almost insidious seeping of Englishmen back into Wales. A court session here, fines paid there, whilst in the background, the English set about rebuilding the castles and fortifications. The Welsh could be forgiven for believing they had not lost. Indeed, the questions, "when?" and "where?" had they lost, have no clear answer. There was no Welsh Culloden, Boyne or Waterloo, and the nagging doubts that the Welsh were defeated remain to this day.

We know Glyn Dŵr did not establish a lasting independent nation, but where did he fall short? It is easy to be critical with hindsight. The reasons for Glyn Dŵr's inability to achieve his goals lie at home and abroad. In Wales, Glyn Dŵr and his men won the battle for the country. The English were reduced to maintaining *"Englishries"*, pockets of Englishness, besieged or ruled by the natives. They clung on to Caernarfon, Pembroke, Tenby, Kidwelly, Brecon and Coity, a handful of impotent foreign enclaves in an otherwise free Wales. English civilian adminstration ceased to function when the Welsh nation rebelled. The civil administration of an occupying force very quickly loses its purchase on a rebel nation and has to rely on its military to retain control.

English forces had no answer for the speed, ferocity and effectiveness of the Welsh in battle. Across the country, Glyn Dŵr's men swept all before them. Welsh tactics in the field were superior to those of the English. This is borne out by the fact that the Welsh were rewarded with years of stunning victories against the English enemy which, on paper, completely outclassed them in numbers and equipment. The Welsh even launched a number of campaigns into England, the summer campaign of 1406 to name but one.

It is true that the Welsh did not confront Henry IV's enormous expeditionary forces head on. In all theatres of war throughout human history, armies, where given a choice, have avoided confronting opposing forces which would destroy them. However, Welsh troops did engage English forces much larger than their own, and, at Hyddgen in 1401 and Bryn Glas in 1402, trounced them. Evidence from English sources, mentioned in the entry for September 1405, show that even the king's armies were not safe and suffered repeated ambush in Wales. These huge columns, too big to destroy, or to tackle head on, were too lumbering to seek out and engage the guerillas, whose attacks reduced Henry's expeditions to almost toothless patrols. The English casualty rate from these expeditions to Wales far exceeded those inflicted on Welsh forces, as the aforementioned extract describes.

At times, English forces sought to evade Glyn Dŵr s army: in July 1403, the sheriff of Hereford, John Bodenham, withdrew his troops from Wales, fled to Hereford and appealed to the king for help. In 1405, Henry IV himself is said to have fled the Allied Franco - Welsh army at Worcester. English towns and communities made treaties with the Welsh, throughout 1405 for example, realising that they could neither fight nor flee Glyn Dŵr's forces and that the King of England could not protect them.

Owain Glyn Dŵr employed what are today considered classic guerilla tactics. In early fifteenth century Europe, they were new and terrifying. Unpredictability was the rebels' trump card - if the enemy knew where they were going to be, and when, it could bring all its might to bear on the rebels. The English had long experience of siege warfare, and the men and equipment to demonstrate their abilities. This explains why the Welsh did not occupy castles or use them as Welsh strongholds. Instead, the Welsh tried to destroy the castles, or render them unusable, in order to deny the enemy.

Some castles, like Harlech, were taken and held, others, such as Criccieth, were razed. Most, however, were abandoned after those inside had been slaughtered, the castle burnt and sections of the walls pulled down. Most Welsh attacks were carried out by horsemen and footmen armed with a terrifying range of hand weapons, but no technical siege equipment capable of destroying fortresses. That so many castles fell to the Welsh onslaught is a great accomplishment; that Glyn Dŵr's men were unable to tear them down with merely hands, swords and ropes is no surprise at all. This meant that the castles, though damaged and abandoned, were still serviceable. Crucially, the English could still make use of them in the future, if an opportunity presented itself.

Welsh tactics and actions confounded and defeated their enemy for years, but this reliance on guerilla warfare as the mainstay of a military strategy also contributed to the eventual demise of the rebel campaign. Welsh forces, though in their thousands, were dispersed throughout Wales and were only concentrated on certain occasions. Rebel assault parties caused enormous damage and achieved amazing successes, but Welsh armies - such as those raised in the summers of 1402, 1403, 1405 and 1406, and that of the winter and spring of 1404, terrified the authorities and threatened crushing victories, both within Wales and east of the border. Had the Welsh driven into England and captured a major town, the history of the war may read very differently today. Taking the horror and slaughter of warfare to English towns could well have led to a more rapid conclusion to hostilities, possibly in the form of a treaty, such as that of Montgomery in 1267, which recognised Wales. Restricting themselves to reconquering Wales and only launching seasonal campaigns into England denied the Welsh more widespread coverage of their campaign, applied less pressure on the English crown, and thus, allowed the shaky Bolingbroke regime more time to get to grips with the rebels.

Was this tactic left unpursued due to a lack of ambition or vision, or because of a lack of manpower ? We will never know for certain. If peace had come with a treaty, it is unlikely to have been a lasting peace. The history of Britain demonstrates the proven inability of the English in accepting independent nations as neighbours.

Glyn Dŵr's hand was forced in critical areas, notably those of manpower and weaponry which, in comparison to those of the English, were severely limited. Had Glyn Dŵr been able to occupy and use the castles effectively, he undoubtedly would have. At least, his actions in so doing at Aberystwyth and Harlech prove this. If he had enough troops to retake the castles, continue sending marauding war parties across the land to ambush the enemy and destroy his resources, as well as launching armies into England, he would have done so. Indeed, his troop deployments hint that this was part of his strategy, and he managed as best he could with the limited numbers available. His military achievements with so few men are astounding, but the simple fact was that Glyn Dŵr did not have enough men to tackle as huge an opponent as England. This proved to be decisive. He knew from the beginning that he would need troops from elsewhere, and duly sought allies. It is to foreign powers that we must turn to gain a complete understanding of the war.

Forces from beyond Wales had a crucial bearing on the outcome of the war. The Welsh had surpassed expectations with their military and political accomplishments. Much weight is given to the military victories, but the political advances are also highly important. That the English administration in Wales was brought down and replaced, and, with the backing of a native Parliament, a nation was reborn, are among the pinnacles of Welsh historical achievement. It should be feted as such, for until recent times, it was the outstanding example of the Welsh nation imposing its will and desire over the English. The native Parliament met at least twice, though probably three times. The apparatus of state was constructed and utilised, a civilian administration reorganised the country into its traditional districts and brought the taxes gleaned from the populace to a Parliament where nobles, clergy and commons were represented. This inclusion of the commons in such an early European Parliament is probably without precedent. English law was set aside, and, for the first time in over a century, the law of the land was not a detriment to the Welsh. The pragmatic and well-developed Welsh law, enlightened enough to recognise women as equals to men for example, was reinstated as Wales' sole legal system for the first time since the murder of Llewelyn II. A native church was born, it held its own synod in March 1406, and, in the Pennal Letter, appealed to a mother church to accept it into the Christian world. Wales created its own tier of diplomatic envoys which represented it, and sought aid abroad. The Welsh military was reawakened, and battered its massive foe for several years. Freedom had been bought with the sword. To attain their final victory, independence, against such a populous, wealthy opponent, they would need foreign help. Catastrophically, all of Wales' allies ultimately failed her.

In England, elements opposed to Henry Bolingbroke lacked co-ordination. Bolingbroke's potential rival claimants to the throne, the Mortimers, were waning from eminence. Their powerbase had been built up by waging war against the Welsh on behalf of Norman kings. Ironically, their leader, the Earl of March, threw his lot in with the Welsh when Mortimer power was broken on 22nd June, 1402, at Bryn Glas. The Mortimers survived and later recovered to positions of eminence, but far too late to help Owain Glyn Dŵr, their ally.

Glyn Dŵr's alliance with the Percy warlords was more promising. The alliance was probably informally negotiated by Hotspur, Worcester and Glyn Dŵr before summer 1403, and formally ratified in the Tripartite Indenture in February 1405 by Northumberland and Glyn Dŵr's bishops. Hotspur's premature, disorganised rebellion in July 1403 was a disaster. Following Percy defeat at the battle of Shrewsbury, the Percy menace and power was effectively broken. Northumberland continued to be problematic for the Lancastrian dynasty until his death in battle against Bolingbroke in February 1408, but was unable to rally enough support to seriously threaten the Crown.

Other anti-Bolingbroke elements in England failed to materialise in support of a third opportunity to bring down the regime in August 1405, when the Allied army threatened the town of Worcester having swept across south Wales and marched through Herefordshire. The French contingent offered those malcontents in England a sure sign that they would be supported from abroad if they rose. They did not rise. This sent the French a message that they would not be able to bring down the English monarch from within.

This knowledge undoubtedly affected French commitment to honouring their treaties and promises to the Welsh.The French repeatedly failed to deliver those promises, despite having the capacity to do so. This proved to be a key factor in Glyn Dŵr's destiny. The French had problems of their own during this period. Charles VI was a weak king, often incapacitated by bouts of mental illness. This led to dangerous instability at court and debilitating factional warfare. Also, a large part of France was occupied by, or allied to, the English. When civil war erupted in France in 1407, after the assassination of the Duke of Orleans, the French were only too eager to conclude a truce guaranteeing English neutrality in the ensuing civil war. The price of that truce was to sell out the Welsh, once more breaking signed and sealed treaties made with Glyn Dŵr and his ambassadors.

Glyn Dŵr's war broke out as Scotland's King Robert III was ailing. Heavy defeat by the English, led by Hotspur, at Homildon Hill in September 1402 crippled the Scots militarily. Promising early signs, achieved through Welsh-Scots diplomacy, evaporated rapidly thereafter and were finally laid to rest in 1406 when Robert III's heir, James, was captured at sea by the English. It is exceptional that both France and Scotland were simultaneously in such weak positions and concluded truces with the English. This left Wales the only country at war with the English. Under these extremely rare conditions, Glyn Dŵr could not succeed. That the rebels accomplished so much without support is a remarkable testament to them and their leader.

The Bretons provided the most consistent foreign military support for Glyn Dŵr. Alone, they could not bring enough force to bear to make a noticeable or lasting impact on the campaign. In the end, they too concluded treaties with the English, completely isolating the Welsh. The Bretons did not do this until January 1408 however, when the balance had swung decidedly in favour of the English who, at that time, were strangling the rebel fortresses of Aberystwyth and Harlech. The outcome of this total failure of foreign support resulted in the subsequent painful ebbing from a victorious position at home. This was the essential factor in deciding the fate of the war.

English nobles, commanders and soldiers found it very hard to make a reputation for themselves in Wales. The terrain was difficult and the opposition tough. The Welsh did not take prisoners or pay ransoms. To an English nobleman, the risks of campaigning in Wales, without an entourage of thousands, were too great, and many only did so reluctantly. English military victories in Wales are few and far between, as previously noted, there is no soul - rending battlefield defeat by the English, such as Waterloo and Culloden, not because the Welsh did not fight - they certainly did, as this account amply reveals - but because they did not fight when and how the English wanted.

Eventually, the authorities reverted to tactics used by Edward I, over a century before. Edward I and his advisors realised that the Welsh could be overcome, not in head to head battle, but by occupation with enormous armies. Forces such as the 16,000 men of 1277, and the 35,000 of 1295 came to Wales not necessarily to fight, but to overwhelm. Edward's commanders realised that the Welsh, in comparison, could only field relatively small forces. When very large armies entered Wales, instead of meeting them in a futile one-day battle, the Welsh reverted to harrying and ambush tactics. Edward and his commanders concluded that the only way of subjugating Wales was by massive sustained military presence. The English armies moved into an area en masse, built fortifications or secure points onto which further constructions could be built, then moved to another area to repeat the process, always with forces too numerous to challenge. Henry IV's royal expeditions, such as the 13, 000 men of 1400, were brief displays of power, not sustained campaigns. During Glyn Dŵr's war, it was not until summer 1407 that Henry IV's forces had the confidence to attempt to capture any military objectives in Wales. Although repeatedly ambushed en route to Aberystwyth and Harlech, these armies pressed on, and played out the final major acts of the war, supported the whole time by warships and relief columns from England. For the Welsh, losing those key fortresses signalled a certain end to potential foreign involvement. With no established capital or urban strongholds, it would be difficult to make a legitimate claim of sovereignty - except sovereignty under occupation, or to identify a site to welcome foreign ambassadors and their armies

The outbreak of the war led to outrage in England. They claimed it was 'treachery' that such a volatile 'people of little reputation' dared to rebel against them. The English Parliament and public were hysterical at the Welsh refusal to lie down. From 1282 onwards they had legislated against a people with no parliamentary representation. More proscriptive laws were added to the statute books during and after Glyn Dŵr's war. In the 1430's, political pamphlets entitled "Beware of Wales" were in circulation, and the Kidwelly Charter of 1443 reaffirmed the old statutes, paying particular attention to the insistence on there being no Welshmen involved in courts, juries or legal action, while accusing the Welsh of 'malice' and blaming them for damage done to the town forty years earlier. Yet for decades, English cruelty and avarice had extorted vast sums in taxation from Wales, and their laws denied even basic rights to the natives.

In the aftermath of Glyn Dŵr's war, the legal and financial pressures on the Welsh had a more crushing effect than the English military. Welshmen, out of necessity and poverty, fought for Henry V in France, most famously at Agincourt in October 1415. The loss of a native noble structure forced Welsh nobles to rethink their futures. Some left Wales forever and went abroad, mainly to Scotland, Brittany, France and Ireland. Others bound themselves tightly to the English. One of the latter group, a grandson of the rebel Maredudd ap Tudor from Anglesey, took the crown of England from Richard III in battle, at Bosworth Field in 1485. When Henry Tudor became King Henry VII of England in 1485, the Tudors were little more than a generation away from being murderous rebels against the crown they now held. Was the

Tudor accession the final Welsh victory over the English that the prophecies foretold? Yet why is Tudor Welshness quietly passed over, when Stewart links to Scotland, or more recent royal lines' distant German heritage, are not ? Is the fact that England was ruled by a Welsh dynasty for more than a century - coincidentally, the same duration as the English occupation from 1282 to 1400 - really so difficult to acknowledge?

The most remarkable thing to emerge from this era was a man who became a national hero. Owain Glyn Dŵr was a man of vision, force and courage. He inspired loyalty, and retained that loyalty and the affection of the people, even when free Wales slipped from his grasp and sank back into subjugation. That he was never defeated, betrayed or captured, elevated him beyond warlord and kingly status to being a hero of his people. He slipped Arthur-like into the hereafter, the seers said that he did not die and no-one could prove otherwise.

It is time that Glyn Dŵr was accorded his rightful place in the pantheon of Welsh heroes. He displayed the warrior prowess of Llewelyn I, Rhys ap Gruffydd, Rhys of Deheubarth and Llewelyn II. He had the vision and humanity of Hywel Dda the Lawgiver and sound kingship of Owain Gwynedd. He also had the international appeal of the adventurer, Owain Lawgoch. The poets and writers, headed perhaps by Dafydd ap Gwilym, can rest easy, for we know of no literary genius to add to Glyn Dŵr's talents. Owain Glyn Dŵr is one of the few Welshmen to gain respect from the English. A number of Englishmen have written favourably of him, not the least of whom was William Shakespeare. 'The Bard' recorded sentiments still common enough to be easily recalled by English audiences two centuries after the war. Apart from keeping with English stereotypes of Welsh verbosity, Shakespeare represented him as a fine rebel leader, cursed but respected by his enemy, a magician with druidic powers over the elements.

Llewelyn ap Gruffudd, Llewelyn II, is widely acclaimed as Wales' last recognised Prince. More recently the name of Owain of the Bloody Hand, Owain Lawgoch, has been advanced as a successor to the title of last Prince of Wales. Surely Owain Glyn Dŵr was Wales' last native Prince? In terms of bloodline alone, he was the foremost of Welsh nobles. His wealth, connections and warrior reputation placed him in the highest echelon of Welsh society. He was fervently acclaimed by his countrymen and crowned Prince of Wales in 1400. His royal status was also recognised by the French, the Scots, the Spanish and the Bretons. Tenaciously he fought his country to freedom, however brief. Thanks to Glyn Dŵr an ancient nation was restored to its own traditions. During his reign, a Welsh state was created. As Prince, he summoned Parliaments, planned for two universities and helped create a national church. He also had his own Royal Seal and Crown Jewels comprising a crown, a sceptre and an orb, - interestingly they were never recovered and may lie lost somewhere, awaiting discovery. In the name of that worthy cause, he lost his family, his home and his lands. The time has come to recognise this man, Owain Glyn Dŵr, as the last true Prince of Wales.

Owain Glyn Dŵr courtesy Martin Green

Summary.

Pre 1282	Independent Wales.
1282	Start of English occupation.
1284	Statute of Wales Act.
1282 to 1400	Various rebellions, resistance, national movements and a cultural flourishing. First English use of title 'Prince of Wales' in 1301.
1346	The Battle of Crecy.
20th September 1349	Possible date of birth of Owain Glyn Dŵr.
28th May 1354	Possible date of birth of Owain Glyn Dŵr.
1356	Battle of Poitiers. Military career of Owain Lawgoch or 'Owain of Wales'.
? 1359	Possible date of birth of Owain Glyn Dŵr.
1369	Lawgoch's first invasion fleet, bound for Wales, delayed by storms.
1372	Lawgoch's second invasion fleet, bound for Wales, recalled by French after capture of Channel islands.
1378	Murder of Owain Lawgoch in France.
Late 1370's to Early 1380's	Glyn Dŵr an Apprentice - at - Law at the Inns of Court at Westminster.
1383	Owain Glyn Dŵr married Margaret Hanmer.
1384	Glyn Dŵr on military duty at Berwick - on - Tweed with a sizeable Welsh contingent and notable English commanders. Glyn Dŵr praised for conduct in battle
1385	Glyn Dŵr on Richard II's expedition to Scotland. Glyn Dŵr again praised for skill at arms and horsemanship. Glyn Dŵr given accolade 'Canwyll Brwydr', the Candle of Battle.
1386	Glyn Dŵr called as a witness at the Grosvenor versus Scrope trial.
1387	Glyn Dŵr heavily involved in naval battle in Channel and subsequent razing of Sluys
1389	Truce between France and England in the Hundred Years war.
1399	Capture at parley of Richard II at Conwy Castle by Bolingbroke. Richard II murdered soon after. Henry Bolingbroke became Henry IV. His son, also Henry, given title 'Prince of Wales' by Henry IV. Friction on the north eastern border and provocation of Glyn Dŵr by Lord Grey of Ruthin and by the English parliament.

1400

Late Summer   Henry IV's campaign summons to Glyn Dŵr withheld by
                           Lord Grey. Glyn Dŵr subsequently branded a traitor by
                           Henry IV.
16th September   The Coronation. Owain Glyn Dŵr proclaimed true Prince of
                           Wales by Welsh nobles.
18th-23rd September   The September Rampage and the Gwynedd Rising, the former
                           led by Glyn Dŵr, the latter led by the Tudors.
28th September to
15th October   Royal Expedition to Wales, led by Henry IV.

1401

January   Parliament passed more anti-Welsh legislation.
1st April   Conwy Castle taken by the Tudors.

Up until early
summer   Infiltration and raiding by Welsh. Rumours concerning
                           planned *'genocide of the English'*.
Early June   The battle of Hyddgen. Glyn Dŵr led 120 men
                           to victory against an English force more than ten times more
                           numerous.
June   The Appeal to the West.
                           The Scots at Bardsey.
24th June   The Tudors hand back Conwy Castle for full pardons.
                           Authorities humbled, nine rebels executed.
August   Slaughter and decapitation of English at Radnor.
1st October to
mid-October   2nd Royal Expedition to Wales, led by Henry IV.
2nd November   The battle of Tuthill. Glyn Dŵr unfurled his new colours,
                           those of Uthr Pendragon.
November
onwards   Welsh and English negotiations. Glyn Dŵr, Hotspur and
                           Worcester.

1402

January   Lord Grey of Ruthin blocked reconciliation attempts between
                           Glyn Dŵr and Henry IV.
January 30th   Glyn Dŵr raided Ruthin and laid waste the county.
Spring   The Great Comet.
April   The battle of Ruthin. English slaughtered by Glyn Dŵr, Lord
                           Grey taken prisoner.
                           Treason trials.
                           Bizarre weather across the country.
22nd June   The battle of Bryn Glas. Glyn Dŵr's summer sweep
                           culminated in this head on clash with the army of March. The
                           Army of March utterly destroyed. English slaughtered and
                           perhaps mutilated in the aftermath by Welsh women.
                           Sir Kinard de la Bere, Sir Walter Devereux, Sir Robert
                           Whitney and their retinues massacred. Only two English
                           nobles, Mortimerand Clanvowe, survived and taken prisoner

	by Glyn Dŵr.The intensity of the whole conflict increased from this point.
August	Glyn Dŵr's late summer chevauchee to the south.
	Welsh and Breton pirates in co-ordinated action in the Celtic sea and the Channel.Burial of Owain Lawgoch's heart in his native soil at Llandybie ?
	English relief columns and fleets in full and frantic action.
Early to mid-September.	3rd Royal Expedition to Wales, led by Henry IV.English massacre of villagers at Llanrwst.
	Town burnt. Freak weather almost killed Henry IV.
November	Grey and Clanvowe freed by payment. Mortimer left in Welsh hands.
	Welsh - English negotiations.
	More anti-Welsh legislation.
30th November	Marriage of Edmund Mortimer and Catrin Glyn Dŵr.

1403

All year	The rebellion, gathering pace since summer 1402, identifiable as full-scale war.
Winter and spring	Heavy fighting throughout Wales. Castles assaulted, English border counties attacked and pillaged by Welsh.
March	Hotspur angrily rebuked parliament for its constant criticism of him.
	Bretons attacked the English at sea.
15th May	Prince Hal wrote of his burning of Glyn Dŵr's homes at Sycharth and Glyndyfrdwy.
	More English rescue missions and relief columns.
1st July	The Tywi Valley Campaign. The rebel army of more than 8000 men swept down the Tywi valley and took castle after castle, including the English capital of south Wales, Carmarthen.
July	English withdrew relief force from Brecon to protect Hereford.
10th July	Hotspur declared himself rebel.
21st July	The battle of Shrewsbury. Henry IV victorious.
	Hotspur killed. Worcester captured. Prince Hal sustained severe wound to face.
23rd July	Execution of 'traitors' taken at Shrewsbury, including Worcester.
August	South-east Wales overrun by rebels.
3rd September	The Archbishop's Diaries.
Mid- to late-September	4th Royal Expedition to Wales, led by Henry IV.
	Reoccupation of Carmarthen. Much cattle stolen. Weather against Henry IV once more.
Late September and October	Rebel action in south-east and south-west Wales. Breton and French land forces in attack Kidwelly.

November	
onwards	Jean D'Espagne and French warships bombarded Caernarfon and marauded the north-west seas.
December	Glyn Dŵr took Cardiff and numerous other towns in the south.

1404

All year	Continuing full-scale war.
January and February	Continuous Welsh campaign brought more victories. Aberystwyth in Welsh hands at this time? Sheriff of Anglesey ambushed. Commander of Harlech captured. Criccieth and other castles fell to the rebels. Brecon refused to submit to Henry IV.
April	Defections to the Welsh cause. Bishops Byford and Lewis joined Glyn Dŵr.
27th April	Death of the peacemaker Philip the Bold, Duke of Burgundy. Orleanist hawks gain control of French court. Jean Sans Peur Duke of Burgundy.
Late spring to early summer	Fall of Harlech to Glyn Dŵr? Fall of Beaumaris to Glyn Dŵr? Treaty with French. The First Rebel Parliament, held at Machynlleth.
June	Cardiff again taken by Welsh. Herefordshire desperately held out against Welsh attacks.
14th July	Treaty of Alliance. Official ratification of the May 1404 agreement between France and Wales, signed in Paris.
July	The battle of Campstone Hill? English victory?
August	Jacques de Bourbon's mission from France. English communities recorded treaties with the Welsh.
20th August	Three-pronged Welsh offensive. Haverford and most of the south-west taken and held. Kidwelly town taken by Henry Don. The battle of Craig-y-Dorth in the south-east. English were massacred and survivors chased to the gates of Monmouth.
Autumn	Two enormous relief armies to Coity.
Winter	The fortresses of Aberystwyth, Harlech and Beaumaris in Welsh hands by the onset of winter.

1405

All year	Constant warfare.
15th February	Lady Despenser captured at Cheltenham with the two Mortimer heirs.
24th February	The Tripartite Indenture:- Wales to go to Glyn Dŵr. The north of England to the Percy dynasty. The south of England to the Mortimer dynasty.
11th March	The battle of Grosmont. English defeated Welsh raiding party.
5th May	The battle of Pwll Melyn. English victory. Tudor Glyn Dŵr and John ap Hywel killed.

	Gruffydd Glyn Dŵr captured. Prisoners executed at Ponfald?
June	Pacification of Anglesey began. The first attack led by English troops in Ireland.
Up to 30th July	2nd Welsh Parliament, held at Harlech. Ambassadors from France, Scotland, Castile and probably Brittany present.
5th August onwards	The French Expedition arrived in Wales. Allied Welsh- French army swept across the whole of south Wales. Culminated with face-off at Worcester.
September	Three relief armies to Coity.
1st November	French nobles returned to France. French and Breton troops left to spend winter near Cardigan.
December	The submission of Glamorgan?

1406

All year	Constant warfare, in particular the battle for Anglesey. Massive two-pronged English attack on Anglesey by naval and land forces launched from English- held Ireland and Chester began in January.
12th January	Ratification of Franco-Welsh Treaty. Earlier treaties also reaffirmed.
8th March	A letter arrived from Charles VI. It said that more French help would be forthcoming if the Welsh supprted the French Pope at Avignon, Benedict XIII.
March	Hywel Gwynedd killed at Halkyn Mountain. Synod of Welsh clergy at Machynlleth and possible first session of Glyn Dŵr's third parliament. Departure of French and Breton troops. Northumberland arrived in Wales.
31st March	The Pennal Letter. A Welsh Declaration of Independence. Outlined plan for independent nation, independent church loyal to Pope at Avignon, and future projects such as establishment of Welsh universities.
July	3rd Welsh Parliament at Harlech ? Hywel Sele's attempted assassination of Glyn Dŵr?
Autumn	North-east Wales attacked, then shortly after devastated by Welsh forces, possibly bent on avenging the actions of a traitorous spy.
9th November	The Submission of Anglesey. Fines and pardons issued. Battle for Anglesey almost over.
December	Bishop Mascall's List. Detailed account of damage done by Welsh raids in England.

1407

Late January or early February	Anglesey finally pacified. Gruffudd Yonge became Bishop of Bangor.
Spring	Heavy fighting in Ceredigion, Merioneth and Gwynedd. Flint and Maelor submitted.

May	English armies equipped with cannons and siege engines broke through to Aberystwyth and began siege. Prince Hal led a host of English nobles and thousands of well - equipped men for the campaign.
July	Oswestry, Bromfield and Yale submitted.
Late summer, early autumn	English laid siege to Harlech. The Talbot brothers and Edward Charlton led a similarly huge, well - equipped army to Harlech, Glyn Dŵr's capital.
September	Rhys Ddu negotiated a truce at Aberystwyth to last until 24th
October,	the final surrender to come on 1st November.
October	Glyn Dŵr visited Aberystwyth and threatened Rhys Ddu with decapitation. Truce broken by Glyn Dŵr. Siege of Aberystwyth recommenced.
23rd November	Assassination of Duke of Orleans in Paris. French civil war resulted.
7th December	French truce with English left Welsh out of peace settlement.
December	Breton peace negotiations with the English.

1408

January	French, and probably Breton, truces with the English came into effect.
Winter	Exceptionally hard winter killed many animals and caused starvation.
19th February	The battle of Bramham Moor, in England. Northumberland killed. Percys broken.
Spring	Sustained English assault on Harlech. Heavy English losses, replaced by massive relief columns.
May	Welsh ambassadors in Paris. French gave vague promises about future help.
September headed	The Fall of Aberystwyth. Many of the garrison escaped and north to join Glyn Dŵr.

1409

February	The Fall of Harlech. Margaret Glyn Dŵr, two of her daughters and four grandchildren captured. Edmund Mortimer killed in siege.
August and early September	The Last Ride. Last mass raid of the war. Scots and French contingent loyal to Glyn Dŵr present? Huge trail of destruction throughout north- east Wales and well into the English border counties. Heavy fighting at Welshpool. Shrewsbury sacked by Welsh with 'much bloodletting' ? Several nobles killed or captured and executed.
November	English communities still making peace treaties with Welsh rebels.

1410

All year	Prosecution and vendettas. The latter continued for at least
40 years	afterwards.

English navy and troops alerted and rushed to Anglesey to suppress rebel activity.
Welsh diplomats in Paris appealing to French.

1411

All year

?Gruffydd Glyn Dŵr died in the Tower of London.
Renewed fighting in Ceredigion and Merioneth.
English taxation and castle reconstruction in Wales recommenced.

1412

April

Dafydd Gam ambushed and captured. Ransomed later in the year by Henry IV.
Rhys ap Tudor executed at Chester for his role in The Last Ride.
English troops to Wales. Continued fighting in Merioneth.

1413

March

Death of Henry IV. Prince Hal became Henry V.
English troops to Wales.

1st December

Catrin Mortimer and her daughters buried in Saint Swithins church in London.

1414

10th March

The Submission of Bala.
English troops to Wales.

1415

All year

Crown officers in Wales refused to gather taxes, fearing the continued threat and occurrence of ambush and murder.

February

Gruffydd Yonge and the Hanmers in Paris pressing the Welsh cause.

5th July

Owain Glyn Dŵr and his son, Maredudd, rejected the royal pardons offered to them by Henry V.

20th/21st
September

The Death of Owain Glyn Dŵr ?

25th October

The battle of Agincourt. Welsh bowmen and foot soldiers secured substantial victory for Henry V against the French, who were massacred. The 'two-fingered salute' first used by bowmen under Henry V's command. Dafydd Gam and the Duke of York killed.

1416

24th February

Pardons offered by the Crown to rebel leaders were again rejected.

February

The Death of Owain Glyn Dŵr? The seers said he did not die.

1417

All year
?Pardon offered to Maredudd Glyn Dŵr alone, who refused.
Report by authorities listed ambushes and attacks in Wales by
rebels on the king's officials, soldiers and others.

1418

?The Hanmers and Gruffydd Yonge in Paris again, still
pressing the Welsh cause with the French, to no avail.
Gruffydd Yonge left for Scotland and became the Bishop of
Ross.

1421

8th April
Maredudd ab Owain, otherwise known as Maredudd Glyn
Dŵr, accepted royal pardon offered by Henry V, and was no
longer considered a rebel.

Publisher's Notes

The following excepts add to our general knowledge of Glyndŵr, and are intended to supplement G.J. Brough's fascinating account of his war:

Excerpts from 'The Secret Vale of Glamorgan' by T.D. Breverton

Iolo Morganwg translated the Lan-y-Lai manuscript of Rev. Thomas Bassett thus:

> '*In the year of Christ, 1400, Owen Glyndŵr came to Glamorgan, and won the castle of Cardiff, and many more: he also demolished the castles of Penlline, Llandough, Flemingston, Dunraven of the Butlers, Tal-y-van, Llanblethian, Llanquian, Malefant, and that of Penmark; and burnt many of the villages and churches about them. He burnt, also, the villages of Llanfrynach and Aberthin; and many houses at Llantwit Major, and other places, the men of which would not join him. But many of the country people collected round him with one accord; and they demolished castles and houses innumerable; laid waste, and quite fenceless, the lands, and gave them, in common, to all. They took away from the powerful and rich, and distributed the plunder among the weak and poor. Many of the higher order and chieftains were obliged to flee to England, under the protection and support of the king. A bloody battle took place on Bryn-Owen mountain* (now called Stalling Down), *near Cowbridge, between Owen and his men, and the king's men, but the latter were put to flight after eighteen hours' hard fighting; during which the blood was up to the horses' fetterlocks, at Pant-y-wennol, that separates both ends of the mountain.*'

There is a local legend at St Athan linking Wales' greatest hero with the Berkerolles family. Edmund, Lord Mortimer, had been imprisoned by **Owain Glyndŵr** after the great victory at Pilleth, and married Owain's daughter Jane in 1402. He died of starvation, fighting to hold Harlech for Glyndŵr in 1409, so the following story comes from between 1402 and 1409. Glyndŵr was travelling alone with Earl Mortimer, and it was customary for travellers in these troubled times to ride from castle to castle, or abbey to abbey, rest free and move on. It seems that Glyndŵr pretended he was a harpist, and stayed with Sir Lawrence Berkerolles at East Orchard Castle. The blind Sir Lawrence told the couple that they might get the chance to see the great Glyndŵr, as he had been sighted in the Vale, and his men were out searching for him. Upon leaving after staying for four nights, Glyndŵr announced that he and his travelling companion had to be on their way, and thanked the Norman knight for his hospitality. Sir Lawrence implored him to stay, as it was only a matter of time before his raiding parties would capture Glyndŵr. Then Glyndŵr introduced himself to the Norman knight, jumped on his horse and rode away. Berkerolles is said to have been struck dumb, and lost his speech for ever. Iolo Morgannwg recounts the version featuring Sir Lawrence Berkerolles, and attributes it to a manuscript of Mr Leision of Prisk, which was then in the hands of Evan of the Farm, Llanblethian.

Excerpt from 100 Great Welshmen by T.D. Breverton
OWAIN GLYNDŴR 1355 or May 28th, 1354 - September 20th 1415
OWAIN AP GRUFFYDD - LORD OF GLYNDRFRDWY, WALES'
GREATEST HERO

For some Welshmen, Millennium Day was be September 16, 2000, Glyndŵr's Day, six hundred years since a company of nobles gathered in his manor at Glyndyfrdwy to proclaim Owain Glyndŵr Prince of Wales. No other Welsh leader is referred to simply by his surname. Owain Glyndŵr is the Welsh leader 'sans pareil', the name a rallying cry for all things Welsh. The group of people who regularly set alight to English holiday homes in remote areas of Wales from the 1960's to the 1980's called themselves *'Meibion Glyndŵr', 'The Sons of Glyndŵr'**. Glyndŵr not only lit up Wales with a united rebellion against overwhelming odds, but also his mysterious disappearance from history left an unbeaten feeling in Welsh hearts. He was the last *'Mab Darogan', 'Son of Prophecy'* for the Welsh bards, before Henry Tewdwr (Tudur, or Tudor) took the English crown in 1485 from the last of the Angevins, Richard Plantagenet.

There are numerous Welsh legends about Glyndŵr's birth. They include the fact that his father's horses were standing in blood up to their fetlocks in their stables, and that the baby would cry at the sight of a weapon, and only stop when he could touch it. The legends are referred to in Shakespeare's *'Henry IV, Part I'*:

> '..........At my birth
> *The front of heaven was full of fiery shapes;*
> The goats ran from the mountains, and the herds
> *Were strangely clamorous to the frighted fields.*
> *These signs have marked me extraordinary,*
> *And all the courses of my life do show,*
> *I am not in the roll of common men.'*

Glyndŵr could trace his heritage back to Rhodri Mawr, who was head of the royal houses of Gwynedd, Powys and Deheubarth. He was born around 1353, and some say he was educated at Oxford. It is known that he studied for seven years at the Inns of Court in Westminster. Later he became squire to the Earl of Arundel and Henry Bolingbroke, later Henry IV. Fluent in Latin, English, French and Welsh, he served King Richard II in his 1385 Scottish campaign. He also may have fought on the Continent for the English King, but records are incomplete. Aged around forty-five, after a life of service to the crown, it appears that he returned to Wales to retire to his great family estates at Glyndyfrdwy (an area of the Dee Valley, between Llangollen and Corwen), and at Cynllaith on the other side of the Berwyn Hills. (Glyndyfrdwy means valley of the river Dee, and was shortened to Glyndŵr, valley of water). At Sycharth, in Cynllaith, was Glyndŵr's chief house, protected by moats, with nine guest rooms, resident minstrels and bards, fishponds, deerpark , dovecot, vineyard, orchards, mill, wheat fields and peacocks. His income from his estates, around £200 a year, had enabled this faithful servant of the English Crown to settle down in 1398 with his wife Margaret, and nine or so children.

But just four years later, in 1402, the English had burnt down both the manor houses at Sycharth and Glyndyfrdwy, of this fifty year-old nobleman. It is difficult to describe the desolation Glyndŵr must have felt about the destruction of Sycharth, in particular - all that is left is the moat, in one of the most beautiful parts of Wales - his family bard Iolo Goch (who died about 1398) has left us a full description, which ends:

> *'Seldom has there been seen there*
> *Either a latch or a lock,*
> *Or someone playing porter,*
> *No lack of bountiful gifts,*
> *No need, no hunger, no shame,*
> *No-one is parched at Sycharth.*
> *The best Welshman, bold leader,*
> *Owns this land, Pywer Lew's line,*
> *Slim strong man, the land's finest,*
> *And owns this court, place to praise.'*
> *(translated by Joseph Clancy)*

1399 had been the turning point in Glyndŵr's existence. King Richard II had sailed to Ireland when he heard that the exiled Henry Bolingbroke, son of John of Gaunt, had landed in England. Richard returned via Milford Haven and made for Conwy, choosing Wales as his base for a battle. However, he was met by Henry Percy, Earl of Northumbria, who assured him that Bolingbroke meant no insurrection, but just wanted to inherit his father's lands and title. Richard rode to Conwy Castle to listen to Bolingbroke's request, but was ambushed, forced to 'abdicate' in favour of Bolingbroke, who became Henry IV. King Richard was spirited away to Pontefract Castle and disappeared from history. Richard's royal baggage train, still at Conwy, was seized by Henry's troops, but then 'liberated' by local Welshmen, who recognised treason when they saw it. Henry IV therefore was not over-enamoured of the Welsh, and it also appears that Glyndŵr might have been a squire to Richard II, as well as to Bolingbroke. Owain Glyndŵr had also in the past fought for King Richard, and Henry Bolingbroke was obviously dubious as to his loyalty to an usurper.

King Richard's abduction and murder ruined Glyndŵr's idyllic existence after just one year of retirement. His income from his estates was around two hundred pounds a year, but in 1399 Reginald Grey, Lord of Ruthin, stole some of his Glyndyfwrdwy lands. Glyndŵr was legally trained, and decided to fight Grey with a lawsuit in the English Parliament. A proud and loyal man, of royal blood, extremely tall for his times, he wore his hair down to his shoulders against the prevailing fashion of cropped hair in London. His case was dismissed with the comment *'What care we for barefoot Welsh dogs !'* Even Shakespeare referred to Glyndŵr as a brave and cultivated man -

> ' a worthy gentleman,
> Exceeding well read, and profited
> In strange concealments, valiant as a lion,
> And wondrous affable, and as bountiful
> As mines of India',

and he gives Glyndŵr these lines:

> 'For I was trained in the English court,
> Where, being but young, I framed to the harp
> Many an English ditty lovely well
> And gave the tongue an helpful ornament.'

We can see that Owain Glyndŵr was not the type of man to be thrown out, and treated like a dog, by an ignorant French-speaking English Parliament. The new king, Henry IV now raised taxes in Wales, and his aggressive (and illiterate) Marcher Lords like Grey urged him to settle the growing unrest there. Henry was preoccupied with Scotland, however, and instructed his barons to offer free pardons to law-breakers, hoping to defuse the situation. Lord Grey offered a pardon and a position as master forester to Gruffydd ap Dafydd, who had stolen some of his horses. The Welshman gave himself up, as requested, at Oswestry, but was lucky to escape alive.

He sent a letter to Grey about the betrayal..........

> 'I was told that you are in purpose to let your men burn and slay in any land which succours me and in which I am taken. Without doubt as many men as you slay for my sake will I burn and slay for yours. And doubt not that I will have bread and ale of the best that is in your Lordship'.

Lord Grey sent a copy to the Prince of Wales, the future Henry V, together with a copy of his reply to Gruffydd, threatening him

> ' I hope we shall do thee a privy thing, a rope, a ladder, and a ryng (noose), high on gallows for to hang. And thus shall be your ending.'

Grey could not be trusted, as we shall see - he desperately wanted more land in Wales. When Henry IV summoned each noble to bring a quota of men to fight in Scotland, Grey did not pass on the message to Owain Glyndŵr His absence from the army, just after the Parliamentary slighting, would hurt Glyndŵr's standing further in Henry's eyes. Henry's army was badly beaten. The king now allowed Grey leave to proceed against his 'treacherous subject', Glyndŵr.

Lord Grey decided that a frontal assault was unlikely to succeed, and therefore arranged a meeting to discuss Glyndŵr's grievances. Glyndŵr agreed, but knowing Grey's record, asked for only a small band of men to accompany the Marcher Lord. Grey agreed, and arrived to open discussions at Sycharth. Luckily, Iolo Goch, the famous house-bard of Glyndŵr, was told of a much larger band of Lord Grey's horsemen, hidden in the woods outside the house, waiting for the signal to attack. Iolo Goch entertained the host, and singing in Welsh alerted Glyndŵr to the threat. Owain made an excuse and fled his beloved Sycharth to his other estate, further west at Glyndyfrdwy, just before Grey's troops arrived.

Here on 16th September 1400, Glyndŵr took the 'Red Dragon' of Cadwaladr and Wales as his standard. This is now celebrated as Glyndŵr Day across Wales, with events and the wearing of red and gold ribbons - his heraldic colours. Aged almost fifty, he was proclaimed Prince of Wales, by Welshmen flocking to Glyndyfrdwy. Students from Oxford and Cambridge, labourers, noblemen and friars came to support him, resenting English wrongs. On 18 September, Glyndŵr's small, poorly armed force rode into Lord Grey's base of Ruthin, looted the fair and fired the town. No-one was killed, but fourteen rebels were captured and hanged. Glyndŵr's band soon learned about fast-moving warfare. By 24 September, they had fired and looted Denbigh, Flint, Hawarden, and Rhuddlan, and were moving on to Welshpool. However, the Sheriff of Shrewsbury had raised men from the Border and Midlands, and beat Glyndŵr's little force decisively on the banks of the Vyrnwy River. On 25 September, Henry IV arrived in Shrewsbury with his army, and dismembered Goronwy ap Tudur, a local nobleman, sending his limbs along the Welsh borders to Chester, Hereford, Ludlow and Bristol, *as an example* to those thinking of supporting Glyndŵr.

Glyndŵr was now in hiding when his aggrieved cousins, Goronwy ap Tudwr's kinsmen on Anglesey, Gwilym and Rhys Tudwr, started a second rebellion. Near Beaumaris, at Rhos Fawr, the Tudur army was defeated but managed to melt away before it was destroyed. Henry IV then destroyed Llanfaes Abbey, as its Franciscan monks had supported the Welsh rebels. Henry marched to the coast at Mawddwy and returned to Shrewsbury. The small Welsh army watched him all the way, not strong enough to face the Plantagenet force. Henry offered a pardon to Glyndŵr's brother, Tudur, which he accepted. However, Owain Glyndŵr was excluded from terms, and all his lands given to the Earl of Somerset, John Beaufort. It looked as if Glyndŵr's days were numbered at the end of the year 1400.

The Marcher Lords were allowed to take any Welsh land that they could by force of arms or subterfuge. On top of this, in 1401, the English Parliament passed laws that no Welsh person could hold official office, nor marry any English person. The Welsh could not live in England, and had to pay for the damage caused by the 1400 rebellions. This racial purity enforcement enraged the Welsh of all classes.

Glyndŵr was back now at Glyndwfrdwy, isolated with few supporters, as Gwynedd had accepted the royal pardon. Other noble Welsh families sent envoys to King Henry, complaining about the brutality and taxes of the Marcher Lords. However, the situation looked bleak until the Tudur brothers once more decided to change the rules of the game. They emerged from hiding in their Anglesey stronghold. While the garrison of Conwy Castle was at church outside the walls, on Good Friday 1401, two of their men posed as labourers, gained access to the castle and killed the two gatekeepers. Gwilym and Rhys Tudur, with a band of just forty men, fired the town and took control of Conwy Castle. Henry Percy, nicknamed Hotspur, controlled North

Wales, and needed to get them out of the castle. After weeks of negotiations, the Welsh were starving. Both sides agreed to a sad compromise. The Tudurs were guaranteed free passage back to Anglesey upon the giving up of some of their force. It is said that Gwilym selected them in their sleep - they were later drawn, hanged, disembowelled and quartered while alive by Hotspur, their remains being scattered about Wales as a warning against further rebellion. However, this piece of history may be later anti-Tudor propaganda.

Many Welshmen again started returning from England to Wales, and were backed by supporters of King Richard (by now probably dead) with donations to the Welsh cause. A man called William Clark had his tongue pulled out for daring to speak against Henry IV, then his hand cut off for writing against him, then he was beheaded. By May 1401, another small band of men had joined Glyndŵr, but he was routed by Hotspur near Cader Idris. He was forced to move South to the slopes of Pumlumon and raised his standard again where Nant-y-Moch reservoir now corrupts the land. With around four hundred men only, he rode down to loot and burn Llandrindod Wells, New Radnor, Cwmhir Abbey and Montgomery. Welshpool resisted and Glyndŵr returned with the remains of his little band (- just one hundred and twenty men, according to Gruffydd Hiraethog), to the safety of the Pumlumon (Plynlimon) foothills and caves.

Unknown to him, an army of fifteen hundred Flemings from the settlements in South-West Wales - the 'Englishry' south of the Preseli Hills - was marching to exterminate this threat to their livelihoods. They surrounded him and charged downhill at Glyndŵr's trapped army at Hyddgen on the Pumlumon foothills. Glyndŵr's army knew that they either died there and then, or would be slowly disembowelled if captured. The incentive was enough, and they halted and reversed the Flemings' charge. News spread all over Wales that the Welsh had won a real battle at last.

Hotspur, disillusioned by a lack of support from Henry in Wales, now took his North Wales peace-keeping army back to Northumberland. This was Glyndŵr's opportunity to traverse all Wales, hitting Marcher Lord possessions and those of their sympathisers. These years are described by Sir John Wynn in his 'History of the Gwydir Family' -

'beginning in Anno 1400, continued fifteen years which brought such a desolation, that green grass grew on the market place in Llanrwst.........and the deer fled in the churchyard'.

'In 1400 Owain Glyndŵr came to Glamorgan and won the castle of Cardiff and many more. He also demolished the castles of Penlline, Landough, Flemingston, Dunraven of the Butlers, Tal-y-Fan, Llanbleddian, Llanquian, Malefant and that of Penmark. And many of the people joined him of one accord, and they laid waste the fences and gave the lands in common to all. They took away from the powerful and rich, and distributed the plunder among the weak and poor. Many of the higher orders and chieftains were obliged to flee to England'.

The king saw that Wales was turning to Glyndŵr, and that his Marcher

Lords could not control any parts of the country. In October 1401, Henry marched to Bangor in North-East Wales, then West to Caernarfon in Gwynedd, then South, looting the abbey at Ystrad Fflur (Strata Florida) near Aberystwyth. Henry carried on to Llandovery, butchering any Welshman he caught, while Glyndŵr's men picked off his outriders and made constant assaults on his baggage train. At Llandovery, Henry *publicly tortured to death* Llywelyn ap Gruffydd Fychan for refusing to betray Glyndŵr's whereabouts. A memorial is to be erected to this loyal Welshman - it is time that Wales celebrated its heroes - how many people know that this event occurred?

While his supporting bands harried the King's army, Glyndŵr unsuccessfully attacked Caernarfon and Harlech castles. Facing a professional army with mere volunteers, and holding no castles of consequence, Glyndŵr made overtures to the Scots, Irish and French for desperately-needed assistance against their mutual *'mortal enemies, the Saxons.'* He even asked Hotspur to try to arrange a peace with Henry IV. The King was inclined to agree, but Lord Grey hated Glyndŵr, and Lord Somerset wanted more Welsh estates, so they agreed to use peace talks as a device to capture Glyndŵr. Fortunately, Hotspur, an honourable Northerner, refused the Norman request to be part of this treacherous charade.

1402 started off well for Owain Glyndŵr. On January 31, he appeared before Ruthin Castle, challenging Grey to fight. Grey was captured, trussed up and carried away to be imprisoned in Dolbadarn Castle. Perhaps Glyndŵr should have killed the man who was the cause of all his troubles, but he immediately ransomed him for £10,000. Some money was raised immediately, and his son was given in surety for the rest. Raising this ransom effectively ruined Grey, who signed an agreement never again to attack the man he had made an outlaw. (If positions had been reversed, the Norman Lord Grey would have tortured Glyndŵr before hanging, drawing and quartering him. The Welsh did not believe in such bestiality. We can also see that when Glyndŵr captured Lord Mortimer in battle, Mortimer eventually married Glyndŵr's daughter in captivity, and died fighting for him against the English.

Soon after, Glyndŵr survived an assassination attempt by his cousin, Hywel Sele of Nannau, probably on the orders of King Henry. An arrow was deflected by the armour under his jerkin, and Hywel Sele was killed and placed in a hollow oak tree. Throughout the rest of the year, Glyndŵr ravaged North Wales (leaving alone Hotspur's estates in Denbigh), and then moved against Powys, controlled by the great Marcher Earls, the Mortimers.

On St Alban's Day, June 22nd, 1402 at the Battle of Pilleth (near Knighton), Edmund Mortimer's English knights and Herefordshire levies charged uphill at Glyndŵr's army. Mortimer's Welsh archers poured volley after volley of deadly arrows into the English charge, apparently in an unrehearsed expression of support for Glyndŵr. (Much of western Herefordshire and Worcestershire was Welsh-speaking at this time). Up to two thousand of Mortimer's troops were killed on the slopes. Rhys Gethin,

Rhys the Fierce, had drawn up his men hidden behind the top of the hill, so Mortimer had underestimated the Welsh force of four thousand, as well as having been unable to control his Welsh archers. Mortimer was captured in the battle, but Henry IV accused him of treason and would not ransom him. Hotspur, Mortimer's brother-in-law, was incensed that a villain like Lord Grey could be ransomed, whereas Henry had set his mind against the innocent Mortimer.

In Shakespeare's 'Henry IV Part I', a horrified courtier recounts

> .... 'the noble Mortimer,
> Leading the men of Hereford to fight
> Against the irregular and wild Glendower,
> Was by the rude hands of that Welshman taken;
> A thousand of his people butchered,
> Upon whose dead corpse there was such misuse,
> Such beastly, shameless transformation
> By those Welsh women done, as may not be,
> Without much shame, retold or spoken of.'

Forget this propaganda against Welsh women - after this event Henry IV passed legislation banning English men marrying Welsh women. Who would have wanted to marry such harridans if the atrocity stories were true ? A contemporary entry in 1402 in the 'Annales Henrici Quarti' tells us of the extent of Glyndŵr's reputation at this time: '(Glyndŵr) almost destroyed the King and his armies, by magic as it was thought, for from the time they entered Wales to the time they left, never did a gentle air breathe on them, but days turned into nights, rain mixed with snow and hail afflicted them with a cold beyond endurance.'

Glyndŵr at last had freedom to do whatever he wanted - he attacked and burnt Abergavenny and Cardiff, and the ruins of his sacking of the Bishop's Palace at Llandaf in Cardiff can still be seen.   He besieged Caernarfon, Cricieth and Harlech castles. This forced Henry IV to totally ignore his Scottish problems and assemble three armies, totalling a massive one hundred thousand men, on the Welsh borders. The bards had been singing of Glyndŵr's supernatural powers, and during Henry's advance into Wales, appalling weather conditions forced all three armies to return to England by the end of September. It was thought at the time that Glyndŵr could command the elements, and well as possessing a magic Raven's stone that made him invisible - even the English troops ascribed magical properties to this guerrilla partisan. Again, this is referred to in Henry IV Part 1:

> 'Three times hath Henry Bolingbroke made head
> Against my power. Thrice from the banks of the Wye
> And sandy-bottomed Severn have I sent
> Him bootless home, and weather-beaten back.'

A 1402 entry in 'Annales Henrici Quarti ', the English recording of the times, reads that Glyndŵr 'almost destroyed the King and his armies, by *magic as it was thought, for from the time they entered Wales to the time they left, never did a gentle air breathe on them, but throughout whole days and nights, rain mixed with snow and hail afflicted them with cold beyond endurance.'*

In 1402, the imprisoned Edmund Mortimer married Owain Glyndŵr's daughter, Jane. Mortimer's nephew, the young Earl of March, had a far better claim to the English throne than Henry IV, and no doubt Glyndŵr was hoping that Henry Bolingbroke would be killed and Wales made safe with an English king as an ally. His big problem was that Hotspur captured the Scots leader, the Earl of Douglas, at the battle of Homildon, securing England's northern border. With his Scottish problems solved, this allowed Henry IV to plan to finally subdue Wales. Glyndŵr, on his part, wanted **complete** control of Wales **before** Henry struck.

In 1403, Owain Glyndŵr kept up his blockade of the Northern Welsh castles, while attacking Brecon and Dinefwr and trying to displace the Flemings from Pembrokeshire. Glyndŵr's able lieutenants were the three Rhys's; Rhys Gethin (the Fierce), Rhys Ddu (the Black), and Rhys ap Llewellyn. The latter had real reason to hate the invading English - it was *his* father, Llewelyn ap Gruffydd Fychan, who had been slowly killed in front of Henry IV at Llandovery in the dark days of 1401, for refusing to lead him to Glyndŵr. Later in 1403, a Welsh army was beaten at Laugharne by Lord Thomas Carew. Glyndŵr also sadly learned of the deliberate demolition of his manors and estates at Sycharth and Glyndfrdwy by the Prince of Wales, Henry of Monmouth, who later won undying fame at Agincourt

Hotspur, meanwhile, wanted to ransom the Earl of Douglas, but Henry demanded him as a prisoner to secure the ransom. Coupling this insult with the argument over Edmund Mortimer's ransom, Hotspur allied with Edmund Mortimer, Douglas and Glyndŵr to form an army near Chester. At the bloody Battle of Shrewsbury, Hotspur was killed, despite the havoc wrought by his Chester archers. This tragedy happened before he could link up with Glyndŵr. Henry then went to Northumberland to suppress a small uprising by Hotspur's father, Earl Percy of Northumberland. Glyndŵr ravaged Herefordshire in Henry's absence.

The enraged King Henry now passed legislation that *any Welshman found in any border town would be executed.* He marched through South Wales to Carmarthen, but like the previous invasion, Glyndŵr did not come to the party. Henry returned to England and within a week Glyndŵr had taken Cardiff, Caerphilly, Newport, Usk and Caerleon. Some French troops were assisting Glyndŵr by now, and his army had grown to at least 10,000 men-at-arms.

By 1404, Owain Glyndŵr's main focus was the taking of the seemingly impregnable 'Iron Ring' of castles in North Wales. He won over the starving Harlech garrison by pardons or bribes when it had only sixteen men left. The great castles of Cricieth and Aberystwyth then fell, and at Machynlleth, in The Parliament House, Owain Glyndŵr held his first Parliament. Envoys came from France and Spain, and an ambassador was sent to France. Dafydd

ap Llewelyn ap Hywel, Davy Gam ('squint-eyed') tried to assassinate him
here for Henry IV, and was surprisingly imprisoned rather than cut to pieces.
(This again demonstrates the humane Welsh attitude of the times towards
prisoners. Davy Gam later was knighted by Henry V as he lay dying at
Agincourt). Another Welsh Parliament was held in Dolgellau in 1404.

Glyndŵr now took a small army to again pillage Herefordshire, but the
Earl of Warwick captured his standard at Campstone Hill near Grosmont
Castle. Glyndŵr just escaped capture. Fortunately, the English did not pursue
the defeated troops, which regrouped and beat Warwick at Craig-y-Dorth,
three miles from Monmouth, and chased them back into the fortified town.
Glyndŵr was in the South-East awaiting a French invasion fleet of 60 vessels
under the Count of March, who for some reason never landed. Glyndŵr
returned to his court at Harlech. In Anglesey, Owain's forces were now
beaten at the battle of Rhosmeirch, and also lost Beaumaris castle.

In 1405, Rhys Gethin burned Grosmont Castle in Monmouthshire, but
was then decisively beaten by Prince Henry, using Welsh archers. Glyndŵr
sent his almost identical brother, Tudur, and his son Gruffydd to restore the
situation by attacking Usk Castle where Prince Henry had established himself.
In the battle of Pwll Melin, two miles away, Tudur and Abbot John ap Hywel
of Llantarnam were killed. Gruffydd ab Owain Glyndŵr was imprisoned in
the Tower of London in disgusting conditions until he soon died. Three
hundred prisoners were beheaded in front of the citizens of Usk, as an
example pour les autres.

After the Welsh defeats at Grosmont and Usk, Henry now offered a pardon
to those who renounced the rebellion, and thereby regained full control of
South-East Wales. He then gathered an army of forty thousand at Hereford
to advance into mid and North Wales. Another English force took Beaumaris
and control of Anglesey in the far North. At this time, Archbishop Scrope of
York led a rebellion in the North of England. Henry diverted his forces to
Shipton Moor where he beat back the Northern rebels. This gave Glyndŵr
some breathing space, and he gathered ten thousand men in Pembrokeshire
to wait for an invasion fleet of one hundred and forty French ships. Around
five thousand Frenchmen arrived at Milford, joined with Glyndŵr and
sacked the English/Fleming town of Haverfordwest, but could not take the
castle. They next looted Carmarthen and then took over Glamorgan, leaving
Glyndŵr back in control of most of Wales.

In August 1405, he moved on to attack England, *its first invasion since
1066.* Henry raced to Worcester to face the threat of Glyndŵr, who was
camped on Woodbury Hill. There were some skirmishes, but Glyndŵr had
no lines of supply, so he retreated back to Wales, following a scorched earth
policy. Henry's starving army was forced to call off the pursuit, freezing as
the bitter winter took hold. Again, the terrible weather was blamed upon
Glyndŵr's supernatural powers. **This had been Henry's *fifth* invasion of
Wales, and still Glyndŵr seemed untouchable.**

1406 began with a treaty between the dead Hotspur's remaining Percy
family of Northumberland, Earl Mortimer and Glyndŵr. This 'Tripartite
Indenture' divided England and Wales between the three Houses, with

Glyndŵr possessing Wales and gaining a 'buffer zone' on its borders. At his second Machynlleth Parliament, Glyndŵr wrote to Charles VI of France, asking for recognition, support and a 'Holy Crusade' against Henry for pillaging abbeys and killing clergymen. In turn, Glyndŵr promised the recognition by St Davids of the French-based Pope Benedict XIII. (Welsh Parliaments were also held in Pennal, Harlech and Dolgellau). Glyndŵr also asked Papal permission to place two universities, one each in North and South Wales, to build a future for his country. This letter was signed *'Owain by the Grace of God, Prince of Wales'*, and is in the French National Archives.

However, Henry IV was wasting away through syphilis or leprosy, which enabled his son Henry, the 'English' Prince of Wales to take control of the Welsh campaigns. He beat a Welsh army, killing yet another of Glyndŵr's sons in March, and retook South Wales, fining the landowners heavily to support his thrust into North Wales. North Wales, being fought over for five years, had neither financial nor manpower reserves to support Glyndŵr, but he still held around two thirds of the land Wales, and castles at Aberystwyth and Harlech. At his time, he almost disappears from history except for bardic references of him roaming the country.

In 1407, Prince Henry besieged Aberystwyth Castle with seven cannon. One, 'The King's Gun' weighed four and a half tons. Rhys Ddu held out and Henry returned to England. Glyndŵr reinforced the castle, while England unfortunately signed a peace treaty with France. In this year, Owain's great ally, Louis of Orleans, was murdered in mysterious circumstances in Paris. It may have been the work of English spies.

1408 saw another blow for Glyndŵr. His ally, the old Earl of Northumberland, Hotspur's father, was killed at the Battle of Braham Moor by Prince Henry's forces. The Prince then re-entered Wales, bombarded Aberystwyth into submission, and by 1409 had also taken Harlech, Glyndŵr's last bastion, capturing his wife and family. Edmund Mortimer, the former enemy who became his son-in-law in captivity, died (probably of starvation) in Harlech, fighting for Glyndŵr. Owain had just managed to escape from Harlech as the besiegers moved in. It must have been a difficult decision to leave his family there, while he tried to round up support rather than be cornered. A sad footnote has been the discovery noted in John Lloyd's 1931 book 'Owen Glendower' – he *'left behind him in the castle one little personal relic which has recently been unearthed in the course of excavations, viz. a gilt bronze boss from a set of horse harness, bearing the four lions rampant which he had assumed as prince of Wales'*. The four lions rampant, counter-changed in gold and red, were the ancient arms of the princes of Gwynedd. Glyndŵr was more a descendant of the Houses of Deheubarth and Powys than Gwynedd, but he had needed that provenance, that in effect died out with the vicious assassination of Owain Llawgoch, to be accepted throughout Wales.

The last gasp of Glyndŵr's revolt occurred near Welshpool Castle when a raiding party under Phillip Scudamore, Rhys Tudur and Rhys Ddu was beaten and the leaders captured. After the usual revolting, slow, barbarous executions, Scudamore's head was placed on a spike at Shrewsbury, Rhys ap Tudur's at London, and Rhys Ddu's at Chester. This disgusting ritual torture was never practised by the Welsh when they captured prisoners, but Normans and Plantagenets believed that payment to the church would get them to heaven, whatever their sins.

In 1413, the Plantagenet Prince of Wales succeeded as Henry V, and in 1415 offered a pardon to Glyndŵr and any of his men. In 1416, he tried again, through Glyndŵr's remaining son Maredudd, who himself accepted a pardon in 1421. It thus appears that Glyndŵr was still alive a few years after his last recorded sighting. Gruffydd Young, in the Council of Constance in France, was still working for Owain Glyndŵr in 1415, stating that Wales was a nation that should have a vote in ending the papal schism. Glyndŵr would have been around sixty-five years old at this time, having spent his last fifteen years in constant warfare against the English crown.

Some say Owain died in a cave in Pumlumon (Plynlimon), where it all started, mourning the death of all but one of his six sons. Other believed he ended his days with his daughter Alice and her husband John Scudamore in Golden Valley in Herefordshire. The present owner of the Great Hall of Kentchurch, Jan Scudamore, has been besieged with people asking permission to search her estate for the remains of Glyndŵr. Many identify him with Sion Cent of Kentchurch (see Magic), a poet, magician and mystic whose grave can still be seen, half in and half out of Grosmont church. Other stories have him dying at Monnington Court, near Kentchurch, at Monnington-on-Wye in 1415, in the deep oakwoods of Glamorgan and on a mountain ridge in Snowdonia. The bards raided Arthurian legend to put him sleeping with his men in a cave to be awakened again in Wales' hour of greatest need. One bard stated that Glyndŵr ' *went into hiding on St Matthew's Day in Harvest (1415) and thereafter his hiding place was unknown. Very many say that he died: the seers maintain that he did not'*. The author's researches confirm that he died at one of his daughter's houses, at Scudamore's mansion or at nearby Monnington, where he had been disguised as a shepherd, upon September 16th, 1415, aged 61, almost exactly fifteen years from the start of his war on September 20th, 1400. Recently in 2000, however, the Scudamore family of Monnington Court revealed that Glyndŵr had been buried on their land, and that the family had divulged to always keep his secret.

Glyndŵr's greatest problem had been that he was up against the greatest soldier of his age, Harry of Monmouth, who within a few years was to win at Agincourt with Welsh archers, and be recognised as the future King of France. Henry cut his teeth against a massively under-resourced Glyndŵr, who had no incomes to pay his troops and relied on volunteers against a vastly superior professional force. However, Owain could still point to a career where he set up his own law-courts and chancery, tried to form the first Welsh universities, summoned parliaments, sent envoys to foreign courts and nominated bishops. However, this last battle between the 'Welsh' Prince of Wales and the 'French-Plantagenet' Prince of Wales could have only one ending.

Repressive laws were enacted after the rebellion to stop any future threat from Wales to the English crown. No-one with Welsh parents could buy land near the Marcher towns, own weapons, become citizens of any towns or hold any offices. *In lawsuits involving a Welshman and an Englishman, the Englishman decided the verdict and the sentence. Gatherings of Welsh people were forbidden, and an Englishman marrying a Welsh woman became legally Welsh, forfeiting all his rights of citizenship. No Welshman could be a juror.* These and many more impositions, on top of the already harsh regime of the Statute of Rhuddlan of 1282, ensured Harri Tewdwr great popular support in his move to gain the crown of England in 1485.

Massive taxes were raised to pay for the invasions of the two Henry's, but Welshmen were not allowed to help each other to harvest their fields, causing major food shortages. If merchants of any towns were robbed in Wales, and the property was not returned within a week, they could retaliate upon *any* Welshman that they could seize. Much of the above is taken from the excellent book by Richard Sale, 'Owain Glyndŵr's Way' (published by Hutchinson), which gives a background to Wales, details of Glyndŵr's life, and a description of the long-distance footpath that commemorates the man. The best summary of Glyndŵr is by the noted English historian, G.M.Trevelyan... *'this wonderful man, an attractive and unique figure in a period of debased and selfish politics'*. The French historian, Henri Martin, calls Glyndŵr a man of courage and genius. Most English encyclopaedias do not mention him - one of the truly great, principled and forward-thinking men in British history. Welsh schools have not taught the history Glyndŵr in any depth whatsoever, for over a hundred years, but his name still inspires Welshmen all over the world.

J.E. Lloyd puts Glyndŵr into his proper perspective in the Welsh national psyche:

'Throughout Wales, his name is the symbol for the vigorous resistance of the Welsh spirit to tyranny and alien rule and **the assertion of a national character which finds its fitting expression in the Welsh language**......... *For the Welshmen of all subsequent ages, Glyndŵr has been a national hero, the first, indeed, in the country's history to command the willing support alike of north and south, east and west, Gwynedd and Powys, Deheubarth and Morgannwg. He may with propriety be called the father of modern Welsh nationalism.'*

I have managed to return to Wales after a career in England and overseas. I bought part of an old barn, part of which was built from the ruins of West Orchard Castle (known locally as 'the humpy field'). The doorway, now a window, has the arch from the old entrance to the castle. According to local legend, Glyndŵr destroyed West Orchard, so my 'East Barn' has now been renamed 'Porth Glyndŵr', and I touch the old stone for good luck every day. He is also said to have stayed at East Orchard Castle. 'Cofiwch Glyndŵr' means ' Remember Glyndŵr' and is a slogan for the Welsh Nationalist movement - he still lives. Glyndŵr is the undefeated symbol of Wales, with his red dragon of Cadwaladr - he is the equivalent of Jeanne d'Arc and William Wallace and el Cid for Welsh people everywhere.

After Owain Lawgoch's (Yvain de Galles) assassination in 1378 on the orders of the English crown, the royal House of Gwynedd was extinct. Glyndŵr was then *'un pen ar Gymru'*, the only head of Wales, as he was the direct descendant and link between the dynasties of Powys and Deheubarth. Glyndŵr symbolically adopted Owain Lawgoch's heraldic device of the four red lions rampant of Gwynedd. As his ambassador had told the French king, Glyndŵr was the 'rightful' heir of Lawgoch, or the princes of Gwynedd and Wales. Owain Glyndŵr united Wales both politically and symbolically. Elen ferch Thomas had a brother, Owain ap Thomas, who died childless in 1360, so the first son of her marriage to Gruffydd Fychan, Owain Glyndŵr, had no rivals as the leader of the Welsh resistance.It was thought that Owain Lawgoch, the sole heir to the Royal House of Gwynedd, had been assassinated before he could marry. (However, the author has found traces of a leader of a French war-band, Edouart d'Yvain who overlapped with Llawgoch's assassination, and the Owain Llawgoch Society believe that he may have married a French-woman, so the Royal House of Gwynedd may still be extant!)

Although Glyndŵr had briefly won political, cultural and ecclesiastical independence, before final defeat and the harshness of the laws of a revenging English king, the wars had been a personal disaster for him. His closest brother Tudur had died at the Battle of Pwll Melyn in 1405. His son Gruffydd was captured there, and spent the remainder of his years imprisoned in the Tower of London and Nottingham Castle. Some sources say that he died of the plague in the Tower of London in 1410 - he just vanished from history, like so many other captured descendants of Welsh princes. Glyndŵr's wife, two daughters and three grand-daughters were taken into imprisonment after the fall of Harlech Castle. His son-in-law, Edmund Mortimer, with a good claim to the English crown, died at Harlech. Mortimer's wife, Owain's daughter Catherine, died in prison with two of her daughters, and all were buried in St Swithin's Church in London around 1413. (Only the churchyard remains, soon to be covered with another office-block for paper-pushers). Her son Lionel, Owain's grandson and a claimant for both Welsh and English crowns, died, where or when is unrecorded. Owain Glyndŵr's closest lieutenants and comrades-in-arms, Rhys Ddu, Rhys ap Llywelyn, Rhys Gethin and Phillip Scudamore had been tortured to death.

It appears that only one relative survived the carnage, his son Maredudd, who had hidden with him when the rebellion was crushed. When Maredudd ab Owain eventually accepted the King's pardon upon 8th April, 1421, it had been twenty years and six months since Owain Glyndŵr had proclaimed himself Prince of Wales. These two decades of fighting against overwhelming odds, of reclaiming Cymru from the Normans, are neglected in all British history books. This British hero has been excised from the history of Britain even more effectively than William Wallace was.

THE TREATY BETWEEN OWAIN AP THOMAS (LAWGÔCH) AND KING CHARLES V, OF FRANCE.
10th MAY 1372
TRANSLITERATION IN MEDIEVAL FRENCH.

A tous ceulx qui ces lectres verront, Yvain de Galles, salut. Comme les roys de Angleterrre, qui ont este es temps passez, meuz de mauvais courage et de convoitise dampnee, a tort et sanz cause et par traisons appensees, aient occis ou fait occirre aucuns de mes predecesseurs roys de Gales et yceulx mis hors et deboutez du dit royaume, et ycellui royaume par force et puissance appliquie a eulx et detenu et ycellui soubzmis avec les subgiez du pais a plusieurs servitutes, lequel est et doit estre et appartenir a moi par la succession et comme plus prochain de sanc et de lignage et en droicte ligne descendant d'iceulx mes predecesseurs roys d'icellui royaume, et pour avoir secours et aide a recouvrer le dit royaume, qui est mon heritage, me soye transportez devers pluseurs roys, princes et seigneurs chrestiens, et leur aye declairie et monstre clerement le droit que je y ay, en leur requerant et suppliant humblement que a ce me voulsissent aydier, et derrainement me soies traiz devers mon tres puissant et tres redoubte seigneur Charles, par la grace de Dieu roy de France, dauphin de Viennoys, et lui ay monstre mon droit que j'ay ou dit royaume et fait les requestes et supplicacions dessus dictes, et ycellui seigneur avent compassion de mon estat, actendu le grant tort que les diz roys d'Angleterre ont eu en leur temps envers mes diz predecesseurs et encores a le roy d'Angleterre qui est a present envers moy, et considere toute la matiere de mon fait de sa benigne et accoustumee clemence, qui est le mirouer singulier et exemple entre les chrestiens de toute justice et de toute grace et misericorde pour touz opprimez relever et conforter, m'ayt octroye son ayde et confort de gens d'armes et de navire pour recouvrer le dit royaume, qui est mon droit heritage, comme dit est; sachent tuit que je, en recongnoissant la grand amour que mon dit seigneur le roy de France m'a monstree et monstre par vray effect en ce fait, ou quel et pour le quel mectre sus a mis et expose du sien trois cens mil francs d'or et plus, tant en gaiges de gens d'armes, d'archiers et d'arlabalestriers comme en navire et en gaiges et despens de marigniers, en hernoiz et eu autres fraiz, missions et despens plusieurs, la quele somme je ne lui puis pas presentement rendre, promet loyaument et par la foy de mon corps et jure aux sains Euvangiles de Dieu, touchees corporelment pour moy et pour mes hoirs et successeurs a tousjoursmaix, que la dicte somme de trois cens mil francs d'or je lui rendray et payeray entierement ou a ses diz hoirs et successeurs ou ceulx qui auront cause d'eulx, ou a leur commandement a leur vos lente, sanz autre terme, et des maintenant ay fait et accorde pour moy, pour mes hoirs et successeurs et tout mon pais et subgiez prepetuelment avec mon dit seigneur le roy de France, pour lui, pour ses hoirs et successeurs roys, pour tout son pais et ses subgiez bonnes et fermes amitiez, confederacions et alliances, si que je les ayderay et conforteray de ma personne, de mes subgiez et pays, de tout mon povoir, loyaument, contre toutes personnes qui pevent vivre et mourir. En testement de ce, j'ay seelle ces lectres de mon seel. Donne a Paris, le Xe jour de may, l'an de grace mil ccc soixante douze

ENGLISH TRANSLATION

Owain of Wales, to all those to whom these letters shall come, greetings. The kings of England in past times having treacherously and covetously, tortuously and without cause and by deliberate treasons, slain or caused to be slain my ancestors, kings of Wales, and others of them have put out of their country, and that country have by force and power appropriated and have submitted it's people to divers servitude, the which country is and should be mine by right of succession, by kindred, by heritage, and by right of descent from my ancestors the kings of that country, and in order to obtain help and succour to recover that country which is my heritage, I have visited several Christian kings, princes and nobles, and have clearly declared and shown unto them my rights therein and have requested and supplicated their aid, and have latterly come to the most puissant and renowned sovereign Charles, by the grace of God, king of France, dauphin of Vienne, and have shown unto him my right in the aforesaid country and have made unto him the aforenamed requests and supplications, and he having had compassion upon my state and understanding the great wrong that the kings of England have done unto my ancestors in former times, and that the present king of England has done unto me, and of his beneficent accustomed clemency in which he is the singular mirror and example amongst Christians of justice, grace and mercy to all those that are oppressed and require comforting, has granted to me his aid and the assistance of his men-at-arms and fleet in order to recover the said realm, which is my rightful heritage, as has been said; know all ye, therefore, that in return for the great love that my said lord the king of France has shown unto me, and is truly showing by his expenditure of three hundred thousand francs of gold, and more, as well in the pay of men-at-arms, archers and arbalisters as in (the provision of) ships and the pay and expenses of the sailors, in harness and in other matters and in various expenses, the which sum I am at the present time not able to furnish, I promise loyally and by my faith and oath upon the holy evangelists, touched corporally by me, and for my heirs and successors for ever, the aforesaid sum of three hundred thousand francs of gold I will return and wholly repay, or my heirs and successors or those who may claim through them (on ceul qui auront cause d'elux), or by their will or command, without any other terms; and I herewith have made and entered into, for me my heirs and successors and for all my country and subjects for ever, with my said lord the king of France, for him his heirs and successors and for all their country and subjects, a good and firm treaty, union and alliance, by which I will aid and assist them by my person, my subjects and my country, to the utmost of my power and loyalty, against all persons alive or dead (contre toutes personnes qui povent vivre et mourir). In witness of which I have sealed these letters with mine own seal. Given at Paris, the 10th day of May, the year of grace, one thousand three hundred and seventy-two.

Glyndŵr had no funeral elegy from the bards – he was probably a broken man – but in Welsh mythology his disappearance from history, rather than his capture and execution, gave the poets and gives the nation a hope for the future – Glyndŵr is THE Welsh hero par excellence. This is a story of culture, humanity, nobility, treachery, courage, bitter defeat, glorious resurgence and a mysterious finale. Can anyone think of a better story for a Hollywood epic ? It was not until 1948 that a Parliamentary Act, declaring Glyndŵr to be a proscribed traitor, was repealed. Perhaps a blockbuster film could start with this scene.

Cymdeithas Owain Glyndŵr has attempted a geophysical survey at the mound at the deserted village of Monnington Straddel, near Monningon Court Farm, an ancestral seat of the Scudamores in Herefordshire's Golden Valley. Afirmation of the site was given by Sir John Scudamore of Kentchurch, a direct descendant of Sir John Scudamore and Alice ferch Owain Glyndŵr. A painting by Jan van Eyck at Kentchurch may be of the mystic poet-priest Sion Cent or his contemporary Owain Glyndŵr.

The Sunday Times ran a poll of 100 world leaders, artists and scientists, published on November 28th, 1999, asking for the names of the most significant figures in the last 1000 years. In 7th place was Owain Glyndŵr. (The list started with Gutenberg, Shakespeare, Caxton, da Vinci, Elizabeth I and Faraday in the first six places. Newton, Lincoln and Galileo followed Glyndŵr in the Top 10). Thus even today he is regarded above Churchill, Mandela, Darwin, Bill Gates and Einstein. Among the voters were President Clinton and Boris Yeltsin.

*The author is not very convinced that many of these attacks on holiday homes were carried out by Meibion Glyndŵr - at this time MI5 was at its most paranoid, and like the Brecon 'bomb-factory' incident, the political inspiration for these events seems to have come the area around Westminster.

FOOTNOTES:
1. From Thomas Pennant's 'Tour in Wales' of 1778 (abridged by David Kirk) we are told that Glyndŵr's father was Gruffudd Fychan and his mother Elena *'(of royal blood and from whom he afterwards claimed the throne of Wales). She was eldest daughter of Thomas ap Llywelyn ap Owain, by his wife Elinor Goch, or Elinor the red, daughter and heiress of Catherine, one of the daughters of Llywelyn last Prince of Wales. She probably was concealed by some friend on the death of her father, otherwise the jealousy of (King) Edward about the succession would have made her share the fate of her sister (Gwenllian) who perforce took the veil in the convent of Shrewsbury.'*

2.Glyndŵr's death date has remained a mystery, but T.D. Breverton has recently come across three separate sources with the same date, in his researches for 'The Book of Welsh Saints' (published September 15th, 2000 by Wales Books, ISBN1-903529-01-8. This information has been passed to the Owain Glyndŵr Society, Cymdeithas Owain Glyndŵr, at 37 Glanyrafon Road, Pontardulais, Swansea SA4 1LT.

T.J. Llywelyn Prichard wrote 'The Heroines of Welsh History' in 1854, in which he quotes the Rev. Thomas Thomas, vicar of Aberporth writing 'The Memoirs of Owain Glyndŵr'.

Our hero terminated his hopes and fears on 20th of September, 1415, on the eve of St Matthew, in the 61st year of his age, at the house of one of his daughters; but whether of his daughter Scudamore or of his daughter Monnington is uncertain. Prichard also mentions Glyndŵr's Life in the Cambrian Plutarch by John Humphreys Parry, but I have been unable as yet to source either book.

Marie Trevelyan of Llanilltud Fawr wrote 'The Land of Arthur' in 1895, dedicated to Llywelyn ap Gruffudd, and states that Glyndŵr was born on May 28th, 1354 (so we also have a birthdate!), and *on September 20th, 1415, this celebrated 15th century leader of the Welsh people, and last hero of Welsh independence, died in Herefordshire. According to the MSS of the Harleian Collection, Glyndŵr's body, which was entire and of "goodly stature" was discovered at Monnington in that shire, during the restoration of the church in 1680. But his resting place remains unmarked and unrecognised.* The May birthdate gives festival opportunities, and the Sept 20th date gives feast-week opportunities to fit in with Glyndŵr Day of Sept 16.

Also, a 'penny booklet' recently acquired by the author is *Hanes Owain Glyndŵr, Tywysog Cymru*, by Thomas Pennant o'r Downing, printed by H. Humphries at Caernarfon around 1900, gives the same death date of September 20th, 1415. It points out that the king sent Sir Gilbert Talbot from Porchester to arrange a pardon for Glyndŵr and his supporters in 1415, but Owain's death delayed its implementation until it was agreed with Meredydd ab Owain Glyndŵr in 1416.

Excerpt from 100 Great Welshwoman by T.D. Breverton
CATRIN GLYNDŴR 1380? - 1413
WALES' LOST PRINCESS

By Isabel Monnington-Taylor [Entries in italics from the author's '100 Great Welshmen']

The greatest of all Welsh heroes was Owain Glyndŵr (May 28th 1354 or 55 - September 20th 1415), a man who fought the English crown for 15 years, repelling no less than three full invasions, and who then vanished from history. Owain's daughter Catrin was probably born at her father's splendid moated manor house at Sycharth, near Oswestry. This grand house had many rooms and pillars, and a tiled roof. It even boasted a chimney, a very modern feature for these times. The bard Iolo Goch wrote of it as:

> "Llys barwn, lle syberwydd
> Lle daw beirdd aml, lle da byd"
> (The court of a baron, a place of courtesy
> Where numerous bards come, a place of the good life)

.....
"Each side full, each house at court,
Orchard, vineyard, white fortress;
The master's rabbit warren;
Ploughs and strong steeds of great frame;
Near the court, even finer,
The deer park within that field;
Fresh green meadows and hayfields;
Neatly enclosed rows of grain;
Fine mill on a smooth-flowing stream;
Dovecot, a bright stone tower;
A fish-pond, enclosed and deep,
Where nets are cast when need be,
Abounding, no argument,
In pike and splendid whiting;
His land a board where birds dwell,
Peacocks, high-stepping herons...

His serfs do the proper work,
Fill the needs of the region,
Bringing Shrewsbury's fine beer,
Whisky, the first-brewed bragget,
All drinks, white bread and wine,
His meat, fire for his kitchen".

And Owain's wife Margaret is described as:
"A knightly line's bright daughter,
Proud hostess of royal blood,
His children come, two by two,
A fine nestful of princes."

Sycharth was indeed a plentiful estate, where Glyndŵr distilled his own 'chwisgi', and his house-bard Iolo Goch delighted in the beer from Shrewsbury. It was set in prosperous and fertile land, with many timbered buildings and nearby market towns.

Through Owain, Catrin Glydŵr was descended from Madog ap Maredudd, last prince of Powys, and also from the princes of Deheubarth. There were also vast family estates at Glyndyfyrdwy near Llangollen, an enclave of Welsh rule in Edeirnion and Dinmael. These were near the ruined remains of the magnificent hilltop castle, Castell Dinas Bran, and also the great Cistercian monastery of Valle Crucis. Here, Catrin could have seen the tomb of her great-great-grandfather Madog ap Gruffudd Fychan, of the dynasty of Powys, under a fine heraldic slab. She could have run her fingers over the carved single lion rampant - the lion of the dynasty of Northern Powys, later taken up by her father as his standard. If she had visited all her father's lands, she would have gained an understanding of the different landscapes of Wales, as Iscoed lay north of the river Teifi, in Ceredigion.

Marriage to English families of the borderlands (The Marches) was quite usual. Owain's grandfather Gruffudd had married Elizabeth leStrange, and

Catrin's own mother Margaret was the daughter of Sir David Hanmer of
Maelor Saesneg. The Hanmers' integration with their Welsh neighbours was
comfortable and complete. Catrin's maternal grandmother, the wife of Sir
David Hanmer, was Angharad ferch Llewelyn Ddu. No doubt these families
were thoroughly bilingual, as shown by the ecclesiastical favour given to
Catrin's mother under her Welsh name Marred ferch Dafydd. Her brothers
were Gruffudd, Philip and John Hanmer. Catrin's was probably an
intellectual household. Her father had received legal training at London's Inns
of Court. Her grandfather Sir David Hanmer was Governor of South Wales
in 1381, and one of the chief justices of the King's Bench by 1383. He was
also retained as a legal advisor to families in the Marcher borders. However,
he died in 1387 and Catrin lost some valuable links and activity with society
across Wales and the borderlands.

After David Hanmer's death, the family must have been marginalised.
Owain Glyndŵr progressively lost influence, a factor in the dispute with his
neighbour Reginald de Grey. De Grey, a notably treacherous character,
claimed land which had been held as common grazing rights for Owain's
Welsh tenants. Owain felt obliged to appeal to the courts and travelled to
London to affirm his rights to this land, on behalf of his tenants. He was 45
years-old, a cultured linguist, legally-trained and had faithfully served the
Franco-English crown in battle. Coming to the end of his years, he had retired
to a life of luxury on his estates. However, this nobleman was sent packing
from the court, with the judge's words ringing in his ears "What care we for
the rights of barefoot Welsh dogs!". Catrin must have seen him leave angry,
but expecting right and legal precedence to prevail. She now saw him return,
exhausted from the journey, frustrated and seething at Norman 'justice'.

The sense of injustice was shared by all his family, and upon September
16th, 1400 (Glyndŵr Day), he was proclaimed Prince of Wales by his
supporters. He adopted on his seal the four lions rampant of Gwynedd, the
arms of the last Prince of Wales, the murdered Llywelyn ap Gruffudd.
Catrin's uncles Gruffudd and Philip Hanmer, and Tewdwr ap Gruffudd
(Glyndŵr) were amongst those whose names were included in the
declaration. Catrin and her brothers and sisters must have experienced a chill
of excitement. The arguments and emotions were strong - there was no choice
but to risk all - the alternative was a slow disintegration of all they valued.
Once fighting had broken out, there was no satisfaction of success in the field
for Catrin and her family, only the watching and hoping for news. Things
must have appeared bleak when Henry IV marched into Sycharth and
destroyed it completely. Everything Catrin had known and loved had gone.

No-one knows where the family spent this time - presumably in the houses
of supporters, never knowing how welcome they might be or when they
might need to move on. Any invading forces of Henry IV followed a
scorched-earth policy. But increasing support and the news of battle successes
must have helped keep their spirits high. And then sometime around late-June
1402 the news must have reahed them - of a superb battle success, both
militarily and psychologically. The 'barefoot Welsh dogs', a volunteer army,

unlike the larger professional forces of Henry and his Marcher Lords, had destroyed the king's army and captured important prisoners, taking them to Owain's 'fortress' of Snowdonia. At the great Battle of Pilleth on June 22nd, over 2000 of the king's men died in a crushing victory. Their commander, Lord Edmund Mortimer was an heir to the throne, and came from one of the most powerful families in the realm. With her connections amongst the Marcher families, Catrin would have known of Edmund and the power and influence of his family. In the brief 3 months that followed, Edmund changed from captive to an important ally. By October 1402, Catrin and Edmund were married*. This may have been a political marriage, but it could also have been a romantic one. Shakespeare suggests this in Henry IV - part 1, where Owain describes his daughter's love and her fighting spirit to Mortimer:

"My daughter weeps; she will not part with you,
She'll be a soldier too; she'll to the wars".

She was "one that no persuasion can do no good upon". So this was a potentially stormy relationship! But in spite of a language problem: "my wife can speak no English, I no Welsh", Shakespeare writes that Mortimer returned her feelings:

"I understand thy looks: that pretty Welsh,
Which thou down-pourest from these swelling heavens"...
"I understand thy kisses, and thou mine."

It was thought at the time that Glyndŵr could command the elements, and well as possessing a magic Raven's stone that made him invisible - even the English troops ascribed magical properties to this guerrilla partisan. Again, this is referred to in Henry IV Part 1:
'Three times hath Henry Bolingbroke made head
Against my power. Thrice from the banks of the Wye
And sandy-bottomed Severn have I sent
Him bootless home, and weather-beaten back.'

A 1402 entry in 'Annales Henrici Quarti ', the English recording of the times, reads that Glyndŵr 'almost destroyed the King and his armies, by magic as it was thought, for from the time they entered Wales to the time they left, never did a gentle air breathe on them, but throughout whole days and nights, rain mixed with snow and hail afflicted them with cold beyond endurance.'

The next few years after her marriage would have been busy for Catrin. She started her family early, but she was still without a permanent home for her young family. By the third year of Catrin's marriage this had all changed. The great, and unconquerable Harlech Castle was captured! The capture was sometime after April 1404 - a major boost to the whole campaign. It was her new home - a home which should have been fit for a royal family. But it was certainly not as luxurious as Sycharth, and the previous occupants had not cared for the castle. Like many of the English castles in Wales, Harlech had fallen into a state of disrepair. Lead had not been replaced, so that the roofs leaked and timbers rotted. There were no stocks of any kind, so Catrin and her children would have to rely on anything that the surrounding country could provide - and blockaded Wales had been ravaged by war and Henry's scorched-earth policy. Provisions were meagre. The traditional trading routes with Herefordshire were badly disrupted and little must have got through to Harlech. But with another home to replace Sycharth and her mother Marred with her to help, Catrin will have started to look forward to a settled future. By the spring of 1405, the family's hopes must have been high. The winter storms and winds in the cold, damp castle, would have passed, and now there was more to eat, and fresh food.

But May 1405 brought terrible news, of the Battle of Pwll Melyn where Catrin lost a brother and an uncle. The family must have been devastated by the news. Her uncle Tewdwr was three years or so younger that Owain. Like Owain, he was a dynamic, experienced knight. Tewdwr and Owain had first fought together at Berwick and in Scotland. Tewdwr was so like Owain that at first it was thought that Owain had been killed in the battle. There was more awful news. Catrin's brother Gruffudd had been captured and taken to the Tower of London (-he was later to die of disease, incarcerated in Nottingham Castle). The news must have had a devastating effect upon Marred, Catrin's mother, who must have started to wonder at the course Owain was taking.

Hopes were now dashed, and there was an increasing sense of foreboding as the summer heat increased. But Owain was determined not to let one setback undermine all the progress he had made. In July, he called for all his supporters to come to an Assembly. The preparations for such a gathering must have been immense, for it took place just a month later in August. Was it on this occasion that Owain wore the royal gilded helmet, cuirass and sword given to him by Charles VI, King of France, just the year before? But in spite of this gift French support was waning, and by the following year was finished. The following spring, with the Pennal Declaration, the family's hopes were high, but mixed with doubt and fear as support diminished. The English siege of Aberystwyth started in early summer 1407. Its defender, Rhys Ddu, was threatened with beheading by Owain himself if he surrendered it. When it finally fell in later 1408, the siege engines (including a massive cannon known as 'The King's Daughter') were brought up to besiege Harlech Cstle.

1408 saw another blow for Glyndŵr. His ally, the old Earl of Northumberland, Hotspur's father, was killed at the Battle of Braham Moor by Prince Henry's forces. The Prince then re-entered Wales, bombarded Aberystwyth into submission, and by 1409 had also taken Harlech, Glyndŵr's last bastion, capturing his wife and family. Edmund Mortimer, the former enemy who became his son-in-law in captivity, died (probably of starvation) in Harlech, fighting for Glyndŵr. Owain had just managed to escape from Harlech as the besiegers moved in. It must have been a difficult decision to leave his family there, while he tried to round up support rather than be cornered. A sad footnote has been the discovery noted in John Lloyd's 1931 book 'Owen Glendower' – he 'left behind him in the castle one little personal relic which has recently been unearthed in the course of excavations, viz. a gilt bronze boss from a set of horse harness, bearing the four lions rampant which he had assumed as prince of Wales'. The four lions rampant, counter-changed in gold and red, were the ancient arms of the princes of Gwynedd. Glyndŵr was more a descendant of the Houses of Deheubarth and Powys than Gwynedd. He had needed that provenance though, which had died out with the vicious assassination of Owain Llawgoch, to be accepted throughout Wales.

The winter of 1408 was exceptionally severe, with an abundance of snow from December to March, so cold that blackbirds and thrushes dropped dead from the trees. At that time, the sea washed right up to the castle crag, and Catrin and her children would have seen the siege engines, men and supplies coming ashore. Wales had no sea power, since the French and Bretons had left them to their fate a few years earlier. Her children saw death and starvation, heard the crashing cannon, and hid from the arrows of longbows and the bolts of crossbows. 1500 crossbow bolts were fired in the sieges of Aberystwyth and Harlech. Llywelyn ap Madog ap Llywelyn, the commander of the castle's defences, was killed, and Catrin's saw her husband, Lord Edmund Mortimer, die of starvation. Through lack of supplies and armaments, and the terrible winter, the castle fell in February 1409. Marred, Catrin and her son Lionel and three daughters were captured by Gilbert Talbot of Goodrich Castle, and transported on a cold, difficult journey to London. The children were potential heirs to the throne, so Catrin knew that their future was bleak. Here she heard of the execution of Owain's bravest lieutenants.

The last gasp of Glyndŵr's revolt occurred near Welshpool Castle when a raiding party under Phillip Scudamore, Rhys Tudur and Rhys Ddu was beaten and the leaders captured. After the usual revolting, slow, barbarous executions, Scudamore's head was placed on a spike at Shrewsbury, Rhys ap Tudur's at London, and Rhys Ddu's at Chester. By 1413, the force of Owain Glyndŵr's uprising was spent, and the new King Henry V took the throne in March. By December, after four long years in captivity, Catrin and two of the children were dead. Their burial, in 1413 at St Swithin's Church in the heart of the City of London, is recorded in Exchequer documents: "To William del Chambre, valet of the said Earl (Arundel). In money paid to his own hands, for expenses and other charges incurred for the burial and exequies of the wife of Edward (sic - Edmund) Mortimer and her daughters, buried within St Swithin's Church London... £1".

For a brief moment in history, Owain Glyndŵr's daughter Catrin might have become Queen of England.

*In 1402, the imprisoned Edmund Mortimer married Owain Glyndŵr's daughter, Catrin. Mortimer's nephew, the young Earl of March, had a far

better claim to the English throne than Henry IV, and no doubt Glyndŵr was hoping that Henry Bolingbroke would be killed and Wales made safe with an English king as an ally. (The nephew was the young son of Roger Mortimer, and he died in 1425, his massive estates passing to Richard, Duke of York. Roger Mortimer had been officially appointed his heir by the childless Richard II. The Welsh people wanted a Mortimer to succeed to the crown, instead of the usurper, Henry Bolingbroke).

Although Glyndŵr had briefly won political, cultural and ecclesiastical independence, before final defeat and the harshness of the laws of a revenging English king, the wars had been a personal disaster for him. His brother Tewdwr had died at the Battle of Pwll Melyn in 1405. His son Gruffydd was captured there, and spent the remainder of his years imprisoned in the Tower of London and Nottingham Castle. Some sources say that he died of the plague in the Tower of London in 1410 - he just vanished from history, like so many other captured descendants of Welsh princes. Glyndŵr's wife, two daughters and three grand-daughters were taken into imprisonment after the fall of Harlech Castle, and all died shortly in captivity. His son-in-law, Edmund Mortimer, with a good claim to the English crown, died at Harlech. Mortimer's wife, Owain's daughter Catherine, died in prison with two of her daughters, and all were buried in St Swithin's Church in London around 1413. Only the churchyard remains. Her son Lionel, Owain's grandson and a claimant for both Welsh and English crowns, died, where or when is unrecorded, but probably by neglect or murder. Owain Glyndŵr's closest lieutenants and comrades-in-arms, Rhys Ddu, Rhys ap Llywelyn, Rhys Gethin and Phillip Scudamore had all been tortured to death Only one son somehow survived the carnage.

Footnote 1: A huge 14-tonne block of bluestone from Gelligaer has been carved as a free-form sculpture by Bryn Chegwidden to stand in the newly landscaped garden around St Swithin's churchyard, as a memorial to Catrin Glyndŵr. Isabel Monnington-Taylor, a direct descendant of Glyndŵr, unveiled the monument upon Glyndŵr Day, September 16th, 2001. The website catringlyndwr.org.uk gives more information on the memorial society.

Footnote 2: There is also information upon Hereford's Wigmore Castle, Mortimer's great base, in the superb website castlewales.com. The Marcher Lords were allowed to raise their own armies, exact taxes and build castles without the king's consent, in return for acting as a defensive cushion between Wales and its adjacent shires, with many Welsh-speakers. By 1328, Roger Mortimer's acquisitions had earned him the title Earl of March, signifying his ownership of lordships all along the Welsh border and in the English enclave of southern Pembrokeshire. Ludlow Castle was the Mortimers' administrative centre, but Wigmore was the family seat, reinforced by the Mortimer endowment of Wigmore Abbey. After Roger Mortimer's liaison with Queen Isabella, and their murder of King Edward II in Berkeley Castle, he became de facto ruler of England until executed by Edward III. The 4th Earl of March, another Roger Mortimer, was named heir to the throne by the childless Richard II. However, the crown was usurped when Henry Bolingbroke captured and murdered Richard II. The new Henry IV held Roger's son Edmund at Windsor, to ensure that his own son, Prince Hal (later Henry V) succeeded him. On Roger Mortimer's death, Edmund Mortimer was in a difficult position. When he was captured by Glyndŵr, Henry IV knew that the powerful uncle to the real heir to the throne was out of the way, and made no attempt to ransom him, as was usual. Declaring his allegiance in the summer of 1402 to Glyndŵr, he married Catrin upon November 30th of that year. His nephew Edmund survived to serve the new king Henry V and was rewarded with the return of the earldom of the March, but died childless and the family's possessions reverted to the crown.

OWAIN GLYN DŴR

1400 ~ 2000

'Pennal Letter'

An important aspect of Owain Glyn Dŵr's attempts to establish himself as the leader of an independent Wales was the formation of alliances with other sovereign nations, especially France. He communicated with the king of France in 1404 and then in 1406 attempted to cement the alliance by declaring his allegiance to the pope of Avignon, Benedict XIII. At this period the papacy was divided, with one pope in Rome and another in Avignon. The King of France, Charles VI, was anxious to win the allegiance of all his allies to the pope of Avignon: the King of England owed allegiance to the Roman pope.

The 'Pennal letter' is in two parts: one brief letter which declares Owain's intention to give obedience to the pope of Avignon, and a formal document sealed with his great seal which sets out the terms of his allegiance, including establishing an independent church and two universities in Wales. The two documents are translated below. A large part of the long document is taken up with a detailed account of the background to the schism in the papacy, and a summary of that portion is given. The English translation is taken from: T. Matthews, *Welsh records in Paris* (Carmarthen, 1910). The original documents are on loan from the Archives nationales de France, J5 16 B. 40 and J5 16. 29.

Most serene prince, you have deemed it worthy on the humble recommendation sent, to learn how my nation, for many years now elapsed, has been oppressed by the fury of the barbarous Saxons; whence because they had the government over us, and indeed, on account of that fact itself, it seemed reasonable with them to trample upon us. But now, most serene prince, you have in many ways, from your innate goodness, informed me and my subjects very clearly and graciously concerning the recognition of the true Vicar of Christ. I, in truth, rejoice with a full heart on account of that information of your excellency, and because, inasmuch from this information, I understood that the lord Benedict, the supreme pontifex, intends to work for the promotion of an union in the Church of God with all his possible strength. Confident indeed in his right, and intending to agree with you as far as is possible for me, I recognize him as the true Vicar of Christ, on my own behalf, and on behalf of my subjects by these letters patent, foreseeing them by the bearer of their communications in your majesty's presence. And because, most excellent prince, the metropolitan church of St. David's was, as it appears, violently compelled by the barbarous fury of those reigning in this country, to obey the church of Canterbury, and de facto still remains in this' subjection. Many other disabilities are known to have been suffered by the church of Wales through these barbarians, which for the greater part are set forth full in the letters patent accompanying. I pray and sincerely beseech your majesty to have these letters sent to my lord, the supreme pontifex, that as you deemed worthy to raise us out of darkness into light, similarly you will wish to extirpate and remove violence and oppression from the church and from my subjects, as you are well able to. And may the Son of the Glorious Virgin long preserve your majesty in the promised prosperity.

Dated at Pennal the last day of March (1406).

Yours avowedly

Owen, Prince of Wales.

Endorsement: To the most serene and most illustrious prince, lord Charles, by the grace of God, King of France.

To the most illustrious prince, the lord Charles, by the grace of God, King of the French, Owen by the same grace, sends the reverence due to such a prince with honour. Be it known to your excellency that we have received from you the articles following, brought to us by Hugh Eddowyer, of the Order of Predicants, and Morris Kery, our friends and envoys, on the eighth day of March, A.D. 1406, the form and tenor of which follow:

In the first place they express the cordial greeting on the part of our lord the king, and of his present letter to our said lord the prince. In this manner, our 'lord the king greatly desires to know of his good state and the happy issue of their negotiations. 'He requests Owen, that he will write as often as an opportunity offers, as he will receive great pleasure, and he will inform him, at length, concerning the good state of the said lord, the king, of the queen, their children, and of the other lords, the princes of the royal family, how my lord the king, and the other princes of the royal family have and intend to have sincere love, cordial friendship, zeal for his honour, the prosperity and well-being of the state of the said prince, and in this the said lord, the prince, can place the most secure faith.

The also explain to the same lord, the prince, how our lord, the king, who esteems him with sincerity and love, greatly desires that, as they are bound and united in temporal matters, so also will they be united in spiritual things, that they may be able to walk to the house of the Lord together. My lord, the king, also requests the same lord, the prince, that he wishes him to consider, With a favourable disposition, the rights of my lord, the pope, Benedict XIII, the supreme pontiff of the universal church, that he may himself learn and cause all his subjects to be informed. Because my lord the king, holds that it shall be to the health of his soul and of the souls of his subjects, to the security and strength of his state, and that their covenants shall be laid in a stronger and more powerfull foundation in the advantage of faith and in the love of Christ. Again, even as all faithful Christians are held to keep themselves well informed concerning the truth of schisms. Princes, however, are so held even more than others, because their opinion can keep many in error, especially their subjects, who must conform with the opinion of their superiors. It is, also, even to their advantage, on account of their duty, to keep themselves informed in all things, that such a schism may be entirely removed and that the Church may have unity in God. Because he, who is the true Vicar of Christ, should be known and acknowledged by all the faithful in Christ, while he, who is an intruder, and known to have by nefarious means usurped the holy apostolic see, shall be expelled and cast aside, by all the faithful, as anti-Christ. To this purpose they should bind themselves to strive, to their utmost, according to the decrees of the holy fathers. To which purpose the said lord, the king, has striven, not without great burdens and e,Expense, and will strive unweariedly.

[The next part of the document explains how the envoys who came from France set about justifying the claims of pope Benedict XIII by giving a detailed history of the papal schism. The King of France appeals to Owain to consider the history and cast his lot in support of Benedict XIII. The King promises to make every effort to ensure that the appointments made by the 'pope of Rome' in Wales will not be threatened if Owain acknowledges Benedict. The last part of the letter is Owain's declaration of intent]

Following the advice of our council, we have called together the nobles of our race, the prelates of our Principality and others called for this purpose, and, at length, after diligent examination and discussion of the foregoing articles and their contents being thoroughly made by the prelates and the clergy, it is agreed and determined that we, trusting in the rights of the lord Benedict, the holy Roman and supreme pontiff of the universal church, especially because he sought the peace and unity of the church, and as we understood daily seeks it, considering the hard service of the adversary of the same Benedict, tearing the seamless coat of Christ, and on account of the sincere love which we specially bear towards your excellency, we have determined that the said lord Benedict shall be recognized as the true Vicar of Christ in our lands, by us and our subjects, and we recognise him by these letters.

Whereas, most illustrious prince, the underwritten articles especially concern our state and the reformation and usefulness of the Church of Wales, we humbly pray your royal majesty that you will graciously consider it worthy to advance their object, even in the court of the said lord Benedict:

First, that all ecclesiastic censures against us, our subjects, or our land, by the aforesaid lord Benedict or Clement his predecessor, at present existing, the same shall by the said Benedict be removed.

Again, that he shall confirm and ratify the orders, collations, titles of prelates, dispensations, notorial documents, and all things whatsoever, from the time of Gregory XI, from which, any danger to the souls, or prejudice to us, or our subjects. may occur, or may be engendered.

Again, that the Church of St. David's shall be restored to its original dignity, which from the time of St. David, archbishop and confessor, was a metropolitan church, and after his death, twenty-four archbishops succeeded him in the same place, as their names are contained in the chronicles and ancient books of the church of Menevia, and we cause these to be stated as the chief evidence, namely, Eliud, Ceneu, Morfael, Mynyw, Haerwnen, Elwaed, Gwmwen, Llewdwyd, Gwrwyst, Gwgawn, Clydâwg, Aman, Elias, Maelyswyd, Sadwmwen, Cadell, Alaethwy, Novis, Sadwmwen, Drochwel, Asser, Arthwael, David II, and Samson; and that as a metropolitan church it had and ought to have the undermentioned suffragan churches, namely, Exeter, Bath, Hereford, Worcester, Leicester, which see is now translated to the churches of Coventry and Lichfield, St. Asaph, Bangor, and Llandaff. For being crushed by the fury of the barbarou,' Saxons, who usurped to themselves the land of Wales, they trampled upon the aforesaid church of St. David's, and made her a handmaid to the church of Canterbury.

Again, that the same lord Benedict shall provide for the metropolitan church of St. David's, and the other cathedral churches of our principality, prelates, dignitaries, and beneficed clergy and curates, who know our language.

Again, that the lord Benedict shall revoke and annul all incorporations, unions, annexions, appropriations of parochial churches of our principality made so far, by any authority whatsoever with English monasteries and colleges. That the true patrons of these churches shall have the power to present to the ordinaries of those places suitable persons to the same or appoint others.

Again, that the said lord Benedict shall concede to us and to our heirs, the princes of Wales, that our chapels, &c., shall be free, and shall rejoice in the privileges, exemptions, and immunities in which they rejoiced in the times of our forefathers the princes of Wales.

Again, that we shall have two universities or places of general study, namely, one in North Wales and the other in South Wales, in cities, towns, or places to be hereafter decided and determined by our ambassadors auld nuncios for that purpose.

Again, that the lord Benedict shall brand as heretics and cause to be tortured in the usual manner, Henry of Lancaster, the intruder of the kingdom of England, and the usurper of the crown of the same kingdom, and his adherents, in that of their own free will they have burnt or have caused to be burnt so many cathedrals, convents, and parish churches; that they have savagely hung, beheaded, and quartered archbishops, bishops, prelates, priests, religious men, as madmen or beggars, or caused the same to be done.

Again, that the same lord Benedict shall grant to us, our heirs, subjects, and adherents, of whatsoever nation they may be, who wage war against the aforesaid intruder and usurper, as long as they hold the orthodox faith, full remission of all our sins, and that the remission shall continue as long as the wars between us, our heirs, and our subjects, and the aforesaid Henry, his heirs, and subjects shall endure.

In testimony whereof we make these our letters patent. Given at Pennal on the thirty-first day of March, A.D. 1406, and in the sixth year of our rule.

Endorsement: The letter by which Owen, Prince of Wales, reduces himself, his lands, and his dominions to the obedience of our lord the Pope Benedict XIII.